SSAT 초빈출 핵심 어휘 완결판

SSATKOREA.COM

한세희의

SSAT®
HIT VOCABULARY

한세희 (SSATKOREA 대표) 지음

For International
Private School Admissions

MUST
HAVE
★★★★★

미국 캐나다
명문 보딩 스쿨
합격을 위한
필수템

SSATKorea
All You Need for Boarding Schools

ERMONHOUSE

한세희의

SSAT®

HIT VOCABULARY

한세희의

SSAT®
HIT VOCABULARY

한세희 (SSATKOREA 대표) 지음

For International
Private School Admissions

MUST
HAVE

★★★★★

미국 캐나다
명문 보딩 스쿨
합격을 위한
필수템

[
큰 꿈에 도전하는
당신의 한 걸음 한 걸음에 위안이 되었으면,
흔들리지 않는 큰 힘이 되었으면 좋겠습니다.
]

첫 SSAT 책을 낼 때부터 전설로 남을 수 있는 어휘 책 하나는 쓰고 싶다는 생각이 있었습니다. 그러다 어느 날 문득 깨달은 것이 있습니다. 끊임없는 변화의 소용돌이 속에서도 중심으로 남는 것들은 그때나 지금이나 항상 그 자리를 지킨다는 것이지요. 그 덕에 시류에 휘둘리지 않는 기본이자, 핵심을 걸러낼 수 있는 안목이 생겼다고나 할까요?

제가 이 책으로 공부하실 여러분께 드리고 싶은 말씀은 세 가지입니다.

첫째, 단어는 매우 강력한 무기입니다. 이제 한 해 한 해 지날 때마다 뼈저리게 느끼실 겁니다. 어휘력이 당신에게 얼마나 큰 힘이 될 수 있는지를 말이지요. 어차피 인생에서 한 번은 제대로 정리해 둬야 하는 어휘. 이제 강한 무기 하나 손에 넣을 때가 되었지요?

둘째, 외우고 잊어버리는 것은 당연한 이치이니 그것으로 괴로워 마십시오. 단, 이것만 기억해 주세요. 운동으로 근육을 단련 시키면 더 큰 힘을 낼 수 있는 것처럼, 여러분의 단어 근육도 훈련을 시키면 시킬수록 더 빨리 외우고, 더 오래 기억하게 만들 수 있습니다. 외우면 외울수록, 더 빨리 더 잘 외우게 됩니다.

셋째, 조급해 하지 말고, 실패했다는 생각이 들 때는 그냥 그 자리에서 다시 일어나서 나아가면 됩니다. 단어는 시간차를 두고 여섯 번 정도 보고, 쓰고, 또 봐야 자기 것이 된다고 합니다. 한 번 외웠는데 생각이 안 난다고 괴로워하지 말고, 그 시간에 한 번만 더 보세요. 불안함은 해야 할 일을 하고 있지 않기 때문에 생기는 것

입니다. SSAT 때문에 너무 걱정되어서 잠도 안 온다고요? 그럼 그냥 책을 펴서 열 개만 외워보세요. 집중해서 하는 그 시간에는 걱정도 불안함도 사라집니다. 그렇게 연습의 횟수가 늘어나면 자신감까지 생겨나게 되죠. 그렇게 불안함을 줄이고 자신감을 키워 나가는 것이죠.

이 책에는 현존하는 SSAT의 가장 중요한 어휘들만을 담았다고 자부합니다. 요리로 치면 아주 싱싱하고 좋은 재료들을 잘 선별해 가져다 놓은 것이죠. 그리고 그 하나하나의 단어에 맞추어 어떤 부분을 꼭 알아야 하는지 포인트를 짚어주는 강의도 따로 준비했습니다. 즉, 맛있는 요리를 위한 조리법도 영상으로 준비해 놓았다는 뜻입니다. 또한 단어를 외울 때는 문제로 나오는 포인트를 연결시킬 줄 알아야 실제 점수 상승으로 연결된다는 점도 잊지 마세요. 마지막으로 재료도 좋고, 요리 비법을 알았다 해도 실제 요리 연습 없이는 좋은 요리를 만들기 어렵겠죠? 단어가 어느 정도 쌓이면 실전 문제 풀이 연습은 선택이 아니라 필수입니다.

이 책으로 공부하고 나면, SSAT가 더 이상 두렵지 않을 것이라고 믿습니다. 그리고 이 작은 책 한 권으로 당신의 인생이 완전히 달라질 수 있기를, 상상도 못했던 좋은 기회를 잡아 더 큰 꿈을 이룰 수 있기를 기대합니다. 큰 꿈에 도전하는 당신의 한 걸음 한 걸음에 위안이 되었으면, 흔들리지 않는 큰 힘이 되었으면 좋겠습니다.

책이 나오기까지 격려와 응원을 아낌없이 보내주신 사랑하는 가족들과 친구들, 함께 일하는 기쁨을 알게 해준 나의 동료들, 좋은 인연으로 힘이 되어주신 헤르몬하우스 여러분들, 그리고 특별히 오랜 시간 애써 주신 이연수 디자이너님께 감사의 말씀을 전합니다.

하나님께 이 모든 영광과 감사를 돌립니다.

한 세 희 드림

[
저에게 Hit Vocab은
보물상자 같더라고요.
]

안녕하세요 후배님들! 저는 이번에 필립스 엑시터 아카데미에 합격한 이예원 입니다. 저는 일반 중학교에서 미국 보딩 스쿨로 간 경우라 도움이 되실 만한 약간의 팁을 이야기해 볼게요.

제 SSAT 첫 주는 말 그대로 혼돈의 카오스였어요. 어느 정도 예상은 했었지만 한세희 선생님의 수업은 그야말로 상상을 초월했어요. 선생님이 던지시는 질문에 아이들 사이에서는 거침없이 답변들이 튀어나오고, Reading을 풀 때는 시, 소설, 연설문, 논설문 등 다양한 스타일의 낯선 지문들이 나와 이해가 잘되지 않았어요. 그러나 뭐니 뭐니 해도 제일 힘들었던 것은 단어였어요. 충격적인 첫 점수를 받고 포기하고 싶었지만 그때마다 선생님과 선배들이 끝까지 버티라고 응원해 준 기억이 떠올라 그렇게 버티며 공부했어요. 두 달 정도 지나니 어느 순간부터 술술 보이기 시작하더라고요. 그래도 여름에 좀 게을리해서인지 첫 시험 점수는 마음에 들지 않았어요. 또 제 주변 친구들 대다수가 외국인 학교나 주니어 보딩 출신으로 첫 시험 한 번에 97~99% 퍼센트 성적을 내는 걸 보고, 일반 중학교에 재학 중이었던 저는 더 주눅이 들었어요. 어느 순간 제가 꿈꿔왔던 탑 보딩들이 너무나도 멀게만 느껴지고, 제가 한 군데라도 붙을 수는 있을까 걱정이 될 정도였어요. 그래도 중간 중간 한세희 선생님께서 할 수 있다고, 내년에 하겠다는 생각은 하지도 말고 끝까지 밀어보라고 해주신 말들이 큰 동기 부여와 힘이 되었어요.

제가 제대로 공부를 시작한 건 학교 인터뷰 후였어요. 인터뷰 투어가 끝날 때쯤

제가 지원했던 너무 좋은 학교들을 보고, 여름에 더 열심히 공부할걸 하고 후회했어요. 그리고 인터뷰 투어의 마지막 날, 제 드림 스쿨인 엑시터에서 온 이메일을 보고 SSAT 2월 성적도 받는다는 것을 알게 되었어요. 인터뷰를 직접 가보니 조금이라도 더 높은 학교에 가고 싶다는 야망과 욕심이 생겼어요. 그래서 저는 다시 2월 시험을 준비하게 됐어요. 이번에는 제발 꼭 한세희 선생님의 Hit Vocab을 제패하자는 마인드로 임했어요. 그렇게 Hit Vocab을 모두 외웠어요. 또 수학에서 약간 점수가 깎인 것이 아까워서 [한세희의 SSAT] 책에 있는 수학 용어도 다시 한번 모조리 외웠어요. 마지막 며칠 동안 한세희 선생님의 모의고사 책을 2-3개씩 풀었어요. 그렇게 해서 본 시험으로 드디어!! 엑시터에 지원할수 있었고, 합격할 수 있었답니다!

저에게 Hit Vocab은 보물 상자 같더라고요. 그것만 외워도 시험에 엄청 많이 나오니까 제발 외워주세요! Hit Vocab을 외우는 것이 Verbal 뿐 아니라, Reading 점수, 나아가 Total 점수까지 올리는 가장 빠른 길이라는 것을 잊지 마세요.

공부를 시작하시는 후배들에게 가장 해주고 싶은 조언은 첫째, Hit Vocab은 기본이니 반드시 꼭 외우기! 둘째, 한세희쌤의 수업 열심히 듣기(실제 시험에서는 수업시간에 한세희 선생님께서 알려 주셨던 세세한 꿀팁들이 완전 도움이 됐어요.)! 그리고 마지막으로 멘탈 관리에요! '포기하고, 내년에 할까? 내가 엑시터를 갈 수는 있을까?'라는 생각은 버리시고, 버티고 버티며 Hit Vocab부터 제패하자는 마인드로 공부하세요! 후배님들 모두 파이팅!

SSAT 99%라는 점수는 나와는
다른 세상 이야기라고만 생각했어요.

안녕하세요! 저는 미국 주니어 보딩에서 Brooks로 진학하게 된 한정원입니다. 처음 한세희 선생님 반에서 SSAT를 시작했을 때는, SSAT 99%라는 점수는 나와는 다른 세상 이야기라고만 생각했어요. 충격적인 첫 모의고사 점수를 보고 정말 앞으로 열심히 해야겠다고 다짐했어요. SSAT와 어드미션 에세이를 같이 준비하다 보니 힘들었지만 한세희 선생님과 꾸준히 상담하며 포기하지 않고 열심히 계속하다 보니 SSAT 99%라는 좋은 결과가 나왔어요.

저는 SSAT를 시작하면서부터 Reading을 집중적으로 했어요. 주니어 보딩에 다니느라 방학이 끝나고 미국에 돌아가면 Reading 문제들을 풀 시간도 없을 것 같고 학교를 다니면서 공부하기가 쉽지 않을 것 같아서요. 선생님 말씀대로 저는 일단 Math를 99%에 맞춰 놓고 Reading을 올리는 데 신경을 썼습니다. 또 Verbal은 상대적으로 Reading 보다 올리기가 쉽기 때문에 선생님이 주시는 Hit Vocab과 [한세희의 SSAT]책에 있는 Analogies 유형들도 잘 정리하면 잘 볼 수 있어요. 선생님과 한 달 정도 공부했을 때 모의고사 점수가 90% 초반이 나와서 힘든 순간도 있었지만 할 수 있다는 선생님의 격려와 선배들의 응원에 포기하지 않고 열심히 했습니다. 미국에 돌아가서는 한세희 선생님께서 만들어 주신 자료들을 복습하고, 오답 노트를 만들어 매일 조금씩 공부하였어요. 단어장을 만들어 학교에서 돌아다니면서 외우고, 시간이 날 때마다 문제들을 풀었어요.

시험 전에는 자주 나오는 시들과 시에 자주 쓰이는 단어들을 외웠어요. 한세희 선생님께서 따로 시에 자주 사용되는 어휘 리스트도 주셔서 그것을 외웠는 데 도움이 많이 되었어요. 선생님께서 종종 말씀해 주셨던 한 가지 팁을 드리자면 SSAT는 Omit을 어떻게 하느냐가 굉장히 중요해요. 저도 처음 시험 볼 때는 Omit을 하나도 하지 않아서 점수가 예상 보다 낮게 나왔었어요. 그 뒤로는 Omit하는 방법을 비롯해 문제풀이 전략을 연습해 좋은 결과를 얻었습니다.

SSAT, GPA, Interview 모두 너무 중요하지만, 제가 하나 더 드리고 싶은 팁은 학교에서 Leadership Position과 Extracurricular 활동에 적극적으로 참여 하라는 것입니다. 저는 다른 부분들은 다 괜찮았는데 학교 활동에서 조금 조용하고 소극적이었던 것이 아쉬웠어요. 또한 Recommendation도 중요하기 때문에 학교에서 친구들, 선생님들과 잘 지내야 하고 수업도 열심히 들어야 해요.

저는 Brooks에 가기로 했습니다. 제가 Brooks 고른 이유는 인터뷰 때문이에요. 인터뷰 때 선생님과 정말 재미있는 시간을 보냈고, 그 이후에도 계속 연락을 주고 받았어요. 지원했던 모든 학교 중에서 Brooks 인터뷰할 때 제일 편했고 가장 저 다웠던 것 같아요.

이 글이 SSAT를 시작하는 많은 후배님들에게 도움이 됐으면 좋겠고, 제가 잘 진학 할 수 있도록 도와주신 모든 분들께 감사드립니다. 아무리 힘들어도 포기하지 마시고 열심히 하셔서 좋은 결과를 보시길 바래요! 후배님들 파이팅!

이 책의 구성

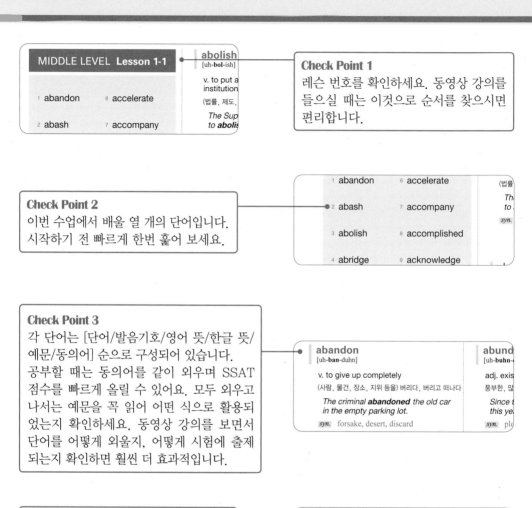

Check Point 1
레슨 번호를 확인하세요. 동영상 강의를 들으실 때는 이것으로 순서를 찾으시면 편리합니다.

Check Point 2
이번 수업에서 배울 열 개의 단어입니다. 시작하기 전 빠르게 한번 훑어 보세요.

Check Point 3
각 단어는 [단어/발음기호/영어 뜻/한글 뜻/예문/동의어] 순으로 구성되어 있습니다. 공부할 때는 동의어를 같이 외우며 SSAT 점수를 빠르게 올릴 수 있어요. 모두 외우고 나서는 예문을 꼭 읽어 어떤 식으로 활용되었는지 확인하세요. 동영상 강의를 보면서 단어를 어떻게 외울지, 어떻게 시험에 출제되는지 확인하면 훨씬 더 효과적입니다.

Check Point 4
배운 열 개의 단어를 이용해 Sentence Completion을 연습해 봅니다. 이때는 왼쪽 페이지에 나왔던 열 개의 단어 리스트를 이용하시면 됩니다.

Check Point 5
정답은 해당 페이지 하단에서 확인하실 수 있습니다.

Analogy 1. Person

Analogy에는 사람 관련 문제가 전체의 10%정도 출제됩니다. 여기서는 가장 중요한 몇
실제 출제되는 문제 유형은 [A is to B]의 형태이지만 여기서는 편의상 [A : B]로 표기 형

A는 B하는 사람

Check Point 1
SSAT Verbal Section에 나오는 Analogy
문제를 유형별로 정리했어요!

Check Point 2
각 세부 유형도 아주 간단하게 보여드리는
형태라 전체 유형 설명과 연습 문제는
[한세희의 SSAT] 책을 보시면 상세하게
보실 수 있어요.

A는 B하는 사람	
mentor : advise 멘토 : 조언하다	nomad : wa 유목민 : 방랑하다
braggart : boast 자랑꾼 : 자랑하다	arbiter : set 결정권자 : 결정ㅎ

POP
QUIZ

1. Abolitionist is to bondage as
(A) iconoclast is to convention
(B) weaver is to weep
(C) superintendent is to manage
(D) glutton is to food
(E) miser is to money

2. Sage
(A) boor
(B) liar is
(C) care
(D) toad
(E) cow

Check Point 3
실전 문제로 Analogy를 연습해 봅시다.
추가적인 유형 설명과 연습 문제는
[한세희의 SSAT] 책에서 확인하실 수
있어요.

Check Point 4
답은 여기서 바로 확인하실 수 있어요.

manage
(B) liar is to candid
(C) caretaker is to solicitous
(D) toady is to unassuming
(E) coward is to gallant

Answer 1. A 2. C

Check-up 1-1

Directions   Each of the following questions consists of one w
You are to select the one word or phrase whose r

1. ABANDON

Check Point 5
SSAT Verbal Section의 Synonym 문제로
배운 단어를 적용해 봅시다.
외운 단어를 문제 풀이에 잘 적용해야
성적 올리기가 쉬워져요!

(B) bulge
(C) mistake
(D) endow
(E) obtain

Check Point 6
정답은 여기서 바로 확인해 보세요.

Answer 1.C 2.E 3.B 4.D 5.A 6.D 7.B 8.B 9.C 10.E

29

MIDDLE LEVEL SSAT VOCABULARY

UPPER LEVEL SSAT VOCABULARY

MIDDLE

한세희의 SSAT HIT VOCABULARY

LEVEL

MIDDLE LEVEL Lesson 1-1

1 abandon

2 abash

3 abolish

4 abridge

5 abundant

6 accelerate

7 accompany

8 accomplished

9 acknowledge

10 acquire

"Be yourself; everyone else is already taken."

- Oscar Wilde

SSATKOREA.com

abandon
[uh-**ban**-duhn]

v. to give up completely

(사람, 물건, 장소, 지위 등을) 버리다, 버리고 떠나다

The criminal abandoned the old car in the empty parking lot.

syn. forsake, desert, discard

abash
[uh-**bash**]

v. to cause another person to feel awkward, embarrassed, or ashamed

(다른 사람을) 당황시키다, 부끄럽게 만들다

The villain vowed to abash his opponent in any way possible.

syn. embarrass, disconcert, confuse

abolish
[uh-**bol**-ish]

v. to put an end to (a system, practice, or institution)

(법률, 제도, 관습 등을) 폐지하다, 없애다

The Supreme Court believed it was time to abolish the outdated law.

syn. cancel, demolish, destroy

abridge
[uh-**brij**]

v. to shorten by omissions while retainig the basic contents

줄이다, 축약하다

The editor wanted to abridge his epic 1000-page history to a 10-page summary instead.

syn. abbreviate, curtail, shorten

abundant
[uh-**buhn**-duhnt]

adj. existing or available in large quantities

풍부한, 많은

Since the apple crops were abundant this year, apple prices are affordable.

syn. plentiful, copious, ample

accelerate
[ak-**sel**-uh-reyt]

v. to increase in speed

가속하다, 속도를 높이다

Many accidents happen when drivers accelerate on sharp curves.

syn. speed up, quicken, expedite

accompany
[uh-**kuhm**-puh-nee]

v. to go along or in company with

(사람과) 같이 가다, 동행하다

I'd like you to accompany me.

syn.   escort, attend, go with go or be with something, attend,

accomplished
[uh-**kom**-plisht]

adj. skilled in activity

숙달된, 노련한, 학식이 깊은

Johann Sebastian Bach had three children who all became highly accomplished musicians.

syn.   skilled, adept, proficient, expert, skillful

acknowledge
[ak-**nol**-ij]

v. to admit to be real or true, to show or express appreciation for

(사실로) 인정하다

The boys acknowledged that they had accidentally broken the window.

syn.   accept, agree, endorse

acquire
[uh-**kwahyuhr**]

v. to obtain or receive

(노력으로) 습득하다, 얻다

Through experience, she acquired a sense of calm in a crisis.

syn.   obtain, get, receive

Sentence Completion 1-1

Directions : Fill in the blanks to complete the sentences.

1. Skilled professionals have to _____ special expertise and knowledge.

2. If your boat is rapidly sinking, then it's time to _____ it.

3. Despite _____ rain throughout the winter, the city is still suffering from a shortage of water.

4. While Lauren sang a song, she asked her friend to _____ her on the piano.

5. Jackie is one of the most _____ designers of her native South Korea.

6. This SSAT vocabulary lessons will improve memory and _____ learning.

7. Praise is a tool meant to _____ an individual's effort and progress.

Answers

1. acquire
2. abandon
3. abundant
4. accompany
5. accomplished
6. accelerate
7. acknowledge

11	acute	16	admirable
12	adaptable	17	adorn
13	adept	18	affirm
14	adequate	19	affront
15	adjoin	20	aggravate

"Do what you can, with what you have, where you are."

- Theodore Roosevelt

SSATKOREA.com

acute
[uh-**kyoot**]

adj. deeply perceptive or very clever
(매우) 예리한

She has an acute understanding of algebra, so she always gets 100% on tests.

syn. sharp, keen, clever

adaptable
[uh-**dap**-tuh-b*uh*l]

adj. able and usually willing to change
(새로운 환경에) 적응할 수 있는

Successful people are highly adaptable to changes.

syn. flexible, versatile, malleable

adept
[uh-**dept**]

adj. very skilled
능숙한, 솜씨 좋은

Carry is an adept speaker; he never loses a debate.

syn. skillful, able, deft, dexterous, proficient

adequate
[**ad**-i-kwit]

adj. fully sufficient or suitable
(특정한 필요에) 충분한, 적절한

Ten dollars is adequate to buy lunch.

syn. sufficient, enough, able

adjoin
[uh-**join**]

v. to be next to
인접하다, 붙어 있다

Reading rooms adjoin the assembly room.

syn. abut, connect

admirable
[**ad**-mer-uh-b*uh*l]

adj. deserving respect or approval
감탄스러운, 존경스러운

She is an admirable teacher, with great power of lucid exposition.

syn. praiseworthy, commendable, laudable

adorn
[uh-**dawrn**]

v. to decorate or add beauty to

꾸미다, 장식하다

*Children **adorn** their Christmas trees with tinsel and lights.*

syn.   embellish, garnish, deck

affirm
[uh-**furm**]

v. to declare the truth of something

단언하다, 확언하다

*I neither **affirm** nor deny the immortality of man.*

syn.   declare, assert, confirm

affront
[uh-**fruhnt**]

n. an insult

모욕, (마음의) 상처

*Revenge for an **affront** massacred all the men capable of bearing arms in the city.*

syn.   insult, indignity, provocation

aggravate
[ag-**ruh**-veyt]

v. to cause to become worse

악화시키다, 더 나쁘게 만들다

*Military intervention **aggravate** regional tensions.*

syn.   worsen, exacerbate, intensify

Sentence Completion 1-2

Directions : Fill in the blanks to complete the sentences.

1. Ryan has many _____ qualities, such as generosity and graciousness.

2. It's essential to devote _____ time to learning and training before you start your task.

3. An _____ is a serious offense o one's dignity or self-respect.

4. The jubilant townspeople _____ trees with yellow ribbons and balloons to celebrate Jay's return to his home.

5. Whatever plans you think about, _____ it in your mouth first, and you will succeed in working it out.

6. The two prisoners whose cells _____ communicate with each other by knocking on the wall.

7. Emma's pain was so _____ that she called 911.

Answers

1. admirable
2. adequate
3. affront
4. adorn
5. affirm
6. adjoin
7. acute

21	agile	26	alias
22	agitate	27	alliance
23	agony	28	allude
24	ailment	29	alter
25	airborne	30	amass

*"If you can dream it,
you can do it."*

- Walt Disney

SSATKOREA.com

agile
[**aj**-*uhl*]

adj. quick and well-coordinated in movement

날렵한, 민첩한

On water skis, she was agile and made sharp turns.

syn. nimble, quick, dexterous

agitate
[**aj**-i-teyt]

v. to move or force into violent, irregular action

(마음을) 뒤흔들다, 불안하게 만들다

When he watched a horror movie at bedtime, he was too agitated to sleep.

syn. provoke, disturb, trouble

agony
[**ag**-uh-nee]

n. extreme and generally prolonged pain

극도의 고통, 괴로움

That level of agony was something he never wanted to go through again.

syn. anguish, suffering, torture

ailment
[**eyl**-m*uh*nt]

n. a physical disorder or illness

병, 질병

The doctor can't find the cause of his sudden ailment.

syn. illness, malady, disease

airborne
[**air**-bawrn]

adj. carried by the air

공기 중에 떠 있는, 비행 중인

The airborne virus infected all of the people on the cruise.

syn. flying, aloft, soaring

alias
[**ey**-lee-*uhs*]

n. an assumed name

가명, 별명

He travelled under an alias: Luke Skywalker.

syn. pseudonym, false name

alliance
[uh-**lahy**-*uh*ns]

n. the act of allying or state of being allied

동맹, 연합

By the tension between the two, their alliance was brittle at best.

syn. association, union, ally

allude
[uh-**lood**]

v. to make an allusion

암시하다, 시사하다, 넌지시 말하다

He alluded to his rival's past failure.

syn. imply, refer, suggest

alter
[**awl**-ter]

v. to cause to change

바꾸다, 고치다

He pronounced the words that would forever alter his life.

syn. change, adjust, modify

amass
[uh-**mas**]

v. to collect as one's own

모으다, 축적하다

His family has amassed great wealth from their investments in real estate.

syn. accumulate, gather, pile

Sentence Completion 1-3

Directions : Fill in the blanks to complete the sentences.

1. Novelty is one of the primary ingredients for keeping the brain _____ and responsive.

2. Once you _____ a basic vocabulary, it would become more comfortable and faster to learn new words and phrases.

3. This feeling will _____ the flow of chemicals differently and generate different physical and mental changes.

4. An _____ is a temporary name that you use for special occasions.

5. Den has suffered from his chronic _____ -a persistent cough.

6. Countries that have an _____ help each other.

7. I don't identify it or mention it specifically - I just _____ it.

Answers

1. agile
2. amass
3. alter
4. alias
5. ailment
6. alliance
7. allude

31	ambiguous	36	antagonistic
32	amiable	37	anticipate
33	ample	38	anxious
34	annex	39	apparatus
35	annoy	40	appease

"Stay hungry, stay foolish."

- Steve Jobs

SSATKOREA.com

ambiguous
[am-big-**yoo**-*uh*s]

adj. open to or having several possible meanings

모호한, 애매한, 불확실한

His answers are intentionally ambiguous.

syn. unclear, equivocal, obscure

amiable
[**ey**-mee-uh-b*uh*l]

adj. having pleasant, good-natured personal qualities

친절한, 쾌활한, 친근한

Her teacher had an amiable personality, always ready with a kind word and a smile.

syn. kind, friendly, agreeable

ample
[**am**-p*uh*l]

adj. plentiful and enough

충분한, 풍부한

His parents have left ample stores of food and water for him.

syn. bountiful, plentiful, abundant

annex
[uh-**neks**]

v. to attach, append, or add

합병하다, 합치다, 더하다

The first ten amendments were annexed to the Constitution.

syn. join, add, adjoin

annoy
[uh-**noi**]

v. to disturb or bother

짜증나게 하다

His attitude often annoys her.

syn. badger, vex, irritate

antagonistic
[an-tag-uh-**nis**-tik]

adj. opposing, especially mutually

적대적인, 반감을 가진

The moral in this story appears to be antagonistic to ideas of monarchy.

syn. hostile, opposing, combative

anticipate
[an-**tis**-uh-peyt]

v. to foretaste or foresee

예상하다, 예측하다

There was every reason to anticipate the success.

syn. foresee, expect, predict

anxious
[**angk**-sh*uh*s]

adj. worried or full of mental distress

불안해하는, 염려하는

At her anxious look, he smiled.

syn. apprehensive, worried, tense

apparatus
[ap-uh-**rat**-*uh*s]

n. a set of instruments, machinery, or tools

기구, 장치

Each set of apparatus works as if it were alone connected to the line.

syn. equipment, implement, gadget

appease
[uh-**peez**]

v. to bring to a state of peace

달래다, 고통을 줄여주다

"Look, you did all you could do," I said trying to appease her.

syn. assuage, soothe, relieve

Sentence Completion 1-4

Directions : Fill in the blanks to complete the sentences.

1. With the _____ instructions, Josh could not assemble the toy.

2. Helen has _____ legroom in her new van that she can stretch her legs.

3. Usually, airline flight attendants tend to be _____ , kind, and friendly.

4. The _____ used for scuba diving includes goggles, flippers, and a breathing tank.

5. Men are _____ to improve their circumstances but are unwilling to improve themselves.

6. The sacrifice of Agamemnon's daughter Iphigenia only could _____ the anger of Artemis.

7. Jack has always been _____ towards his sister Jasmin, never sharing his things or spending any time with her.

 Answers

1. ambiguous	
2. ample	5. anxious
3. amiable	6. appease
4. apparatus	7. antagonistic

41	appliances	46	arid
42	approve	47	arouse
43	apt	48	ashamed
44	arable	49	aspire
45	arduous	50	assert

"Good is the enemy of great."

- Jonathan Ive

SSATKOREA.com

appliances
[uh-**plahy**-*uh*ns]

n. machine, usually with domestic purpose

가전제품

All household appliances, such as a stove, fan, or refrigerator, are now on sale.

syn.   device, instrument, gear

approve
[uh-**proov**]

v. to consent or agree to

찬성하다, 승인하다, 인정하다

The committee approved the proposed budget.

syn.   accept, ratify, approve

apt
[apt]

adj. quick to learn

~를 잘하는, 적성이 있는

He was apt at dancing.

syn.   able, adept, skillful

arable
[**ar**-uh-b*uh*l]

adj. suitable for farming

농사지을 수 있는, 경작 가능한

In Great Britain, 15% of all arable land is unproductive.

syn.   farmable, cultivable, tillable

arduous
[**ahr**-joo-*uh*s]

adj. difficult, needing a lot of effort and energy

몹시 힘든, 고된

It was a long and arduous trip.

syn.   onerous, burdensome, harsh

arid
[**ar**-id]

adj. extremely dry

매우 건조한

An arid stony plateau lacks water.

syn.   desiccated, dehydrated, parched

arouse
[uh-**rouz**]

v. to stir to action or strong response

(느낌이나 태도를) 불러일으키다

A warm touch began to arouse him.

syn. induce, excite, awaken

ashamed
[uh-**sheymd**]

adj. feeling shame

부끄러운, 수치스러운

He was ashamed that he'd made so little effort.

syn. abashed, embarrassed, humiliated

aspire
[uh-**spahy***uhr*]

v. to be eagerly desirous

바라다, 열망하다

As an actor, he aspired to work on Broadway.

syn. desire, dream, pine

assert
[uh-**surt**]

v. to state strongly or positively

주장하다, 확고히 말하다

The defense attorney asserted that he believed strongly in his client's innocence.

syn. declare, insist, maintain

Sentence Completion 1-5

Directions : **Fill in the blanks to complete the sentences.**

1. Most deserts feature _____ climates.

2. I realize this Himalayan trekking will be a long and _____ journey.

3. Teachers should _____ curiosity to ask quality questions in class.

4. The settlers found an ideal location with plenty of _____ land for farming.

5. Leadership is a relationship between those who _____ to lead and those who choose to follow.

6. Ashley is _____ to ignore small things she considers unimportant.

7. A toaster is one of the most common home _____ designed to expose various sliced bread types to radiant heat.

Answers

1. and
2. arduous
3. arouse
4. arable
5. aspire
6. apt
7. appliances

Analogy 1. Person

Analogy에는 사람 관련 문제가 전체의 10%정도 출제됩니다. 여기서는 가장 중요한 몇가지 유형과 자주 출제되는 단어를 살펴 보도록 합시다. 실제 출제되는 문제 유형은 [A is to B]의 형태이지만 여기서는 편의상 [A : B]로 표기 합니다.

A는 B하는 사람

mentor : advise
멘토 : 조언하다

nomad : wander
유목민 : 방랑하다

braggart : boast
자랑꾼 : 자랑하다

arbiter : settle
결정권자 : 결정하다

A의 특징이 B

acrobat : agile
곡예사 : 민첩한

philanthropist : benevolent
박애주의자 : 인정 많은

boor : vulgar
시골뜨기 : 상스러운

sage : wise
현명한 사람 : 현명한

B는 A가 좋아하거나 추구하는 것

glutton : food
대식가 : 음식

miser : money
구두쇠 : 돈

bibliophile : book
애서가 : 책

hedonist : pleasure
쾌락주의자 : 쾌락, 기쁨

B는 A가 싫어하거나 피하려는 것

vegetarian : meat
채식주의자 : 고기

pacifist : violence
평화주의자 : 폭력

iconoclast : convention
인습타파주의자 : 관습

anarchist : government
무정부주의자 : 정부

POP QUIZ

1. Abolitionist is to bondage as

(A) iconoclast is to convention
(B) weaver is to weep
(C) superintendent is to manage
(D) glutton is to food
(E) miser is to money

2. Sage is to wise as

(A) boor is to refined
(B) liar is to candid
(C) caretaker is to solicitous
(D) toady is to unassuming
(E) coward is to gallant

Check-up 1-1

Directions Each of the following questions consists of one word followed by five words or phrases.
You are to select the one word or phrase whose meaning is closest to the word in capital letters.

1. ABANDON
(A) impact
(B) convene
(C) desert
(D) revitalize
(E) veil

2. ABASH
(A) donate
(B) handle
(C) reflect
(D) resolve
(E) embarrass

3. ABOLISH
(A) generate
(B) cancel
(C) stare
(D) doze
(E) liberate

4. ABRIDGE
(A) protest
(B) locate
(C) quote
(D) shorten
(E) annoy

5. ABUNDANT
(A) plentiful
(B) artistic
(C) noble
(D) fatal
(E) hasty

6. ACCELERATE
(A) take over
(B) hand in
(C) count on
(D) speed up
(E) let up

7. ACCOMPANY
(A) detect
(B) escort
(C) determine
(D) produce
(E) discourage

8. ACCOMPLISHED
(A) athletic
(B) skilled
(C) clumsy
(D) structural
(E) obsolete

9. ACKNOWLEDGE
(A) achieve
(B) protest
(C) accept
(D) demand
(E) steal

10. ACQUIRE
(A) falter
(B) ask
(C) demand
(D) endow
(E) obtain

Check-up 1-2

1. ACUTE
- (A) lively
- (B) empty
- (C) sharp
- (D) inborn
- (E) dull

2. ADAPTABLE
- (A) versatile
- (B) generous
- (C) merciful
- (D) messy
- (E) unkempt

3. ADEPT
- (A) inept
- (B) able
- (C) tamed
- (D) insane
- (E) magnanimous

4. ADEQUATE
- (A) excellent
- (B) sufficient
- (C) redundant
- (D) distinct
- (E) obese

5. ADJOIN
- (A) abut
- (B) detach
- (C) lessen
- (D) ponder
- (E) agree

6. ADMIRABLE
- (A) sacred
- (B) proud
- (C) miserable
- (D) inclement
- (E) praiseworthy

7. ADORN
- (A) embellish
- (B) disband
- (C) change
- (D) worsen
- (E) create

8. AFFIRM
- (A) garnish
- (B) repulse
- (C) convert
- (D) reject
- (E) assert

9. AFFRONT
- (A) nobility
- (B) strength
- (C) depth
- (D) pleasure
- (E) insult

10. AGGRAVATE
- (A) retract
- (B) worsen
- (C) bellow
- (D) ameliorate
- (E) compensate

Check-up 1-3

Directions Each of the following questions consists of one word followed by five words or phrases. You are to select the one word or phrase whose meaning is closest to the word in capital letters.

1. AGILE
(A) fierce
(B) soiled
(C) breathless
(D) nimble
(E) spiritual

2. AGITATE
(A) humiliate
(B) provoke
(C) disagree
(D) endure
(E) furnish

3. AGONY
(A) anguish
(B) truce
(C) approval
(D) initiate
(E) expound

4. AILMENT
(A) era
(B) gear
(C) malady
(D) concede
(E) retailer

5. AIRBORNE
(A) articulate
(B) genteel
(C) contagious
(D) flying
(E) cluttered

6. ALIAS
(A) stranger
(B) accomplice
(C) pseudonym
(D) backer
(E) patron

7. ALLIANCE
(A) avalanche
(B) ally
(C) blizzard
(D) rebellion
(E) worker

8. ALLUDE
(A) vend
(B) conflict
(C) inspire
(D) imply
(E) save

9. ALTER
(A) invest
(B) change
(C) peddle
(D) investigate
(E) insinuate

10. AMASS
(A) accumulate
(B) conspire
(C) aggress
(D) refer
(E) attack

31

Check-up 1-4

1. AMBIGUOUS
(A) contented
(B) unclear
(C) conflicting
(D) obvious
(E) evident

2. AMIABLE
(A) happy
(B) kind
(C) dim
(D) clever
(E) satisfied

3. AMPLE
(A) ingenious
(B) sincere
(C) comical
(D) bountiful
(E) frivolous

4. ANNEX
(A) classify
(B) scold
(C) underestimate
(D) add
(E) evaluate

5. ANNOY
(A) badger
(B) appease
(C) soothe
(D) reveal
(E) call

6. ANTAGONISTIC
(A) welcoming
(B) hospitable
(C) balmy
(D) dominant
(E) hostile

7. ANTICIPATE
(A) foresee
(B) ascend
(C) publish
(D) communicate
(E) release

8. ANXIOUS
(A) essential
(B) jubilant
(C) exclusive
(D) apprehensive
(E) valuable

9. APPARATUS
(A) courier
(B) jalopy
(C) hovel
(D) chauffer
(E) equipment

10. APPEASE
(A) impair
(B) ameliorate
(C) deceive
(D) mar
(E) assuage

Check-up 1-5

Directions Each of the following questions consists of one word followed by five words or phrases.
You are to select the one word or phrase whose meaning is closest to the word in capital letters.

1. APPLIANCES
(A) gear
(B) plot
(C) charger
(D) ruse
(E) battery

2. APPROVE
(A) dishearten
(B) ratify
(C) determine
(D) produce
(E) detect

3. APT
(A) fainthearted
(B) inept
(C) mousy
(D) skillful
(E) various

4. ARABLE
(A) farmable
(B) soggy
(C) ache
(D) parched
(E) mountainous

5. ARDUOUS
(A) replaced
(B) smug
(C) harsh
(D) uncovered
(E) distinguished

6. ARID
(A) desiccated
(B) soaked
(C) financial
(D) drowned
(E) pecuniary

7. AROUSE
(A) whisper
(B) stare
(C) glare
(D) fret
(E) awaken

8. ASHAMED
(A) incognito
(B) lackluster
(C) peevish
(D) humiliated
(E) pout

9. ASPIRE
(A) address
(B) pine
(C) accost
(D) aggress
(E) perspire

10. ASSERT
(A) emancipate
(B) inspire
(C) improvise
(D) declare
(E) insert

51	assist	56	authentic
52	associate	57	authority
53	assure	58	avid
54	astounding	59	baffle
55	astute	60	banish

"You only live once, but if you do it right, once is enough."

- Mae West

SSATKOREA.com

assist
[uh-**sist**]

v. to give support or aid to
도와주다, 돕다

She had the sudden urge to assist her friend.

syn. aid, help, support

associate
[uh-**soh**-shee-eyt]

v. to connect in the mind
연관을 짓다, 연상하다

Even a prisoner was unwilling to associate with him.

syn. connect, correlate, combine

assure
[uh-**shoor**]

v. to make certain
보증하다, 장담하다, 단언하다

'It'll be all right,' Meg assured her sister.

syn. convince, ensure, persuade

astounding
[uh-**stoun**-ding]

adj. causing surprise and wonder
크게 놀라게 하는, 놀라운

She made an astounding success.

syn. amazing, astonishing, surprising

astute
[uh-**stoot**]

adj. showing an ability to accurately assess situations or people
통찰력 있는, 기민한, 날카로운

He is an astute businessman who is skillful at using his knowledge to his own advantage.

syn. shrewd, sharp, acute

authentic
[aw-**then**-tik]

adj. not false or copied
진짜의, 진품의

The expert doesn't know if the painting is authentic.

syn. genuine, real, reliable

authority

[uh-**thawr**-i-tee]

n. the power or right to give orders, make decisions, and enforce obedience

권위, 권력, 권한, 직권

Only the principal has the authority to sign this document.

syn. power, authorization, control

avid

[**av**-id]

adj. showing a great interest in or desire for something

몹시 탐내는, 열심인, 열광적인

He is an avid reader.

syn. eager, enthusiastic, ardent

baffle

[**baf**-*uhl*]

v. to confuse, frustrate, or perplex

당황하게 하다, 꺾어버리다, 좌절시키다

A boy's awkward behavior baffles his mom.

syn. perplex, puzzle, bewilder

banish

[**ban**-ish]

v. to force to leave

추방하다, 유배를 보내다

Roger Williams was banished from Massachusetts Bay Colony.

syn. exile, expel, deport

Sentence Completion 2-1

Directions : Fill in the blanks to complete the sentences.

1. As an _____ reader, Louis reads as much as he can.

2. Min saw the _____ sight of a dog walking on one leg.

3. When you buy a diamond ring, you want an _____ diamond and not a fake one.

4. Ella has an _____ on that issue, so she has the right or power to do it.

5. You might _____ the smell of lemons with summer memories of selling lemonade.

6. Ben was an _____ proofreader who always finds all the typos in manuscripts.

7. The council members thought very carefully before they _____ someone from their group.

  Answers

1. avid
2. astounding
3. authentic
4. authority
5. associate
6. astute
7. banish

61 barrier	66 bestow
62 barter	57 bland
63 bellow	68 blatant
64 beneficial	69 bleak
65 benign	70 bliss

"Be the change that you wish to see in the world."

- Mahatma Gandhi

SSATKOREA.com

barrier
[**bar**-ee-er]

n. anything that restrains or obstructs progress or access

장애물, 장벽

The police put a barrier across the road to stop the traffic.

syn.   obstacle, obstruction, barricade

barter
[**bahr**-ter]

v. to trade by exchange of commodities

물물교환하다, 물건을 교환하다

The Native Americans bartered not only with natural resources, but also with handcrafted goods.

syn.   trade, exchange, haggle

bellow
[**bel**-oh]

v. to emit a hollow, loud, animal cry as a bull or cow

(우렁찬 소리로) 고함치다, 소리 지르다

The boss was bellowing into the phone, giving orders to his employees.

syn.   roar, holler, yell

beneficial
[ben-uh-**fish**-uhl]

adj. advantageous or helpful

도움이 되는, 이익이 되는

Ladybugs are beneficial insects, eating the pesky aphids.

syn.   helpful, advantageous, profitable

benign
[bih-**nahyn**]

adj. having a kindly disposition

상냥한, 유순한, 양성의

The gracious king was benign and generous.

syn.   benevolent, kind, mild

bestow
[bih-**stoh**]

v. to present as a gift

수여하다, 부여하다

The trophy was bestowed upon the winner.

syn.   endow, give, allot

bland
[bland]

adj. pleasantly gentle or agreeable
부드러운, 단조로운, 재미없는

Avocado's bland taste and creamy texture make it easy to add to almost any salad.

syn. mild, temperate, dull

blatant
[bleyt-nt]

adj. brazenly obvious
명백하고 뻔뻔한

The math prodigy made a blatant error in simple addition

syn. flagrant, obvious, conspicuous

bleak
[bleek]

adj. bare and desolate
차가운, 쓸쓸한

In the winter the landscape is bleak and the house is drafty.

syn. desolate, dreary, barren

bliss
[blis]

n. supreme happiness
행복, 환희

Follow your bliss and the universe will open doors where there were only walls.

syn. happiness, euphoria, ecstasy

Sentence Completion 2-2

Directions : **Fill in the blanks to complete the sentences.**

1. Exercise is _____ to your health.

2. The _____ food means dull, flavorless, and unappealing.

3. Judy's dad _____ at her to come over at once.

4. Swimming on a hot summer day is sheer _____.

5. His situation is _____ that he has looked for work and no one will hire him.

6. People continue to _____ for goods and services although this method of commerce is no longer widespread.

7. You should _____ more time to work and less to daydreaming.

Answers

1. beneficial
2. bland
3. bellow
4. bliss
5. bleak
6. barter
7. bestow

71 blunder   76 brash

72 bolster   77 brawl

73 boon   78 brazen

74 boundary   79 breach

75 bounteous   80 brittle

"Without music,
life would be a mistake."
- Friedrich Nietzsche

SSATKOREA.com

blunder
[**bluhn**-der]

n. a huge, stupid or careless mistake
큰 실수, 실책

Blessed are the forgetful, for they get the better even of their blunders.

syn. mistake, error, blooper

bolster
[**bohl**-ster]

v. to support with or as with a pillow or cushion
북돋다, 개선하다, 강화하다

Mom's hug bolstered the kid's confidence.

syn. boost, help

boon
[boon]

n. something to be thankful for
유용한 것, 요긴한 것, 도움이 되는 것

This mobile battery is a boon for cellphone users.

syn. advantage, godsend, blessing

boundary
[**boun**-duh-ree]

n. something that indicates bounds or limits
경계, 한계, 제한점

The two neighbors had a violent dispute on the boundary.

syn. barrier, limit, border

bounteous
[**boun**-tee-*uhs*]

adj. generous and abundant
너그러운, 풍부한

The king gave bounteous gifts to the poor.

syn. abundant, generous, liberal

brash
[brash]

adj. impulsive and brazen
성급한, 자신만만한, 경솔한

The brash young man was too confident and aggressive.

syn. bold, hasty, rash, impetuous

brawl
[brawl]

n. a noisy fight
싸움, 소동

Josh had been in a drunken street brawl.

syn. scuffle, quarrel, wrangle

brazen
[**brey**-*zuhn*]

adj. bold and without shame
철면피의, 뻔뻔스런

The crime was so brazen and daring.

syn. unashamed, shameless, unabashed

breach
[breech]

v. to break or act contrary to a law
(법을) 위반하다, (약속을) 져버리다

The company unilaterally breached a contract.

syn. violate, break

brittle
[**brit**-l]

adj. fragile and breakable
약한, 깨지기 쉬운, 불안정한

As a man ages, his bones grow more brittle.

syn. fragile, frail, feeble

Sentence Completion 2-3

Directions : Fill in the blanks to complete the sentences.

1. He'd spent his last dollar, so it was a real _____ to find a ten-dollar bill.

2. A _____ guest disputed the strict rules for admission to the club.

3. With _____ disregard for the sign that said, "No Cellphones," the girl took a long call in the library.

4. Osteoporosis causes bones to become _____ that even mild stresses can cause a fracture.

5. He celebrated her birthday by bringing her a _____ armful of flowers.

6. Earth has its _____, but human stupidity is limitless.

7. He sued his neighbor for _____ of contract.

81	camouflage	86	clumsy
82	candor	87	coarse
83	capitulate	88	colossal
84	chaotic	89	combative
85	clarify	90	combine

"Nothing can substitute experience."

- Paulo Coelho

SSATKOREA.com

camouflage
[**kam**-uh-flahzh]

v. to disguise by means of camouflage
위장하다, 변장하다

They camouflaged ships by painting them gray.

syn. disguise, cover, conceal

candor
[**kan**-der]

n. the quality of being frank, open, and sincere
솔직함, 신실함

He spoke with candor about his past life.

syn. honesty, straightforwardness, frankness

capitulate
[kuh-**pich**-uh-leyt]

v. to surrender unconditionally or on stipulated terms
항복하다, 복종하다, 굴복하다

The city capitulated after a three-month siege.

syn. surrender, concede, defeat

chaotic
[key-**ot**-ik]

adj. utterly confused
대혼란의, 무법의

Chaotic conditions followed the war.

syn. anarchic, disorganized, lawless

clarify
[**klar**-uh-fahy]

v. to make clear and intelligible
명확하게 하다, 분명히 말하다

She was unable to clarify her situation.

syn. explain, expound, elucidate

clumsy
[**kluhm**-zee]

adj. awkward in movement or action
솜씨없는, 손재주가 없는, 어색한

His accent was pretty good, but his speech pattern was really clumsy.

syn. awkward, uncoordinated, ungainly

coarse
[kohrs]

adj. not fine or rude

거친, 상스러운, 굵은

*She prefers **coarse** grind to fine grind coffee.*

syn.   crude, vulgar, rough

colossal
[kuh-**los**-*uhl*]

adj. extraordinarily great in size, extent, or degree

거대한, 광대한, 대량의

*It was a **colossal** bronze image of Athena, which was visible far out at sea.*

syn.   huge, massive, enormous

combative
[k*uh*m-**bat**-iv]

adj. ready or inclined to fight

호전적인, 싸우기 좋아하는

*His **combative** disposition led him to numerous difficulties.*

syn.   pugnacious, aggressive, warlike

combine
[kuhm-**bahyn**]

v. to bring into or join in a close union or whole

결합하다, 조합하다

*The choreography **combines** artistry and athletics.*

syn.   unite, integrate, connect

Sentence Completion 2-4

Directions : Fill in the blanks to complete the sentences.

1. The _____ pyramids made the overwhelmed tourists say, "Whoa!"

2. The soldiers _____ with the leaf-colored and patterned uniforms.

3. Because the realtor was an honest man, he replied with _____ about the damage to the house.

4. The _____ people drop things, trip a lot, and stumble always.

5. _____ your intention, otherwise others will not understand it clearly.

6. The teacher found it _____ inside the bus on the way home from a field trip.

7. The _____ man licks his dinner plate and wipes his nose on his sleeve.

Answers

1. colossal
2. camouflage
3. candor
4. clumsy
5. clarify
6. chaotic
7. coarse

91 comfort	96 conceal
92 commotion	97 concede
93 companion	98 condemn
94 compliment	99 condense
95 composed	100 confide

"Always forgive your enemies;
nothing annoys them so much."
- Oscar Wilde

SSATKOREA.com

comfort
[**kuhm**-fert]

v. to soothe, console, or reassure
위로하다, 애도하다

There was no use to try to comfort her.

syn. condole, console, assuage

commotion
[kuh-**moh**-shuhn]

n. a violent or tumultuous motion
난동, 소란

What's all the commotion in the study hall?

syn. tumult, furor, uproar

companion
[kuhm-**pan**-yuhn]

n. a person who is frequently in the company of
친구, 동료, 동반자

The little pup was his best companion.

syn. colleague, friend, comrade

compliment
[**kom**-pluh-muhnt]

v. to praise or express admiration
칭찬하다

Her sincere compliment boosts his morale.

syn. applaud, praise, commend

composed
[kuhm-**pohzd**]

adj. having one's feelings and expression under control
침착한, 조용한, 차분한

The captain's composed face reassured the nervous passengers.

syn. calm, collected, serene

conceal
[kuhn-**seel**]

v. to hide, to keep secret
감추다, 비밀로 하다

He was always trying to conceal that passion.

syn. hide, cover, disguise

concede
[kuhn-**seed**]

v. to acknowledge as true, just, or proper

(마지못해) 인정하다, 수긍하다

*Dad finally **conceded** that mom was right.*

syn. admit, accept, acknowledge

condemn
[kuhn-**dem**]

v. to indicate strong disapproval of

비난하다, 규탄하다

*Don't **condemn** him before you hear the evidence.*

syn. criticize, blame, convict

condense
[kuhn-**dens**]

v. to make more dense or compact

줄이다, 응결되다

*She **condensed** her answer into a few words.*

syn. abridge, compress, shorten

confide
[kuhn-**fahyd**]

v. to tell confidentially

비밀을 털어놓다

*Lucy dared not **confide** the secret to her family.*

syn. divulge, reveal, confess

Sentence Completion 2-5

Directions : **Fill in the blanks to complete the sentences.**

1. She was upset about her brother's unkind remark, but her _____ face doesn't give away her feelings.

2. As Ian tried to concentrate on reading papers, he wouldn't want the person to cause a _____ .

3. Jason worked hard to _____ his disappointment at the outcome of the match.

4. Whether it's travel or card-playing, your _____ is the one who does it with you.

5. As anti-fur activists, they _____ someone for wearing fur.

6. The publisher asked the editor to _____ a 1000-page novel into a 2-page summary.

7. Matte tried to _____ his best friend to shore up the mood.

 Answers

1. composed
2. commotion
3. conceal
4. companion
5. condemn
6. condense
7. comfort

Analogy 2. Tools & Function

Tools & Function은 도구와 그 기능을 연결짓는 관계입니다.

A는 B하기 위한 것	
loom : weave 베틀 : 천을 짜다	**locomotive : travel** 증기 기관차 : 이동하다
magnifying glass : enlarge 돋보기 : 확대하다	**lamp : illuminate** 램프 : 밝히다
tripod : support 삼각대 : 지지하다	**buffer : polish** 버퍼 : 광내다
colander : drain 물기 빼는 체 : 물기를 빼다	**drill : bore** 드릴 : 구멍 뚫다
mortar : grind 절구 : 갈다	**awl : pierce** 송곳 : 구멍 뚫다
cleaver : cut 큰 식칼 : 자르다	**jack : raise** 잭(자동차 타이어를 갈 때처럼 무거운 것을 들어 올릴 때 쓰는 기구) : 들어올리다
chisel : carve (조각용) 끌 : 조각하다	**shovel : dig** 삽 : 파다
stove : cook 스토브 : 요리하다	**blade : cut** 칼날 : 자르다
vessel : contain 용기, 담는 그릇 : 담다, 포함하다	**hammer : pound** 망치 : 두드리다

POP
QUIZ

1. Tripod is to support as

   (A) razor is to fix
   (B) blade is to cut
   (C) shears is to cull
   (D) tongs is to tweezers
   (E) podium is to speech

2. Magnifying glass is to enlarge as

   (A) telescope is to prolong
   (B) stethoscope is to physician
   (C) ladder is to rung
   (D) vessel is to contain
   (E) crater is to apple

Check-up 2-1

Directions   Each of the following questions consists of one word followed by five words or phrases.
You are to select the one word or phrase whose meaning is closest to the word in capital letters.

1. ASSIST
(A) aid
(B) preserve
(C) add
(D) odd
(E) annex

2. ASSOCIATE
(A) appease
(B) connect
(C) smuggle
(D) falsify
(E) muffle

3. ASSURE
(A) hoard
(B) sanction
(C) validate
(D) disapprove
(E) convince

4. ASTOUNDING
(A) grimy
(B) soiled
(C) sooty
(D) astonishing
(E) sullen

5. ASTUTE
(A) stout
(B) meandering
(C) acute
(D) dull
(E) blunt

6. AUTHENTIC
(A) intrepid
(B) deafening
(C) bogus
(D) practical
(E) genuine

7. AUTHORITY
(A) elite
(B) power
(C) complexion
(D) knack
(E) reaper

8. AVID
(A) tepid
(B) enthusiastic
(C) opinionated
(D) flexible
(E) supple

9. BAFFLE
(A) puzzle
(B) crumble
(C) banish
(D) fabricate
(E) collapse

10. BANISH
(A) concede
(B) accelerate
(C) deport
(D) invert
(E) descend

Check-up 2-2

1. BARRIER
(A) timber
(B) obstacle
(C) risk
(D) pastime
(E) nectar

6. BESTOW
(A) cultivate
(B) distract
(C) reap
(D) comply
(E) endow

2. BARTER
(A) donate
(B) negotiate
(C) tear
(D) rip
(E) trade

7. BLAND
(A) essential
(B) constructive
(C) available
(D) mild
(E) destructive

3. BELLOW
(A) frown
(B) compose
(C) roar
(D) dent
(E) clash

8. BLATANT
(A) flagrant
(B) cordial
(C) belligerent
(D) illicit
(E) surreptitious

4. BENEFICIAL
(A) extinct
(B) sparse
(C) sluggish
(D) hostile
(E) helpful

9. BLEAK
(A) torrid
(B) contiguous
(C) desolate
(D) candid
(E) mammoth

5. BENIGN
(A) illustrate
(B) forecast
(C) benevolent
(D) anticipate
(E) compete

10. BLISS
(A) folly
(B) artisan
(C) happiness
(D) apprentice
(E) ignorance

Check-up 2-3

Directions   Each of the following questions consists of one word followed by five words or phrases.
You are to select the one word or phrase whose meaning is closest to the word in capital letters.

1. BLUNDER
(A) mischief
(B) mission
(C) mishap
(D) mislead
(E) mistake

2. BOLSTER
(A) boost
(B) slide
(C) credit
(D) debate
(E) submit

3. BOON
(A) nest
(B) stroke
(C) label
(D) discipline
(E) advantage

4. BOUNDARY
(A) harness
(B) limit
(C) disgust
(D) scheme
(E) result

5. BOUNTEOUS
(A) opaque
(B) sleeve
(C) lucid
(D) abundant
(E) wanting

6. BRASH
(A) bold
(B) sheepish
(C) embarrassed
(D) omnipotent
(E) lithe

7. BRAWL
(A) fictitious
(B) scuffle
(C) indirect
(D) pungent
(E) tasty

8. BRAZEN
(A) pungent
(B) incendiary
(C) toothsome
(D) pliable
(E) unashamed

9. BREACH
(A) derive
(B) violate
(C) render
(D) institute
(E) remain

10. BRITTLE
(A) callous
(B) evanescent
(C) congenial
(D) fragile
(E) vicarious

Check-up 2-4

1. CAMOUFLAGE
(A) illustrate
(B) forecast
(C) scrub
(D) disguise
(E) compete

2. CANDOR
(A) honesty
(B) fidelity
(C) faithfulness
(D) sympathy
(E) detachment

3. CAPITULATE
(A) anticipate
(B) surrender
(C) entitle
(D) recede
(E) infer

4. CHAOTIC
(A) gruesome
(B) ungainly
(C) tattered
(D) discursive
(E) disorganized

5. CLARIFY
(A) cower
(B) decorate
(C) explain
(D) intimidate
(E) pollute

6. CLUMSY
(A) awkward
(B) belligerent
(C) hilarious
(D) unlawful
(E) stealthy

7. COARSE
(A) crude
(B) deft
(C) fanciful
(D) beneficial
(E) massive

8. COLOSSAL
(A) tiny
(B) conflicting
(C) enormous
(D) impetuous
(E) colloquial

9. COMBATIVE
(A) torrid
(B) warlike
(C) peripheral
(D) candid
(E) mammoth

10. COMBINE
(A) integrate
(B) muffle
(C) compensate
(D) acquit
(E) commence

Check-up 2-5

Directions   Each of the following questions consists of one word followed by five words or phrases.
You are to select the one word or phrase whose meaning is closest to the word in capital letters.

1. COMFORT
(A) dwindle
(B) soar
(C) wither
(D) console
(E) translate

2. COMMOTION
(A) emphasis
(B) tumult
(C) option
(D) game
(E) distinction

3. COMPANION
(A) foe
(B) colleague
(C) protagonist
(D) villain
(E) bandit

4. COMPLIMENT
(A) delusion
(B) consternation
(C) hallucination
(D) addition
(E) praise

5. COMPOSED
(A) ardent
(B) consecutive
(C) dense
(D) collected
(E) edible

6. CONCEAL
(A) employ
(B) hide
(C) envelop
(D) locate
(E) ebb

7. CONCEDE
(A) refuse
(B) admit
(C) leak
(D) stir
(E) pardon

8. CONDEMN
(A) endorse
(B) frustrate
(C) criticize
(D) purchase
(E) fascinate

9. CONDENSE
(A) gratify
(B) flee
(C) abridge
(D) oppose
(E) hew

10. CONFIDE
(A) usurp
(B) bellow
(C) retract
(D) taper
(E) divulge

49

101 confound	106 conspicuous
102 confront	107 conspire
103 congenial	108 constant
104 conjecture	109 constraint
105 conquest	110 contemporary

"Don't cry because it's over,
smile because it happened."

- Oscar Wilde

SSATKOREA.com

confound
[kon-**found**]

v. to cause confusion or surprise

당황하게 하다

The sudden rise of the Arctic temperature has confounded many meteorologists.

syn.   confuse, baffle, puzzle

confront
[ku*h*n-**fruhnt**]

v. to oppose directly and openly

직면하다, 대면하다, 대결하다

The girl had to confront her fears.

syn.   challenge, stand up to, oppose

congenial
[ku*h*n-**jeen**-yu*h*l]

adj. agreeable, suitable, or pleasing in nature or character

마음이 맞는

She wants to be back in the more congenial company.

syn.   hospitable, pleasant, amiable

conjecture
[ku*h*n-**jek**-cher]

n. inference formed without proof or sufficient evidence

추측, 짐작

He tried to make a conjecture on her intentions.

syn.   guess, surmise, supposition

conquest
[**kon**-kwest]

n. the act of invading, taking over, and ruling another area or group

정복, 극복

He continued to expand his kingdom by conquest.

syn.   defeat, takeover, seizure

conspicuous
[ku*h*n-**spik**-yoo-u*h*s]

adj. very noticeable

눈에 잘 띄는, 남의 눈을 끄는

Her red hair made her conspicuous in her class.

syn.   remarkable, noticeable, discernible

conspire
[kuhn-**spahy***uh*r]

v. to make secret plans with others to do something that is illegal or harmful

음모를 꾸미다, 공모하다

*They **conspired** to rebel.*

syn. plot, scheme, unite

constant
[**kon**-st*uh*nt]

adj. not changing or varying, continuing without pause

불변의, 변함없는, 계속되는

*Toddlers need **constant** attention.*

syn. steady, regular, unceasing

constraint
[k*uh*n-**streynt**]

n. a limit or restriction on actions or ideas

제한점, 한계

*The project team has suffered from **constraints** of time and money.*

syn. restriction, limitation, inhibition

contemporary
[k*uh*n-**tem**-puh-rer-ee]

adj. of or relating to present and recent time

동시대의, 현세의

*He was **contemporary** with the Alexander the Great.*

syn. modern, present-day, current

Sentence Completion 3-1

Directions : Fill in the blanks to complete the sentences.

1. A number of stars in the universe is still a matter of

_____.

2. Hugh made _____ drumming sound on the table with his fingers.

3. Alexander the Great's famous _____ of the Persian Empire was an act of conquering.

4. The _____ tower could be seen at a great distance.

5. Catie's _____ friend is easy to get along with.

6. If one famous person was a _____ of another, that means they lived at the same time.

7. Rather than letting things go, when people are rude to you, you should _____ them.

Answers

1. conjecture
2. constant
3. conquest
4. conspicuous
5. congenial
6. contemporary
7. confront

---

111 contend	116 convenient
112 contented	117 conventional
113 continuous	118 converse
114 contract	119 cooperate
115 contrive	120 coordinate

"That which does not kill us makes us stronger."

- Friedrich Nietzsche

SSATKOREA.com

contend
[k*uh*n-**tend**]

v. to strive in rivalry

겨루다, 다투다, 주장하다

The governor contends with great difficulties.

syn. compete, fight, argue

contented
[k*uh*n-**ten**-tid]

adj. satisfied or showing satisfaction with things as they are

(자기 삶에) 만족해 하는

Whenever he returns to his home, he is happy and contented.

syn. happy, satisfied, at ease

continuous
[k*uh*n-**tin**-yoo-*uhs*]

adj. uninterrupted in time

연속적인, 끊임없는

Success is a continuous journey.

syn. unceasing, uninterrupted, constant

contract
[kon-trakt]

n. a formal or legal, written agreement between two or more people

계약

The contract gives a female executive maternity leave rights.

syn. pact, agreement, deal

contrive
[k*uh*n-**trahyv**]

v. to plan with ingenuity

고안하다, 설계하다

The rebel contrived a plot to seize power.

syn. invent, devise, plan

convenient
[kuhn-**veen**-y*uh*nt]

adj. well suited to a person's needs, plans, or comfort

편리한, 알맞은, 사용하기 쉬운

Put things where they will be most convenient for you.

syn. handy, appropriate, suited

conventional

[ku*h*n-**ven**-shuh-nl]

adj. common, traditional, or accepted by most people

습관적인, 관습에 따른

Conventional symbols are universally used.

syn.   traditional, customary, accustomed

converse

[ku*h*n-**vurs**]

v. to carry on a conversation

대화하다

She speaks several languages fluently, so people want to meet and converse with her.

syn.   discourse, talk, chat

cooperate

[koh-**op**-uh-reyt]

v. to work or act together for a common purpose or benefit

협력하다

The two companies agreed to cooperate with each other.

syn.   collaborate, work together

coordinate

[koh-**awr**-dn-it]

v. to bring order and organization to

조정하다, 조화를 이루게 하다

When you dance, try to coordinate your steps.

syn.   match, harmonize, integrate

Sentence Completion 3-2

Directions : Fill in the blanks to complete the sentences.

1. People used to _____ that the earth was flat, but the round theory won.

2. Do you believe that you will be able to _____ well with this person into your old age?

3. As Rita lives close to her job, it's _____ to get there and get home.

4. When you rent a condo, you and your future landlord sign a rental _____.

5. She made a _____ smile showing satisfaction with things.

6. The batteries provide enough power for two hours of _____ uses.

7. _____ weapons mean not using, making, or involving nuclear weapons.

Answers

1. contend
2. converse
3. convenient
4. contract
5. contented
6. continuous
7. conventional

---

121 cordial	126 crawl
122 corroborate	127 crouch
123 counteract	128 crucial
124 courtesy	129 cultured
125 cower	130 cunning

"A room without books is like a body without a soul."

- Marcus Tullius Cicero

SSATKOREA.com

cordial
[**kawr**-juh]

adj. diffusing warmth and friendliness

다정한, 친근한, 친절한

He was cordial to his friends.

syn. friendly, sociable, affectionate

corroborate
[kuh-**rob**-uh-reyt]

v. to make more certain

확인하다, 확증하다

The story was corroborated by evidence.

syn. confirm, validate, endorse

counteract
[koun-ter-**akt**]

v. to reduce the effect by doing something that produces an opposite effect

(나쁜 영향에) 대응하다, 반작용하다

Volunteering is a good way to counteract loneliness.

syn. counterbalance, neutralize, offset

courtesy
[**kur**-tuh-see]

n. showing politeness in how one behaves with others

예의, 공손함

You could at least have had the courtesy to let me know.

syn. politeness, manners, etiquette

cower
[**kou**-er]

v. to crouch, as in fear or shame

움츠리다, 위축하다

A shot went off, and people cowered under tables.

syn. cringe, shrink, crouch

crawl
[krawl]

v. to move on one's hands and knees close to the ground

기다, 기어가다

In a panic, she began to crawl toward the back door.

syn. creep, inch, squirm

crouch
[krouch]

v. to stoop or bend low

쭈그리다, 움츠리다, 웅크리다

He crouched down to avoid being seen.

syn. squat, bend, stoop

crucial
[**kroo**-sh*uh*l]

adj. very important or significant

결정적인, 매우 중요한

The meetings are crucial for the success of the plan.

syn. essential, vital, decisive

cultured
[**k*uh*l**-cherd]

adj. enlightened or refined

교양 있는, 세련된, 고상한

You all seem so elegant and cultured, and you've even written books.

syn. enlightened, refined, cultivated

cunning
[**kuhn**-ing]

adj. able to use cleverness to trick others

교활한, 간사한

He is cunning as a fox.

syn. crafty, wily, sly

Sentence Completion 3-3

Directions : Fill in the blanks to complete the sentences.

1. Holding the door open for someone is the common _____.

2. The antidote will _____ the poison.

3. She was moved by her colleague's _____ welcome.

4. The diplomat played a _____ role in the negotiations.

5. The _____ plan involves setting traps for the innocent prey.

6. _____ people have good manners and etiquette.

7. The witness in court will _____ the testimony of others.

Answers

1. courtesy
2. counteract
3. cordial
4. crucial
5. cunning
6. cultured
7. corroborate

131	damp	136	deceive
132	daring	137	deceptive
133	dawdle	138	declare
134	dearth	139	defiance
135	debacle	140	dejected

"Well done is better than well said."

- Benjamin Franklin

SSATKOREA.com

damp
[damp]

adj. slightly wet

축축한, 젖은

The rain had made the floors damp.

syn. saturated, humid, soaked

daring
[**dair**-ing]

adj. disposed to venture or take risks

담대한, 용감한, 겁 없는

The daring artist is willing to do which might shock or anger other people.

syn. audacious, venturesome, bold

dawdle
[**dawd**-l]

v. to waste time

시간을 낭비하다, 빈둥빈둥 지내다

He knew that he might not live for another six months, so there was no time to dawdle.

syn. delay, linger, loiter

dearth
[durth]

n. an inadequate supply

부족, 결핍

There was a dearth of reliable information on the issue.

syn. shortage, paucity, insufficiency

debacle
[dey-**bah**-k*uh*l]

n. a general breakup or dispersion

파괴, 붕괴, 재해

His first performance was a debacle.

syn. disaster, ruin, fiasco

deceive
[dih-**seev**]

v. to mislead by a false appearance or statement

기만하다, 사기 치다

We easily deceive ourselves.

syn. mislead, swindle, defraud

deceptive

[dih-**sep**-tiv]

adj. apt or tending to deceive

남을 속이는, 믿을 수 없는, 현혹하는

Appearances can be deceptive.

syn. delusive, fallacious, specious

declare

[dih-**klair**]

v. to make known or state clearly, to announce officially

선언하다, 단언하다, 밝히다

They had unilaterally declared a ceasefire.

syn. proclaim, announce, assert

defiance

[dih-**fahy**-*uh*ns]

adj. daring or bold resistance to authority or to any opposing force

과감한 저항, 대담한 반항

He held up a clenched fist in defiance.

syn. resistance, opposition, noncompliance

dejected

[dih-**jek**-tid]

adj. depressed in spirits

기가 죽은, 풀 죽은, 의기소침한

He was thoroughly dejected and miserable.

syn. discouraged, despondent, dispirited

Sentence Completion 3-4

Directions : Fill in the blanks to complete the sentences.

1. A _____ person will lead you to believe something other than the truth.

2. The _____ knight dares to do things that are risky and even dangerous.

3. His mom seems to be _____ but trying to look cheerful.

4. If you'd like to get to the class on time, don't _____ along the way.

5. He bluffed at poker in order to _____ the other players.

6. This entire _____ has prompted some people to question the reliability of the government.

7. The lawn might be _____ with dew in the morning.

Answers

1. deceptive
2. daring
3. dejected
4. dawdle
5. deceive
6. defiance
7. damp

MIDDLE 1 2 3 4 5 6 7 8 9 10

UPPER 1 2 3 4 5 6 7 8 9 10

SSAT MIDDLE LEVEL **57**

141 **delegate**   146 **denounce**

142 **deliberate**   147 **deplete**

143 **delicacy**   148 **detach**

144 **deluge**   149 **detailed**

145 **demolish**   150 **device**

"No one can make you feel inferior without your consent."

- Eleanor Roosevelt

SSATKOREA.com

delegate
[**del**-i-git]

n. a person appointed or elected to represent others

대표자

*The **delegates** voted to support the resolution.*

syn. representative, deputy, envoy

deliberate
[dih-**lib**-er-it]

adj. carefully thought out in advance

신중한, 찬찬한

*It was a calculated and **deliberate** move.*

syn. intentional, measured, calculated

delicacy
[**del**-i-kuh-see]

n. fineness of texture or quality

섬세함, 깨지기 쉬움, 연약함

*His voice has both warmth and **delicacy**.*

syn. fragility, elegance, sensitivity

deluge
[**del**-yooj]

n. the rising of a body of water and its overflowing onto normally dry land

홍수, 범람

*The **deluge** was caused by a huge amount of rainfall in a day.*

syn. flood, inundation, overwhelm

demolish
[dih-**mol**-ish]

v. to destroy or ruin

파괴하다, 부수다

*A new café was built where the old house was **demolished**.*

syn. destroy, bulldoze, wreck

denounce
[dih-**nouns**]

v. to condemn or censure openly or publicly

비난하다, 고발하다

*The governor publicly **denounced** the president's handling of the crisis.*

syn. condemn, criticize, censure

deplete
[dih-**pleet**]

v. to decrease seriously or exhaust the abundance or supply of

고갈시키다, 다 써버리다

Water pollution depletes the world of natural resources.

syn. exhaust, use up, reduce

detach
[dih-**tach**]

v. to unfasten and separate

떼다, 분리하다, 분리되다

The skis should detach from the boot when you fall on the ground.

syn. unfasten, disconnect, disengage

detailed
[dih-**teyld**]

adj. having many details

상세한

She needs the witness' detailed report on the accident.

syn. specific, precise, thorough

device
[dih-**vahys**]

n. a thing made for a particular purpose

장치, 기구

Please turn off your electronic devices.

syn. implement, gadget, gear

Sentence Completion 3-5

Directions : **Fill in the blanks to complete the sentences.**

1. In presidential primaries in the United States, people vote for a _____ whose job is to vote for that candidate at a convention.

2. The _____ of a spider web fascinated the little kid.

3. _____ the lower part of the form and return it with your payment.

4. Many people _____ the politician as morally corrupt.

5. If you _____ your body of water after a lot of exercises, be sure to replete yourself with a nice glass of water.

6. Do not bring a smartphone or any other electronic _____ into the testing site.

7. The accomplished writer is renowned for a _____ description of people.

Analogy 3. Degree

Degree는 강도의 차이를 구별하는 관계를 말합니다. 크게 그 품사에 따라 Noun/ Adjective / Verb 의 세 가지 유형으로 구분됩니다. 매우 자주 출제되는 유형이므로 단어를 외울때 이 Degree 유형에 자주 출제되는 것인 경우에는 뜻과 함께 강도의 여부도 함께 기억해야 합니다.

Adjective ﹤ Adjective 형용사 degree

happy < ecstatic
행복한 < 황홀한

sad < inconsolable
슬픈 < 너무 슬픈

singed < charred
그을린, 살짝 태운 < 새까맣게 탄, 숯이 된

shocked < traumatic
충격받은 < 정신적으로 큰 외상을 입은

Verb ﹤ Verb 동사 degree

nudge < shove
쿡쿡 찌르다 < 거칠게 밀치다

glance < stare
흘끗 보다 < 노려보다

request < command
요청하다 < 명령하다

embarrass < humiliate
당황하게 하다 < 수치스럽게 하다

Noun ﹤ Noun 명사 degree

daydream < hallucination
공상 < 환각

sleep < coma
잠 < 혼수상태

tweezers < tongs
족집게 < 집게

gully < canyon
도랑 < 협곡

POP
QUIZ

1. Singed is to charred as
(A) happy is to jubilant
(B) warm is to mild
(C) frigid is to algid
(D) shocked is to surprised
(E) sad is to inconsolable

2. Request is to command as
(A) shove is to nudge
(B) humiliate is to abash
(C) idolize is to worship
(D) admonish is to berate
(E) commend is to suggest

3. Ripple is to wave as
(A) coma is to sleep
(B) canyon is to gully
(C) breeze is to squall
(D) cello is to viola
(E) tongs is to tweezers

4. Sleepy is to comatose as
(A) detestable is to abominable
(B) hideous is to dreary
(C) embarrassed is to humiliated
(D) inflated is to deflated
(E) abridged is to abbreviated

Check-up 3-1

Directions Each of the following questions consists of one word followed by five words or phrases. You are to select the one word or phrase whose meaning is closest to the word in capital letters.

1. CONFOUND
- (A) tickle
- (B) confuse
- (C) illustrate
- (D) snip
- (E) accost

2. CONFRONT
- (A) chatter
- (B) trip
- (C) rage
- (D) fling
- (E) challenge

3. CONGENIAL
- (A) feasible
- (B) boring
- (C) fair
- (D) amiable
- (E) prevented

4. CONJECTURE
- (A) guess
- (B) overlook
- (C) recall
- (D) absorb
- (E) swipe

5. CONQUEST
- (A) display
- (B) spite
- (C) bump
- (D) delegate
- (E) defeat

6. CONSPICUOUS
- (A) jocular
- (B) remarkable
- (C) cogent
- (D) empirical
- (E) inherent

7. CONSPIRE
- (A) scheme
- (B) frown
- (C) spit
- (D) complain
- (E) grant

8. CONSTANT
- (A) hilarious
- (B) solitary
- (C) unceasing
- (D) feisty
- (E) loathsome

9. CONSTRAINT
- (A) aim
- (B) restriction
- (C) object
- (D) stream
- (E) pace

10. CONTEMPORARY
- (A) dangerous
- (B) filthy
- (C) modern
- (D) conspicuous
- (E) manifold

Answer 1.B 2.E 3.D 4.A 5.E 6.B 7.A 8.C 9.B 10.C

Check-up 3-2

1. CONTEND
- (A) strengthen
- (B) cultivate
- (C) replace
- (D) consume
- (E) argue

2. CONTENTED
- (A) shapeless
- (B) happy
- (C) gloomy
- (D) finicky
- (E) amorphous

3. CONTINUOUS
- (A) decrepit
- (B) sparse
- (C) aforementioned
- (D) uninterrupted
- (E) noxious

4. CONTRACT
- (A) agreement
- (B) comment
- (C) subject
- (D) input
- (E) strap

5. CONTRIVE
- (A) instruct
- (B) address
- (C) devise
- (D) equip
- (E) devote

6. CONVENIENT
- (A) tepid
- (B) superfluous
- (C) discordant
- (D) fallacious
- (E) handy

7. CONVENTIONAL
- (A) fallow
- (B) customary
- (C) sanguine
- (D) comatose
- (E) seminal

8. CONVERSE
- (A) chat
- (B) subtract
- (C) rouse
- (D) enlarge
- (E) fasten

9. COOPERATE
- (A) prove
- (B) crush
- (C) collaborate
- (D) inherit
- (E) abuse

10. COORDINATE
- (A) stimulate
- (B) harmonize
- (C) imply
- (D) allow
- (E) acknowledge

Check-up 3-3

Directions Each of the following questions consists of one word followed by five words or phrases. You are to select the one word or phrase whose meaning is closest to the word in capital letters.

1. CORDIAL

(A) friendly
(B) greedy
(C) philanthropic
(D) treacherous
(E) indifferent

2. CORROBORATE

(A) imitate
(B) validate
(C) solve
(D) describe
(E) split

3. COUNTERACT

(A) civilize
(B) neutralize
(C) establish
(D) punch
(E) industrialize

4. COURTESY

(A) lid
(B) mess
(C) curve
(D) dye
(E) politeness

5. COWER

(A) approve
(B) accomplish
(C) hesitate
(D) cringe
(E) heal

6. CRAWL

(A) squeeze
(B) creep
(C) provoke
(D) contribute
(E) eliminate

7. CROUCH

(A) snoop
(B) eavesdrop
(C) stoop
(D) spy
(E) stretch

8. CRUCIAL

(A) vital
(B) urbane
(C) parochial
(D) fulsome
(E) profuse

9. CULTURED

(A) cultivated
(B) clandestine
(C) impious
(D) freaky
(E) seemly

10. CUNNING

(A) furtive
(B) sly
(C) destitute
(D) illustrious
(E) rife

Check-up 3-4

1. DAMP
- (A) tortuous
- (B) conscious
- (C) exemplary
- (D) omnivorous
- (E) saturated

2. DARING
- (A) audacious
- (B) humid
- (C) narrow-minded
- (D) versatile
- (E) prosperous

3. DAWDLE
- (A) bounce
- (B) reinforce
- (C) damn
- (D) prohibit
- (E) linger

4. DEARTH
- (A) status
- (B) statute
- (C) shortage
- (D) surplus
- (E) excess

5. DEBACLE
- (A) fiasco
- (B) survey
- (C) landscape
- (D) curse
- (E) favor

6. DECEIVE
- (A) cope
- (B) mislead
- (C) deal
- (D) flee
- (E) sympathize

7. DECEPTIVE
- (A) delusive
- (B) felicitous
- (C) canine
- (D) arrogant
- (E) pretentious

8. DECLARE
- (A) invest
- (B) suffer
- (C) congratulate
- (D) spur
- (E) assert

9. DEFIANCE
- (A) resistance
- (B) malfunction
- (C) delegate
- (D) comparison
- (E) commencement

10. DEJECTED
- (A) akin
- (B) bovine
- (C) constructive
- (D) despondent
- (E) complicit

Check-up 3-5

Directions Each of the following questions consists of one word followed by five words or phrases.
You are to select the one word or phrase whose meaning is closest to the word in capital letters.

1. DELEGATE
(A) stature
(B) rim
(C) orbit
(D) contrast
(E) representative

2. DELIBERATE
(A) winsome
(B) covetous
(C) dismal
(D) pompous
(E) intentional

3. DELICACY
(A) prestige
(B) fragility
(C) hazard
(D) stature
(E) audacity

4. DELUGE
(A) conduct
(B) ambition
(C) flood
(D) border
(E) cable

5. DEMOLISH
(A) destroy
(B) convey
(C) drift
(D) attract
(E) amaze

6. DENOUNCE
(A) accompany
(B) define
(C) enable
(D) criticize
(E) deposit

7. DEPLETE
(A) digest
(B) examine
(C) regret
(D) mystify
(E) reduce

8. DETACH
(A) arouse
(B) coast
(C) disconnect
(D) pause
(E) surrender

9. DETAILED
(A) additional
(B) arctic
(C) bold
(D) cunning
(E) thorough

10. DEVICE
(A) ordeal
(B) respect
(C) version
(D) outcome
(E) gear

65

Answer 1.E 2.E 3.B 4.C 5.A 6.D 7.E 8.C 9.E 10.E

MIDDLE LEVEL Lesson 4-1

151	devious	156	disclose
152	dexterous	157	disgrace
153	dignified	158	disguise
154	dilemma	159	dishearten
155	diligence	160	dismay

"If you tell the truth, you don't have to remember anything."

- Mark Twain

SSATKOREA.com

devious
[**dee**-vee-*uh*s]

adj. departing from the most direct way

정직하지 못한, 속이는

*She has **devious** ways of making money.*

syn. underhanded, deceitful, dishonest

dexterous
[**dek**-str*uh*s]

adj. attracting notice or attention, worthy of notice

손재주가 매우 좋은, 솜씨 좋은

*Power users are **dexterous** at using new gadgets.*

syn. agile, nimble, adroit

dignified
[**dig**-nuh-fahyd]

adj. characterized or marked by dignity of aspect or manner

위엄 있는, 품위 있는

*She maintained a **dignified** silence as a queen.*

syn. glorified, stately, majestic

dilemma
[dih-**lem**-uh]

n. a situation requiring a choice between equally undesirable alternatives

딜레마, 곤경, 궁지

*The ranchers often face the **dilemma** of feeding themselves or their cattle.*

syn. quandary, predicament, plight

diligence
[**dil**-i-j*uh*ns]

n. constant and earnest effort to accomplish what is undertaken

근면, 성실, 부지런함

***Diligence** is the mother of success.*

syn. conscientiousness, assiduousness, assiduity

disclose
[dih-**sklohz**]

v. to make known

밝히다, 폭로하다

*She **disclosed** her rival's gossips to the press.*

syn. reveal, debunk, unveil

disgrace
[dis-**greys**]

n. the loss of respect, honor, or esteem
불명예, 망신, 수치

He's a disgrace to his family.

syn. ignominy, dishonor, shame

disguise
[dis-**gahyz**]

v. to hide an opinion, a feeling, etc.
변장하다, 가장하다

He tried to disguise his voice with holding a handkerchief to the mouthpiece.

syn. camouflage, conceal, hide

dishearten
[dis-**hahr**-tn]

v. to make a person lose confidence, hope, and energy
낙심시키다, 실망시키다

He was very disheartened by the results of the test.

syn. discourage, dispirit, demoralize

dismay
[dis-**mey**]

v. to break down the courage of completely, as by sudden danger or trouble
실망하게 하다, 경악하게 만들다

They were dismayed by the condition of the hotel.

syn. appall, horrify, shock

Sentence Completion 4-1

Directions : Fill in the blanks to complete the sentences.

1. A player's _____ ball handling and footwork mesmerized young soccer fans.

2. _____ credit card companies lure younger people into debt with offers of low interest rates.

3. The government faces this awful _____ : raise interest rates and slow the economy or lower them and risk serious inflation.

4. His reckless behaviors _____ the entire family.

5. They worked with _____ to paint a wall.

6. Fine clothes may _____, but silly words will disclose a fool."

7. Hardship may _____ at first, but every hardship passes away.

Answers

1 dexterous
2 Devious
3 dilemma
4 disgrace
5 diligence
6 disguise
7 dishearten

161	disregard	166	distraction
162	dissuade	167	distress
163	distasteful	168	divisive
164	distend	169	docile
165	distort	170	dominant

"A friend is someone who knows all about you and still loves you."

- Elbert Hubbard

SSATKOREA.com

disregard
[dis-ri-**gahrd**]

v. to pay no attention to
무시하다, 묵살하다

The evidence is too substantial to disregard.

syn.   snub, ignore, overlook

dissuade
[dih-**sweyd**]

v. to deter by advice or persuasion
(~을 하지 않도록) ~를 설득하다

Her family tried to dissuade him from studying abroad.

syn.   discourage, foil, frustrate

distasteful
[dis-**teyst**-fuhl]

adj. unpleasant, offensive, or causing dislike
불쾌한, 혐오스러운

People complained about the distasteful odor.

syn.   unpleasant, disagreeable, obnoxious

distend
[dih-**stend**]

v. to expand by stretching, as something hollow or elastic
팽창시키다, 부풀리다

Air is introduced into the stomach to distend it.

syn.   swell, dilate, bulge

distort
[dih-**stawrt**]

v. to twist awry or out of shape, to give a false, perverted, or disproportionate meaning to
비틀다, 왜곡시키다

The pipe will distort as you bend it.

syn.   garble, twist, falsify

distraction
[dih-**strak**-shuhn]

n. the act of distracting
집중을 방해하는 것

Her kids drive her to distraction at times.

syn.   diversion, interruption, disturbance

distress
[dih-**stres**]

n. great pain, anxiety, or sorrow

고통, 괴로움

Ted was obviously in distress after the bankruptcy.

syn. trouble, suffering, affliction

divisive
[dih-**vahy**-siv]

adj. forming or expressing division or distribution

분열을 초래하는

The highly divisive issues cause disagreement or hostility between people.

syn. dissenting, alienating, discordant

docile
[**dos**-*uh*l]

adj. easily managed or handled

고분고분한, 유순한

The docile workers were ready to accept control or instruction.

syn. compliant, obedient, pliant

dominant
[**dom**-uh-n*uh*nt]

adj. occupying or being in a commanding or elevated position

우세한, 지배적인

The company is in the most dominant position in the market.

syn. presiding, ruling, governing

Sentence Completion 4-2

Directions : **Fill in the blanks to complete the sentences.**

1. She complains that her family has a complete _____ for her privacy.

2. Discussing politics usually leads _____ talk at your family's Thanksgiving dinner.

3. A _____ movie disturbed her so much that she left the theater before it's over.

4. When cell phones first came out, their _____ use was for making calls.

5. When she saw his broken leg, she tried to _____ him from going to the Europe.

6. A pregnancy would cause a stomach to _____.

7. A _____ student is willing to be taught.

Answers

1 disregard
2 divisive
3 distasteful
4 dominant
5 dissuade
6 distend
7 docile

---

171 domineering 176 dynamic

172 drought 177 eager

173 drowsy 178 economical

174 durable 179 edible

175 dwindle 180 efficient

"If you judge people, you have no time to love them."
- Mother Teresa

SSATKOREA.com

domineering
[dom-uh-**neer**-ing]

adj. inclined to rule arbitrarily or despotically
거만한, 지배하려 드는, 폭군적인

She found him arrogant and domineering.

syn. overbearing, authoritarian, imperious

drought
[drout]

n. a period of dry weather, especially a long one that is injurious to crops
가뭄

The rain ended a six-month drought.

syn. scarcity, deficiency, aridity

drowsy
[**drou**-zee]

adj. half-asleep
졸리는, 나른하게 만드는

A glass of wine can make her drowsy.

syn. sleepy, lethargic, soporific

durable
[**door**-uh-b*uh*l]

adj. able to resist, wear, decay, etc.
내구성이 있는, 오래가는

Gold is strong and durable.

syn. resistant, lasting, imperishable

dwindle
[**dwin**-dl]

v. to become smaller and smaller
줄어들다, 작아지다

Traffic dwindled when the construction was over.

syn. diminish, decrease, reduce

dynamic
[dahy-**nam**-ik]

adj. pertaining to or characterized by energy or effective action
정력적인, 활발한

His performance is dynamic and passionate in every move.

syn. active, energetic, vigorous

eager
[**ee**-ger]

adj. keen or ardent in desire or feeling

열렬한, 간절히 바라는

*The young boys are **eager** for new knowledge.*

syn. enthusiastic, avid, fervent

economical
[ek-uh-**nom**-i-k*uh*l]

adj. avoiding waste or extravagance

경제적인, 절약하는

*This pipe is **economical** in metal and therefore light in weight.*

syn. frugal, prudent, careful

edible
[**ed**-uh-b*uh*l]

adj. fit to be eaten as food

먹을 수 있는, 식용의

*They tried to find **edible** mushrooms.*

syn. consumable, digestible, palatable

efficient
[ih-**fish**-*uh*nt]

adj. performing or functioning in the best possible manner with the least waste of time and effort

능률적인, 효율적인

*LED lamps are **efficient** at converting electricity into light.*

syn. effective, adept, able

Sentence Completion 4-3

Directions : Fill in the blanks to complete the sentences.

1. The _____ dictator is strong-willed and overbearing.

2. When there is a _____, there's not enough rainfall.

3. He was so _____ after a big lunch.

4. All can _____, or shrink away, if we don't handle them properly.

5. Even the most exciting rural town won't be as _____ as a big city.

6. To his relief, they all seemed _____ to speak to him.

7. If it's _____, you can eat it.

181	egress	186	enact
182	elaborate	187	enclose
183	emergent	188	encounter
184	empower	189	endurance
185	emulate	190	enhance

"Live as if you were to die tomorrow.
Learn as if you were to live forever."
- Mahatma Gandhi

SSATKOREA.com

egress
[**ee**-gres]

n. the act or an instance of going, especially from an enclosed place

출구, 떠남, 나감

The passengers go through a narrow egress.

syn. exit, out

elaborate
[ih-**lab**-er-it]

adj. worked out with great care and nicety of detail

정교한, 정성들인

It requires more elaborate procedures than those just described.

syn. complicated, complex, intricate

emergent
[ih-**mur**-*juh*nt]

adj. coming into view or notice

신생의, 새로 생겨난

The emergent democracies of eastern Europe are the beginning of this change.

syn. appearing, developing, rising

empower
[em-**pou**-er]

v. to give power or authority to

권한을 주다

Nobody was empowered to sign checks on the boss's behalf.

syn. authorize, entitle, permit

emulate
[**em**-yuh-leyt]

v. to try to equal or excel

모방하다, 따라가다

Only a few people tried to emulate his greatness.

syn. imitate, copy, mirror

enact
[en-akt]

v. to make into an act or statue

제정하다, 법으로 만들다

This new legislation was enacted in 2012 to attract foreign investments.

syn. legislate, approve, perform

enclose
[en-**klohz**]

v. to shut or hem in

두르다, 에워싸다

Pure darkness enclosed space.

syn.   surround, hem, encompass

encounter
[en-**koun**-ter]

v. to come upon or meet with, especially unexpectedly

우연히 만나다, 맞닥뜨리다

You will encounter numerous problems.

syn.   meet, experience

endurance
[en-**door**-uhns]

n. the ability or strength to continue or last

인내, 참을성

Sean showed great endurance in the face of pain.

syn.   persistence, tenacity, perseverance

enhance
[en-**hans**]

v. to raise to a higher degree

높이다, 향상시키다

He refused to do more things to enhance his reputation.

syn.   improve, reinforce, intensify

Sentence Completion 4-4

Directions : **Fill in the blanks to complete the sentences.**

1.   After Michael Jordan retired from the NBA, player after player tried to _____ Jordan's game and success.

2.   An _____ lace pattern reveals the artisan's diligence.

3.   The number of doors needs to be reviewed as the means of _____ for emergencies.

4.   When you believe in someone, you _____ them to go after their dreams.

5.   The Internet was an _____ technology in the early 1990s.

6.   The Congress is going to _____ a new statute.

7.   If you practice more, you can _____ your chance to win.

Answers

1 emulate
2 elaborate
3 egress
4 empower
5 emergent
6 enact
7 enhance

191	enlarge	196	eradicate
192	enormous	197	erratic
193	entice	198	essential
194	entreat	199	evade
195	epoch	200	evident

*"What we dwell on
who we become."*
- Oprah Winfrey

SSATKOREA.com

enlarge
[en-**lahrj**]

v. to make larger
확장하다, 확대하다

We enlarged our swimming pool.

syn. extend, expand, swell

enormous
[ih-**nawr**-m*uh*s]

adj. greatly exceeding the common size, extent, etc.
거대한, 매우 큰

Your possibilities are enormous.

syn. colossal, mammoth, gigantic

entice
[en-**tahys**]

v. to lead on by exciting hope or desire
유도하다, 유인하다

The performance group needs to entice a new audience into the theater.

syn. tempt, lure, allure

entreat
[en-**treet**]

v. to ask (a person) earnestly
간청하다, 애원하다

Her husband entreated her not to leave.

syn. implore, beg, plead

epoch
[**ep**-*uh*k]

n. a particular period of time marked by distinctive features, events, etc.
시대, 기간

The art style is very common in the Victorian epoch.

syn. era, age, period

eradicate
[ih-**rad**-i-keyt]

v. to remove or destroy utterly
근절하다, 뿌리뽑다

This disease has been eradicated from the world.

syn. eliminate, remove, obliterate

erratic
[ih-**rat**-ik]

adj. deviating from the usual or proper course in conduct or opinion

불규칙한, 일정치 않은

*The old man's breath was **erratic**.*

syn. unpredictable, inconsistent, idiosyncratic

essential
[uh-**sen**-sh*uh*l]

adj. absolutely necessary

필수적인

*A filament is an **essential** part in a light bulb.*

syn. vital, crucial, indispensable

evade
[ih-**veyd**]

v. to escape from by trickery or cleverness

피하다, 모면하다

*He tried to kiss her, but she **evaded** him.*

syn. elude, avoid, dodge

evident
[**ev**-i-duhnt]

adj. plain or clear to the sight

명백한, 분명한

*Queen's frown made it **evident** to all that she was displeased.*

syn. apparent, clear, obvious

Sentence Completion 4-5

Directions : **Fill in the blanks to complete the sentences.**

1. The office decided not to undertake the project because of the _____ costs involved.

2. My friend tried to _____ me by offering to buy me popcorn and a soda to go to the movie together.

3. It's _____ that public health is part of national security.

4. The Civil War era was an _____ in 19th-century U.S. history.

5. His unpredictable and _____ behaviors baffled me.

6. The mayor has decided to _____ corruption, poverty, or diseases rampant in the city.

7. To prevent fires, it's _____ to turn off appliances before leaving the house.

Answers

1 enormous
2 entice
3 evident
4 epoch
5 erratic
6 eradicate
7 essential

SSAT MIDDLE LEVEL **75**

Analogy 4. Study

학문과 연구대상 또는 학자와 연구 대상을 연결짓는 관계입니다.

학문 : 연구대상

botany : plant
식물학 : 식물

zoology : animal
동물학 : 동물

aesthetics : beauty
미학 : 아름다움

petrology : rock
암석학 : 암석

phonetics : sound
음성학 : (언어의) 소리

semantics : meaning
의미론 : (언어의) 의미

학자 : 연구대상

archeologist : artifact
고고학자 : 유물

ornithologist : birds
조류학자 : 새, 조류

meteorologist : weather
기상학자 : 날씨

physicist : physics
물리학자 : 물리학

astronomer : space
천문학자 : 우주

spelunker : cave
동굴 탐험가 : 동굴

POP QUIZ

1. Entomology is to insects as
- (A) etymology is to words
- (B) aesthetic is to sedatives
- (C) petrology is to oil
- (D) phonetics is to telephone
- (E) abacus is to computer

2. Archeologist is to artifact as
- (A) astronomer is to sun
- (B) physician is to physics
- (C) meteorologist is to space
- (D) analyst is to finance
- (E) spelunker is to cave

Check-up 4-1

Directions Each of the following questions consists of one word followed by five words or phrases.
You are to select the one word or phrase whose meaning is closest to the word in capital letters.

1. DEVIOUS
(A) apparent
(B) deceitful
(C) fatal
(D) obvious
(E) irresistible

2. DEXTEROUS
(A) vacant
(B) intelligent
(C) nimble
(D) suitable
(E) primary

3. DIGNIFIED
(A) opposite
(B) current
(C) jagged
(D) finicky
(E) glorified

4. DILEMMA
(A) definition
(B) quandary
(C) curiosity
(D) objective
(E) cycle

5. DILIGENCE
(A) assiduity
(B) misery
(C) graduate
(D) indifference
(E) similarity

6. DISCLOSE
(A) govern
(B) promote
(C) grasp
(D) reveal
(E) doze

7. DISGRACE
(A) conference
(B) ignominy
(C) survey
(D) attitude
(E) nursery

8. DISGUISE
(A) camouflage
(B) confess
(C) tackle
(D) drift
(E) credit

9. DISHEARTEN
(A) launch
(B) arrange
(C) steer
(D) crumple
(E) dispirit

10. DISMAY
(A) scatter
(B) horrify
(C) injure
(D) vanish
(E) frustrate

Answer 1.B 2.C 3.E 4.B 5.A 6.D 7.B 8.A 9.E 10.B

Check-up 4-2

Each of the following questions consists of one word followed by five words or phrases. You are to select the one word or phrase whose meaning is closest to the word in capital letters.

1. DISREGARD
(A) stress
(B) urge
(C) ignore
(D) volunteer
(E) starve

2. DISSUADE
(A) defend
(B) flutter
(C) tan
(D) influence
(E) discourage

3. DISTASTEFUL
(A) mental
(B) unpleasant
(C) vigorous
(D) positive
(E) gradual

4. DISTEND
(A) contain
(B) rely
(C) elect
(D) swell
(E) thrive

5. DISTORT
(A) amaze
(B) twist
(C) arouse
(D) memorize
(E) reverse

6. DISTRACTION
(A) cocoon
(B) diversion
(C) prank
(D) tentacle
(E) talent

7. DISTRESS
(A) dangle
(B) smuggle
(C) trouble
(D) forsake
(E) humiliate

8. DIVISIVE
(A) dissenting
(B) novel
(C) average
(D) marine
(E) individual

9. DOCILE
(A) transparent
(B) frail
(C) compliant
(D) sufficient
(E) mature

10. DOMINANT
(A) exceptional
(B) recessive
(C) obstinate
(D) ruling
(E) eager

Check-up 4-3

Directions Each of the following questions consists of one word followed by five words or phrases.
You are to select the one word or phrase whose meaning is closest to the word in capital letters.

1. DOMINEERING
(A) deliberate
(B) overbearing
(C) amiable
(D) artificial
(E) parallel

2. DROUGHT
(A) feature
(B) spine
(C) scarcity
(D) court
(E) cylinder

3. DROWSY
(A) spacious
(B) eventual
(C) vast
(D) ancient
(E) lethargic

4. DURABLE
(A) scarce
(B) lasting
(C) flexible
(D) annual
(E) abreast

5. DWINDLE
(A) behold
(B) diminish
(C) deprive
(D) detest
(E) pierce

6. DYNAMIC
(A) energetic
(B) stout
(C) vain
(D) active
(E) crude

7. EAGER
(A) humble
(B) petty
(C) enthusiastic
(D) familiar
(E) temporary

8. ECONOMICAL
(A) frugal
(B) precious
(C) entire
(D) threadbare
(E) famished

9. EDIBLE
(A) instant
(B) prompt
(C) shallow
(D) digestible
(E) frequent

10. EFFICIENT
(A) utter
(B) foremost
(C) apt
(D) considerable
(E) adept

79

Check-up 4-4

Each of the following questions consists of one word followed by five words or phrases. You are to select the one word or phrase whose meaning is closest to the word in capital letters.

1. EGRESS
   (A) fanatic
   (B) exit
   (C) lack
   (D) entrance
   (E) entry

2. ELABORATE
   (A) mammoth
   (B) content
   (C) severe
   (D) intricate
   (E) fortunate

3. EMERGENT
   (A) furious
   (B) capital
   (C) developing
   (D) stingy
   (E) external

4. EMPOWER
   (A) authorize
   (B) despise
   (C) increase
   (D) attend
   (E) observe

5. EMULATE
   (A) wander
   (B) imitate
   (C) chord
   (D) consider
   (E) applaud

6. ENACT
   (A) ail
   (B) cherish
   (C) legislate
   (D) coax
   (E) develop

7. ENCLOSE
   (A) implore
   (B) approach
   (C) refine
   (D) surround
   (E) astonish

8. ENCOUNTER
   (A) intend
   (B) permit
   (C) revise
   (D) astound
   (E) meet

9. ENDURANCE
   (A) forlorn
   (B) keen
   (C) widespread
   (D) persistence
   (E) distant

10. ENHANCE
   (A) utilize
   (B) recognize
   (C) intensify
   (D) arrest
   (E) seize

Check-up 4-5

Directions   Each of the following questions consists of one word followed by five words or phrases. You are to select the one word or phrase whose meaning is closest to the word in capital letters.

1. ENLARGE
- (A) achieve
- (B) expand
- (C) separate
- (D) approve
- (E) obtain

2. ENORMOUS
- (A) melancholy
- (B) destructive
- (C) exquisite
- (D) sensitive
- (E) colossal

3. ENTICE
- (A) allure
- (B) slay
- (C) plead
- (D) distribute
- (E) ensure

4. ENTREAT
- (A) represent
- (B) implore
- (C) confirm
- (D) shun
- (E) forbid

5. EPOCH
- (A) tour
- (B) hamlet
- (C) era
- (D) fare
- (E) trio

6. ERADICATE
- (A) eliminate
- (B) eject
- (C) boast
- (D) summon
- (E) create

7. ERRATIC
- (A) idiosyncratic
- (B) tragic
- (C) hearty
- (D) crafty
- (E) apparent

8. ESSENTIAL
- (A) drowsy
- (B) sentimental
- (C) sole
- (D) crucial
- (E) shrewd

9. EVADE
- (A) inhale
- (B) exclaim
- (C) alter
- (D) occupy
- (E) avoid

10. EVIDENT
- (A) charming
- (B) disillusioned
- (C) muddled
- (D) staunch
- (E) apparent

81

201	excessive	206	expand
202	exclude	207	expert
203	exemplary	208	explicit
204	exhaust	209	expound
205	exhort	210	exquisite

"Every strike brings me closer to the next home run."
- Babe Ruth

SSATKOREA.com

excessive
[ik-**ses**-iv]

adj. going beyond the usual, necessary, or proper limit or degree

지나친, 과도한

She was drinking excessive amounts of wine.

syn. immoderate, intemperate, imprudent

exclude
[ik-**sklood**]

v. to keep from being a part of something

제외하다, 빼다

Women had been excluded from many scientific societies.

syn. expel, forbid, ban, boycott

exemplary
[ig-**zem**-pluh-ree]

adj. worthy of imitation

모범적인

Her works are exemplary of certain feminist arguments.

syn. admirable, perfect, ideal

exhaust
[ig-**zawst**]

v. to drain of strength or energy

(에너지나 기력을) 다 써버리다

This long journey had exhausted her.

syn. consume, fatigue, deplete

exhort
[ig-**zawrt**]

v. to urge, advise, or caution earnestly

열심히 권하다, 촉구하다

The social media has been exhorting people to turn out for the showing.

syn. urge, encourage, enjoin

expand
[ik-**spand**]

v. to make larger in size, amount, volume, or scope

넓히다, 확장하다

Baby birds cannot expand and contract their lungs.

syn. extend, augment, broaden

expert
[**ek**-spurt]

n. a person who has a lot of knowledge about a subject

전문가

They are accredited as experts in legal and financial advice.

syn. veteran, master, specialist, authority

explicit
[ik-**splis**-it]

adj. clear, direct, and specific as to leave no doubt about the meaning

명백한, 확실한

The writer's intentions were not made explicit.

syn. obvious, apparent, clear

expound
[ik-**spound**]

v. to set forth or state in detail

자세히 설명하다

She declined to expound on her decision.

syn. present, explain, interpret

exquisite
[ik-**skwiz**-it]

adj. of special beauty of charm, or rare and appealing excellence

매우 아름다운, 정교한

They were surprised with her exquisite taste in painting.

syn. elegant, magnificent, excellent

Sentence Completion 5-1

Directions : Fill in the blanks to complete the sentences.

1. You can blow into a balloon and make it _____.

2. If you want to be an _____ in certain areas, you need more hands-on experience.

3. She is an _____ skater who is an excellent example to others.

4. Wearing a ball gown for a casual lunch is so _____; it is too much.

5. Miners deplete a mineral deposit and _____ the resource.

6. She has somewhat _____ taste, so she is able to make fine distinctions.

7. When you try to teach the kids, you need to give them _____ instructions.

Answers

1 expand
2 expert
3 exemplary
4 excessive
5 exhaust
6 exquisite
7 explicit

211	extend	216	famine
212	exuberant	217	fascinate
213	factor	218	ferocious
214	fallacy	219	fertile
215	falsify	220	fervent

"Some people want it to happen,
some wish it would happen,
others make it happen."

- Michael Jordan

SSATKOREA.com

extend
[ik-**stend**]

v. to stretch out
늘이다, 더 길게 만들다

Middle schools may consider extending the class day from five to seven periods.

syn.   expand, enlarge, increase

exuberant
[ig-**zoo**-ber-*uh*nt]

adj. effusively and almost uninhibitedly enthusiastic
활기 넘치는

This type of arch is a flamboyant and exuberant architectural invention.

syn.   ebullient, buoyant, cheerful

factor
[**fak**-ter]

n. a fact or circumstance that contributes to a result
요인, 요소

His health problem was not a factor in his decision.

syn.   determinant, cause, element

fallacy
[**fal**-uh-see]

n. a deceptive, misleading, or false notion or belief
오류, 틀린 생각

The most common fallacy is to suppose that wealth brings happiness.

syn.   illusion, misconception, falsehood

falsify
[**fawl**-suh-fahy]

v. to make false or incorrect,
속이다, 위조하다

The hypothesis is falsified by the evidence.

syn.   misrepresent, fake, counterfeit

famine
[**fam**-in]

n. extreme and general scarcity of food purpose, intent, etc.
기근, 기아

Widespread famine had triggered this violent protest.

syn.   starvation, hunger, drought

fascinate
[**fas**-uh-neyt]

v. to attract and hold attentively by a unique power, personal charm, unusual nature, or some other special quality

마음을 사로잡다, 매혹하다

He has always been fascinated by other cultures.

syn. interest, captivate, engross

ferocious
[fuh-**roh**-sh*uh*s]

adj. savagely fierce, as a wild beast, person, action, or aspect

흉포한, 맹렬한, 격렬한

The puma is nature's most ferocious and violent animal.

syn. fierce, savage, brutal

fertile
[**fur**-tl]

adj. bearing or capable of bearing offspring

비옥한, 기름진

He decided to buy some fields along the fertile flood-plains of the river.

syn. fecund, fruitful, productive

fervent
[**fur**-v*uh*nt]

adj. having or showing great warmth or intensity of spirit, feeling, enthusiasm, etc.

열렬한, 강렬한

The government confronted a fervent opposite of tax reform.

syn. zealous, passionate, intense

Sentence Completion 5-2

Directions : Fill in the blanks to complete the sentences.

1. Due to her _____ desire to become an actress, she could not give up her stage.

2. Money is probably a big _____ in the travel plans under a shoestring budget.

3. The wolverine is nature's most _____ and violent animal.

4. When the bell rang on the last section of the test, she was _____ .

5. It's a common _____ to suppose that wealth brings happiness.

6. Rabbits are famously _____ creatures; they can have several generations in a matter of months.

7. She _____ her hand as she offered to shake.

Answers

1 fervent
2 factor
3 ferocious
4 exuberant
5 fallacy
6 fertile
7 extend

MIDDLE LEVEL Lesson 5-3

221	fierce	226	fledgling
222	fiery	227	flippant
223	flamboyant	228	flounder
224	flatter	229	focus
225	flawless	230	foible

"Dare to err and to dream."

- Friedrich Schiller

SSATKOREA.com

fierce
[feers]

adj. very violent or powerful

사나운, 험악한

A tiger is a fierce predator.

syn. ferocious, aggressive, intense

fiery
[**fahy***uh***r**-ee]

adj. burning brightly and strongly

불타는 듯한, 불의

The crowd was agitated by the fiery speech.

syn. passionate, blazing, flaming

flamboyant
[flam-**boi**-*uh*nt]

adj. strikingly bold or brilliant

이색적인, 대담한

Her flamboyant fashion styles are brightly colored, oddly patterned, or unusual.

syn. showy, extravagant, ostentatious

flatter
[**flat**-er]

v. to give a compliment, especially for the purpose of gaining something

아첨하다, 알랑거리다

She was flattering him to avoid doing what he wanted.

syn. compliment, adulate, fawn

flawless
[**flaw**-lis]

adj. having no defects or faults, especially none that diminish the value of something

흠 하나 없는, 나무랄 데 없는

She greeted him in almost flawless English.

syn. perfect, impeccable, unblemished

fledgling
[**flej**-ling]

n. a young bird that has grown feathers and is learning to fly or a beginner

(막 날기 시작한) 어린 새, 신출내기, 초보자

The fledgling has just developed wings not enough for flight.

syn. greenhorn, novice, rookie, tyro

flippant

[**flip**-*uh*nt]

adj. frivolously disrespectful, shallow, or lacking in seriousness

경솔한, 건방진

He frowned as he heard the boy's flippant remark.

syn.   frivolous, facetious, disrespectful

flounder

[**floun**-der]

v. to struggle with stumbling, or plunging movements

몸부림치다, 허우적거리다, 허둥대다

The little boy was floundering at the edge of the shallow brook.

syn.   struggle, stumble, wallow

focus

[**foh**-k*uh*s]

n. the center of one's attention

초점, 관심의 중심점

Our focus is on the customer's complaints.

syn.   focal point, spotlight, center

foible

[**foi**-b*uh*l]

n. a minor weakness or failing of character

약점

Family members have to tolerate each other's little foibles.

syn.   defect, flaw, weakness, shortcoming

Sentence Completion 5-3

Directions : Fill in the blanks to complete the sentences.

1. A fuzzy _____ has just learned to fly.

2. A _____ performer dressed up with feathers, sequins, and beads.

3. Despite their loss, his team put up a _____ fight against the strongest opponents.

4. Most people have an idiosyncrasy, but interestingly, a person rarely sees his or her own characteristic _____.

5. Because I want my mom to offer me a ride, I _____ her by telling her she's the best driver in the world.

6. She was as _____ as the impeccable marble statues.

7. His _____ reply was casual to the point of sarcasm and disrespect.

MIDDLE LEVEL Lesson 5-4

231 force	236 fragment
232 forthright	237 frenzied
233 fortify	238 fretful
234 foundation	239 frugal
235 fragile	240 fruitful

"Whatever you are,
be a good one."

- Abraham Lincoln

SSATKOREA.com

force
[fawrs, fohrs]

v. to compel or oblige to do something

강요하다, 억지로 하게 하다

The police officer forced a suspect to confess.

syn. coerce, impel, compel

forthright
[fawrth-rahyt]

adj. going straight to the point

솔직 담백한

His forthright manner can be mistaken for rudeness.

syn. straightforward, honest, frank

fortify
[fawr-tuh-fahy]

v. to protect or strengthen against attack

강화하다, 요새처럼 만들다

The bright intellect was fortified by the profound knowledge.

syn. strengthen, reinforce, toughen

foundation
[foun-dey-shuhn]

n. the beginning point and support from which something develops

기초, 기반, (건물의) 토대

No good building exists without a good foundation.

syn. basis, base, groundwork, infrastructure

fragile
[fraj-uhll]

adj. easily broken, shattered, or damaged

부서지기 쉬운, 손상되기 쉬운

Be careful not to drop it; it's very fragile.

syn. frail, feeble, brittle

fragment
[frag-muhnt]

n. a part broken off or detached

조각, 파편

I heard only a fragment of their conversation.

syn. piece, bit, particle

frenzied
[**fren**-zeed]

adj. wildly excited or enthusiastic

광분한, 매우 화난, 미친듯한

There was no getting away from his frenzied assault.

syn. frantic, wild, frenetic

fretful
[**fret**-*fuhl*]

adj. irritable or peevish

안달하는, 초조해하는, 짜증 잘내는

Babies soon become fretful when they are tired or hungry.

syn. fidgeting, irritable, distressed

frugal
[**froo**-*guhl*]

adj. economical in use or expenditure

절약하는, 검소한

She lived a very frugal life, avoiding all luxuries.

syn. thrifty, economical, careful

fruitful
[**froot**-*fuhl*]

adj. producing good results

생산적인, 유익한

He lived a fruitful life as a man can only die once.

syn. fertile, productive, prolific

Sentence Completion 5-4

Directions : **Fill in the blanks to complete the sentences.**

1. My _____ aunt lives her life simply and economically.

2. As one of the most popular rock stars, he has enjoyed a _____ crowd at his concerts.

3. A business is _____ if it creates profits and expands.

4. The glass vase is so _____ and easily broken.

5. Written goals can exert a _____ or have a strong influence on your achievement.

6. As he was waiting to hear whether or not he's been accepted into the prestigious boarding school, he was upset and _____.

7. He always welcomes any _____ advice; He really appreciates it.

Answers

1	frugal
2	frenzied
3	fruitful
4	fragile
5	force
6	fretful
7	forthright

241	frustrate	246	futile
242	fulfill	247	gallant
243	fumble	248	genesis
244	furnish	249	genre
245	furtive	250	genuine

*"Energy and persistence
conquer all things."*

- Benjamin Franklin

SSATKOREA.com

frustrate
[**fruhs**-treyt]

v. to disappoint or thwart
좌절감을 주다, 불만스럽게 만들다

The failure didn't frustrate him.

syn. thwart, foil, dissuade

fulfill
[fool-**fil**]

v. to carry out, or bring to realization,
as a prophecy or promise
(의무나 약속을) 다하다, 이루다

I have a promise to fulfill as well.

syn. achieve, attain, realize, satisfy

fumble
[**fuhm**-b*uhl*]

v. to feel or grope about clumsily
(찾느라고 손으로) 더듬거리다

*He bit his lip and began to fumble
with his tie.*

syn. grope for, mishandle, bumble

furnish
[**fur**-nish]

v. to put furniture and other needed
items in a building
(가구를) 비치하다

*I'll furnish my own place according
to my own taste.*

syn. supply, provide, equip

furtive
[**fur**-tiv]

adj. done in a quiet and secretive way
은밀한, 엉큼한

He cast a furtive glance at her.

syn. secretive, surreptitious, clandestine

futile
[**fyoot**-l]

adj. incapable of producing any result
헛된, 소용없는

*The teacher described these activities
as futile.*

syn. useless, vain, fruitless

gallant
[**gal**-*uh*nt]

adj. brave, spirited, noble-minded, or chivalrous

용감한, 용맹한

The general is famous for his gallant and successful defense in the war.

syn. valiant, brave, valorous

genesis
[**jen**-uh-sis]

n. an origin, creation, or beginning

시작, 창조, 기원

It was the genesis of the Great Empire.

syn. origin, source, formation

genre
[**zhahn**-ruh]

n. a class or category of artistic endeavor having a particular form

장르, 분야, 카테고리

What genre does the movie fall into - fantasy or action?

syn. category, class, sort

genuine
[**jen**-yoo-in]

adj. possessing the claimed or attributed character, quality, or origin

진짜의, 진품의

Is it genuine or fake?

syn. authentic, real, actual, sincere

Sentence Completion 5-5

Directions : Fill in the blanks to complete the sentences.

1. The treasure chests were filled with _____ gold bars.

2. The princess would be grateful for the knight's _____ actions to rescue her.

3. The _____ of jazz was West African cultural and musical expression including blues and ragtime.

4. Pouring water into a leaky bucket is _____.

5. The robbers exchanged a _____ glance when they realized their actions had been caught.

6. What _____ do you like to read the most?

7. We should accept ourselves as we are and try to _____ whatever dreams are within our capability.

Answers

1 genuine
2 gallant
3 genesis
4 futile
5 furtive
6 genre
7 fulfill

Analogy 5. Doctors

의학을 다루는 여러 의사와 그들이 연구하거나 치료하는 대상을 연결짓는 관계입니다.

cardiologist : heart
심장 전문의 : 심장

psychiatrist : mind
정신과 전문의 : 정신, 심리

dermatologist : skin
피부과 의사 : 피부

oculist : eyes
안과의사 : 눈

geriatrician : elderly
노인병 의사 : 노인들

pediatrician : children
소아과 의사 : 아이들

anatomist : dissection
해부학자 : 해부

chiropractor : spine
척추 지압사 : 척추

orthodontist : teeth
치과 교정 의사 : 치아

orthopedist : skeleton
정형외과 의사 : 뼈대, 골격

physician : medical practice
내과의사 : 의료

surgeon : surgery
외과의사 : 수술

POP QUIZ

1. Psychiatrist is to mind as
- (A) husbandry is to farmer
- (B) surgeon is to rehabilitation
- (C) dermatologist is to skin
- (D) pollster is to garment
- (E) physiatrist is to operation

2. Geriatrician is to elderly as
- (A) neurologist is to liver
- (B) oculist is to stomach
- (C) coroner is to specimen
- (D) podiatrist is to brain
- (E) pediatrician is to children

Check-up 5-1

Directions   Each of the following questions consists of one word followed by five words or phrases.
             You are to select the one word or phrase whose meaning is closest to the word in capital letters.

1. EXCESSIVE
(A) abrupt
(B) quaint
(C) immoderate
(D) modest
(E) typical

2. EXCLUDE
(A) expel
(B) elevate
(C) decay
(D) intrude
(E) cease

3. EXEMPLARY
(A) dreary
(B) sullen
(C) ideal
(D) fragile
(E) dejected

4. EXHAUST
(A) ease
(B) conclude
(C) blend
(D) consume
(E) recommend

5. EXHORT
(A) relent
(B) dispute
(C) urge
(D) console
(E) encircle

6. EXPAND
(A) cower
(B) parch
(C) banish
(D) locate
(E) extend

7. EXPERT
(A) elder
(B) veteran
(C) benefit
(D) terror
(E) torment

8. EXPLICIT
(A) obvious
(B) valiant
(C) provocative
(D) approximate
(E) evident

9. EXPOUND
(A) explain
(B) communicate
(C) persuade
(D) afford
(E) recite

10. EXQUISITE
(A) capable
(B) complete
(C) essential
(D) recent
(E) magnificent

Answer 1.C 2.A 3.C 4.D 5.C 6.E 7.B 8.A 9.A 10.E

Check-up 5-2

Each of the following questions consists of one word followed by five words or phrases. You are to select the one word or phrase whose meaning is closest to the word in capital letters.

1. EXTEND
- (A) paralyze
- (B) prune
- (C) descend
- (D) enlarge
- (E) somber

2. EXUBERANT
- (A) ebullient
- (B) drab
- (C) overdue
- (D) dormant
- (E) animated

3. FACTOR
- (A) chamber
- (B) passage
- (C) element
- (D) feud
- (E) venture

4. FALLACY
- (A) treachery
- (B) profundity
- (C) falsehood
- (D) trickery
- (E) perfidy

5. FALSIFY
- (A) evaporate
- (B) reject
- (C) reveal
- (D) misrepresent
- (E) vary

6. FAMINE
- (A) bent
- (B) starvation
- (C) provision
- (D) incumbency
- (E) stipulation

7. FASCINATE
- (A) replace
- (B) suspect
- (C) migrate
- (D) captivate
- (E) dismay

8. FEROCIOUS
- (A) brutal
- (B) dormant
- (C) obscure
- (D) bland
- (E) major

9. FERTILE
- (A) primitive
- (B) rigid
- (C) fruitful
- (D) intense
- (E) dense

10. FERVENT
- (A) alert
- (B) zealous
- (C) substantial
- (D) overdue
- (E) feeble

Check-up 5-3

Directions   Each of the following questions consists of one word followed by five words or phrases. You are to select the one word or phrase whose meaning is closest to the word in capital letters.

1. FIERCE
(A) formal
(B) methodical
(C) somber
(D) ferocious
(E) tropical

2. FIERY
(A) tempestuous
(B) absurd
(C) puny
(D) ample
(E) passionate

3. FLAMBOYANT
(A) bland
(B) puny
(C) compatible
(D) tropical
(E) showy

4. FLATTER
(A) ban
(B) adulate
(C) scurry
(D) invade
(E) forecast

5. FLAWLESS
(A) perfect
(B) meager
(C) painstaking
(D) bracing
(E) carnivorous

6. FLEDGLING
(A) crew
(B) milestone
(C) novice
(D) landmark
(E) chasm

7. FLIPPANT
(A) obsolete
(B) frivolous
(C) previous
(D) equivalent
(E) edible

8. FLOUNDER
(A) mope
(B) stumble
(C) release
(D) insert
(E) depend

9. FOCUS
(A) limit
(B) structure
(C) freight
(D) border
(E) center

10. FOIBLE
(A) shaft
(B) rod
(C) gust
(D) flaw
(E) gulf

95

Check-up 5-4

Each of the following questions consists of one word followed by five words or phrases. You are to select the one word or phrase whose meaning is closest to the word in capital letters.

1. FORCE
(A) coerce
(B) falsify
(C) implicate
(D) burnish
(E) verify

2. FORTHRIGHT
(A) akin
(B) related
(C) straightforward
(D) optional
(E) aforementioned

3. FORTIFY
(A) nourish
(B) reinforce
(C) hibernate
(D) engage
(E) affect

4. FOUNDATION
(A) basis
(B) tournament
(C) cable
(D) nation
(E) process

5. FRAGILE
(A) compassionate
(B) brittle
(C) notable
(D) rebellious
(E) monstrous

6. FRAGMENT
(A) piece
(B) habit
(C) moisture
(D) recreation
(E) pattern

7. FRENZIED
(A) optimistic
(B) solitary
(C) frantic
(D) meddlesome
(E) harsh

8. FRETFUL
(A) nostalgic
(B) compatible
(C) significant
(D) irritable
(E) superior

9. FRUGAL
(A) thrifty
(B) burly
(C) ridiculous
(D) stupendous
(E) foolhardy

10. FRUITFUL
(A) nonchalant
(B) productive
(C) brilliant
(D) jubilant
(E) visible

Check-up 5-5

1. FRUSTRATE
(A) exceed
(B) trudge
(C) persist
(D) extinguish
(E) thwart

2. FULFILL
(A) plunge
(B) yield
(C) attain
(D) mock
(E) confuse

3. FUMBLE
(A) lean on
(B) give in
(C) grope for
(D) call up
(E) take over

4. FURNISH
(A) concern
(B) equip
(C) repent
(D) prepare
(E) recall

5. FURTIVE
(A) premature
(B) steadfast
(C) secretive
(D) minor
(E) desperate

6. FUTILE
(A) patient
(B) scalding
(C) vertical
(D) vain
(E) obscure

7. GALLANT
(A) evasive
(B) flimsy
(C) hilarious
(D) numerous
(E) brave

8. GENESIS
(A) malice
(B) interval
(C) span
(D) origin
(E) resident

9. GENRE
(A) deed
(B) cathedral
(C) myriad
(D) category
(E) carnival

10. GENUINE
(A) cumbersome
(B) boisterous
(C) authentic
(D) moral
(E) subsequent

251	gimmick	256	gracious
252	glare	257	greedy
253	glow	258	grotesque
254	gossip	259	guarded
255	graceful	260	guile

"This world is but a canvas to our imagination."

- Henry David Thoreau

SSATKOREA.com

gimmick
[**gim**-ik]

n. an ingenious or novel device or scheme

속임수 장치, 책략

Some food companies give small gifts with children's meals as a sales gimmick.

syn. finesse, scheme, trick

glare
[glair]

v. to stare with a fiercely or angrily piercing look

노려보다, 쏘아보다

He glared at his opponent with an angry face.

syn. stare, frown, gape

glow
[gloh]

v. to shine like something intensely heated

빛나다, 타다

The pebbles around the bonfire glowed red with the heat.

syn. burn, radiate, blaze

gossip
[**gos**-uhp]

n. idle talk or rumor, especially about the personal or private affairs of others

소문

The magazine was full of gossip about celebrities.

syn. rumor, scandal, news

graceful
[**greys**-fuhl]

adj. characterized by elegance or beauty of form, manner, movement, or speech

우아한, 매우 솜씨 좋은

Her movements were graceful and elegant.

syn. skilled, agile, charming

gracious
[**grey**-shuhs]

adj. pleasantly kind, benevolent, and courteous

친절한, 품위 있는

The gracious lady was very well-mannered and kind.

syn. courteous, polite, elegant, civil

greedy
[**gree**-dee]

adj. excessively or inordinately desirous of wealth, profit, etc.

욕심 많은, 탐욕스러운

The greedy merchant wants to have more money than is fair.

syn. gluttonous, ravenous, voracious

grotesque
[groh-**tesk**]

adj. odd or unnatural in shape, appearance, or character

모습이 이상하고 무서운, 기괴한

The grotesque statue was so unnatural and unpleasant.

syn. malformed, deformed, misshapen

guarded
[**gahr**-did]

adj. cautious and careful

조심스러운, 신중한

The guarded inspector was so careful not to show his feelings.

syn. cautious, careful, circumspect

guile
[gahyl]

n. insidious cunning in attaining a goal

속임수

I love children's innocence and lack of guile.

syn. cunning, craftiness, craft, artfulness

Sentence Completion 6-1

Directions : **Fill in the blanks to complete the sentences.**

1. Acting like a millionaire when you're actually unemployed would take a lot of _____.

2. The _____ ice skater's elegant move, great timing and well-chosen choreography seem to come naturally to some.

3. A gluttonous person is _____ for food.

4. He is a _____ person careful, restrained, and maybe a little bit wary.

5. The _____ host wants every guest to be comfortable.

6. She has seen all the celebrity _____ featured in the tabloids.

7. The _____ statues near the entrance make them feel very strange and ugly in an unnatural way.

Answers

1 guile
2 graceful
3 greedy
4 guarded
5 gracious
6 gossip
7 grotesque

261	harass	266	heed
262	hasten	267	heinous
263	hazard	268	herculean
264	heave	269	hibernate
265	hectic	270	hindrance

"Nature never gives everything at once."

- Samuel Johnson

SSATKOREA.com

harass
[huh-**ras**]

v. to disturb persistently

괴롭히다, 못살게 굴다

*They **harassed** him by attacking him repeatedly.*

syn.　badger, vex, irritate

hasten
[**hey**-su*h*n]

v. to move or act with haste

재촉하다, 서두르다

*"Not me," I **hasten** to add.*

syn.　accelerate, expedite, precipitate

hazard
[**haz**-erd]

n. an unavoidable danger or risk, even though often foreseeable

위험

*His casual remark was a real **hazard** to his reputation.*

syn.　danger, risk, peril

heave
[heev]

v. to raise or lift with effort or force

들어올리다

*They push, pull and **heave** the luggage.*

syn.　raise, lift, hoist

hectic
[**hek**-tik]

adj. characterized by intense agitation, excitement, confused and rapid movement, etc.

정신 없이 바쁜, 빡빡한

*I had a **hectic** schedule for the last two weeks.*

syn.　frantic, crazy, frenzied

heed
[heed]

v. to give careful attention to

(남의 충고에) 주의를 기울이다

*It is important to **heed** the lessons of failure.*

syn.　care, listen, observe

heinous
[**hey**-nu*h*s]

adj. extremely evil or horrible

악랄한, 매우 사악한

*That **heinous** crime is extremely evil and horrible.*

syn.   egregious, wicked, evil

herculean
[hur-kyuh-**lee**-*uh*n]

adj. requiring the great strength of a Hercules, having enormous strength, courage, or size

엄청나게 힘든

*The **herculean** task required extremely great strength or effort.*

syn.   arduous, grueling, hard

hibernate
[**hi**-ber-neyt]

v. to sleep through cold weather

동면하다, 겨울잠 자다

*Bats migrate to a warmer climate or **hibernate** in a cold season.*

syn.   sleep, lie dormant, hole up

hindrance
[**hin**-dr*uh*ns]

n. an impeding, stopping, preventing, or the like

방해, 장애

*To be honest, he was more of a **hindrance** than a help.*

syn.   obstruction, deterrent, impediment

Sentence Completion 6-2

Directions : Fill in the blanks to complete the sentences.

1.   An untied shoelace is an annoying _____ to running.

2.   Balloons are fun, but they're a choking _____ for little kids.

3.   In winter, grizzly bears _____ to take a season-long snooze.

4.   She did not realize how fat her pet cat has become until she has to _____ him.

5.   Take _____ of the instructions for the magic potion will work only by the moonlight.

6.   Finishing all the assignments in such a short time is a _____ task that takes tremendous strength and endurance.

7.   A _____ crime is very evil or wicked one.

Answers

1   hindrance
2   hazard
3   hibernate
4   heave
5   heed
6   herculean
7   heinous

271 hollow	276 hue
272 honorable	277 humble
273 horde	278 hurl
274 hospitable	279 hypnotic
275 hostile	280 hypocritical

"Life is too short
for long-term grudges."

- Elon Musk

SSATKOREA.com

hollow
[**hol**-oh]

adj. having a space or cavity inside
빈, 속이 움푹 꺼진

Most bones are hollow to provide the light and strong body.

syn. empty, void, unfilled

honorable
[**on**-er-uh-b*uh*l]

adj. in accordance with or characterized by principles of honor
명예로운, 고상한

We will end this war with an honorable peace.

syn. reputable, principled, virtuous

horde
[hawrd]

n. a large group, multitude, number
무리, 떼

A horde of children ran over the office building.

syn. throng, pack, crowd

hospitable
[**hos**-pi-tuh-b*uh*l]

adj. receiving or treating guests or strangers warmly and generously
친절한, 환대하는

The hospitable host is friendly, generous, and welcoming to guests.

syn. cordial, congenial, friendly

hostile
[**hos**-tl]

adj. of, relating to, or characteristic of an enemy
적대적인, 강력히 반대하는

Their hostile looks showed that he was unwelcome.

syn. antagonistic, adverse, belligerent

hue
[hyoo]

n. a gradation or variety of a color
색채, 색

Black will take no other hue.

syn. color, shade, tone

humble
[**huhm**-b*uhl*]

adj. not proud or arrogant

겸손한

Knowledge makes humble; ignorance makes proud.

syn. modest, unassuming, unpretentious

hurl
[hurl]

v. to throw forcefully

던지다

The mob hurled a brick violently and with a love of force.

syn. fling, throw, lob

hypnotic
[hip-**not**-ik]

adj. inducing sleep or hypnosis

최면의, 최면을 거는

He has been hypnotized deeply, so he was in a total hypnotic state.

syn. spellbinding, sleep-inducing

hypocritical
[hip-uh-**krit**-i-k*uhl*]

adj. of the nature of hypocrisy, or pretense of having virtues, beliefs, principles, etc.

위선적인, 가식적인

She accused the statesman of being hypocritical.

syn. deceitful, pretending, duplicitous

Sentence Completion 6-3

Directions : Fill in the blanks to complete the sentences.

1. The voice of a powerful public speaker could be _____.

2. A rainbow shows the melting of one _____ into another, from red to violet, and all shades in between.

3. "The universe seems neither benign nor _____, merely indifferent."
- Carl Sagan

4. The landlady is _____ person providing a warm and friendly environment.

5. A _____ of fans followed the movie star as he left the airport.

6. When you lose a game, it's _____to shake hands.

7. His _____ drunk driving made people dumbfounded with the fact that he was the president of a club against drunk driving.

Answers

1 hypnotic
2 hue
3 hostile
4 hospitable
5 horde
6 honorable
7 hypocritical

281	illuminate	286	implied
282	illustrious	287	improvise
283	impassive	288	impulse
284	impeccable	289	inadequate
285	impetuous	290	inadvertent

"I am a slow walker,
but I never walk back."

- Abraham Lincoln

SSATKOREA.com

illuminate
[ih-**loo**-muh-neyt]

v. to supply or brighten with light
비추다, 밝히다

The red glow of the sunset illuminated the sky.

syn. lighten, brighten, radiate

illustrious
[ih-**luhs**-tree-*uhs*]

adj. highly distinguished
유명한, 저명한

The composer was one of many illustrious visitors to the town.

syn. renowned, eminent, acclaimed

impassive
[im-**pas**-iv]

adj. without emotion, apathetic
무표정한, 아무런 감정이 없는

His impassive face is not showing any emotion.

syn. aloof, callous, apathetic

impeccable
[im-**pek**-uh-b*uh*l]

adj. without fault or error
흠 잡을 데 없는, 완벽한

Her appearance was impeccable, showing perfect taste.

syn. flawless, faultless, unblemished

impetuous
[im-**pech**-oo-*uh*s]

adj. likely to do something suddenly, without considering the results of the actions
성급한, 충동적인

It would be foolish and impetuous to resign over such a small matter.

syn. impulsive, rash, hasty

implied
[im-**plahyd**]

adj. involved, indicated, or suggested without being directly or explicitly stated
함축된, 은연중의, 암시적인

There was an implied promise between the two partners.

syn. implicit, hidden, tacit

improvise
[**im**-pruh-vahyz]

v. to compose and perform or deliver without previous preparation

(연주나 연설 등을) 즉흥적으로 하다

The jazz pianist improvised on the melody without having planned it in advance.

syn.　extemporize, contrive, devise

impulse
[**im**-p*uh*ls]

n. the influence of a particular feeling, mental state, etc.

(갑작스러운) 충동

She is likely to decide on impulse without being careful.

syn.　impetus, stimulus, throb

inadequate
[in-**ad**-i-kwit]

adj. not adequate or sufficient

불충분한, 부적당한

Undernutrition is a condition of malnutrition caused by inadequate food supply.

syn.　insufficient, deficient, incompetent

inadvertent
[in-*uh*d-**vur**-tnt]

adj. unintentional

고의가 아닌, 우연의, 의도하지 않은

Most mistakes are 'inadvertent' and 'unintentional.'

syn.　unwitting, accidental, unintentional

Sentence Completion 6-4

Directions : **Fill in the blanks to complete the sentences.**

1.　The business mogul's _____ career is full of impressive achievements and celebrated contributions to society.

2.　With an _____ gesture he swept the vase off the table.

3.　She speaks _____ French fluently and confidently.

4.　The boy's height is _____ for riding the big roller coaster.

5.　There is an _____ agreement between Josh and Sarah.

6.　The teacher may now be regretting her _____ promise not to give any homework.

7.　The jazz musicians _____ their plays for an audience without having a rehearsal.

MIDDLE 1 2 3 4 5 6 7 8 9 10

UPPER 1 2 3 4 5 6 7 8 9 10

291	inane	296	industrious
292	incentive	297	inept
293	incident	298	initiate
294	incognito	299	inquire
295	indomitable	300	insanity

"Excellence is not an act, but a habit."

- Aristotle

SSATKOREA.com

inane
[ih-**neyn**]

adj. lacking sense, significance, or ideas
어리석은, 무의미한

His behavior was inane, silly and stupid.

syn. silly, foolish, stupid

incentive
[in-**sen**-tiv]

n. something that incites or tends to incite to action or greater effort
(어떤 행동을 장려하기 위한) 유도책, 유인책

Tax-refund incentives encourage tourist to buy more products.

syn. inducement, lure

incident
[**in**-si-d*uh*nt]

n. an individual occurrence or event
(특이하거나 불쾌한) 일, 사건

An error in the translation nearly caused a diplomatic incident.

syn. event, accident, occurrence

incognito
[in-kog-**nee**-toh]

adj. having one's identity concealed
자기 신분을 숨기고, 가명으로

The film star is incognito using a false name to make a reservation.

syn. anonymous, disguised, concealed

indomitable
[in-**dom**-i-tuh-b*uh*l]

adj. that cannot be subdued or overcome, as person's will or courage
불굴의, 절대 굴복하지 않는

She has an indomitable spirit, never giving up.

syn. invincible, unconquerable, unbeatable

industrious
[in-**duhs**-tree-*uh*s]

adj. working energetically and devotedly
근면한, 부지런한

He was an industrious worker working very hard.

syn. diligent, assiduous, conscientious

inept
[in-**ept**]

adj. without skill or aptitude for a particular task or assignment

솜씨 없는, 서투른

The green politician was inept at dealing with people.

syn. unskilled, clumsy, ungainly

initiate
[ih-**nish**-ee-eyt]

v. to begin, set going, or originate

시작하다, 착수하다

The school has initiated a program of higher education.

syn. commence, launch, inaugurate

inquire
[in-**kwahy**uhr]

v. to seek information by questioning

묻다, 알아보다

The detective kept inquiring about a neighbor.

syn. ask, investigate, probe

insanity
[in-**san**-i-tee]

n. a foolish or senseless action, policy, statement, etc.

정신이상, 무모한 짓

The crimes against humanity are so primitive that to allow such insanity to happen at this turn of the century is incomprehensible.

syn. lunacy, frenzy, foolishness

Sentence Completion 6-5

Directions : Fill in the blanks to complete the sentences.

1. Bonus payments provide an _____ to work harder.

2. The parents of all students got an email about the _____ at school.

3. Celebrities often try to go out or travel _____ so that they may have some privacy.

4. As she works hard and tirelessly, her _____ attitude affects all of her classmates.

5. He is _____ at Math and Science but is quite strong in English and History.

6. His _____ spirit does not need pep talks or energy drink.

7. There are too many _____ reality TV shows these days.

Answers

1 incentive
2 incident
3 incognito
4 industrious
5 inept
6 indomitable
7 inane

Analogy 6. Part & Whole

전체와 부분 간의 관계도 꼭 알아야 할 유형이죠? 이 때 포인트는 부분의 위치도 같은 것이 더 가까운 관계가 된다는 것입니다. 문제가 전체에서 앞쪽을 가리키면, 답도 전체의 앞쪽 부분에 있는 것이 된다는 것이죠.

A는 B의 Front 앞 부분

preface : book
서문 : 책

Preamble : Constitution
헌법 서문 : 헌법

overture : opera
서곡 : 오페라

prologue : novel
프롤로그 : 소설

A는 B의 Ending 끝 부분

finale : opera
피날레 : 오페라

epilogue : novel
에필로그 : 소설

dessert : meal
디저트 : 식사

postscript : letter
추신 : 편지

같은 기능이나, 같은 위치를 하는 것을 연결한 관계

candle : wick
양초 : 심지

bulb : filament
전구 : 필라멘트

pinnacle : mountain
산봉우리 : 산

crest : wave
물마루: 파도

POP QUIZ

1. Preamble is to constitution as
(A) overture is to opera
(B) epilogue is to novel
(C) frigid is to algid
(D) intermission is to play
(E) recess is to school

2. Postscript is to letter as
(A) salutation is to greeting
(B) finale is to class
(C) appetizer is to banquet
(D) epilogue is to novel
(E) caliber is to gun

3. Gill is to fish as
(A) shark is to fish
(B) talon is to eagle
(C) poem is to stanza
(D) chapter is to book
(E) lung is to man

4. Bulb is to filament as
(A) candle is to wick
(B) bear is to claw
(C) harpsichord is to piano
(D) sentence is to paragraph
(E) rind is to watermelon

Check-up 6-1

Directions   Each of the following questions consists of one word followed by five words or phrases.
You are to select the one word or phrase whose meaning is closest to the word in capital letters.

1. GIMMICK
(A) finesse
(B) cadence
(C) lull
(D) platoon
(E) helix

2. GLARE
(A) appall
(B) stare
(C) resist
(D) quiver
(E) submit

3. GLOW
(A) regain
(B) nestle
(C) radiate
(D) pounce
(E) isolate

4. GOSSIP
(A) trophy
(B) barrier
(C) fortress
(D) advantage
(E) rumor

5. GRACEFUL
(A) fascinating
(B) immense
(C) gracious
(D) skilled
(E) available

6. GRACIOUS
(A) sensational
(B) unwieldy
(C) courteous
(D) prosperous
(E) remote

7. GREEDY
(A) grim
(B) gluttonous
(C) gigantic
(D) heroic
(E) elegant

8. GROTESQUE
(A) malformed
(B) exultant
(C) former
(D) urban
(E) exasperating

9. GUARDED
(A) terse
(B) cautious
(C) reluctant
(D) celebrated
(E) obedient

10. GUILE
(A) delicate
(B) confident
(C) cunning
(D) barren
(E) durable

Check-up 6-2

Directions Each of the following questions consists of one word followed by five words or phrases. You are to select the one word or phrase whose meaning is closest to the word in capital letters.

1. **HARASS**
   (A) liberate
   (B) revive
   (C) badger
   (D) slither
   (E) decrease

2. **HASTEN**
   (A) taper
   (B) pledge
   (C) transform
   (D) expedite
   (E) convalesce

3. **HAZARD**
   (A) blossom
   (B) limb
   (C) frontier
   (D) fringe
   (E) peril

4. **HEAVE**
   (A) celebrate
   (B) bask
   (C) raise
   (D) prosper
   (E) pardon

5. **HECTIC**
   (A) massive
   (B) stationary
   (C) crazy
   (D) benevolent
   (E) deft

6. **HEED**
   (A) taper
   (B) care
   (C) elevate
   (D) glisten
   (E) adore

7. **HEINOUS**
   (A) minute
   (B) perpetual
   (C) resourceful
   (D) solar
   (E) egregious

8. **HERCULEAN**
   (A) wide
   (B) arduous
   (C) esteemed
   (D) unruly
   (E) eloquent

9. **HIBERNATE**
   (A) sleep
   (B) accumulate
   (C) excel
   (D) degrade
   (E) shed

10. **HINDRANCE**
    (A) bough
    (B) request
    (C) prospect
    (D) obstruction
    (E) tower

Check-up 6-3

1. **HOLLOW**
   (A) pretentious
   (B) doleful
   (C) engrossing
   (D) empty
   (E) squalid

2. **HONORABLE**
   (A) elaborate
   (B) straightforward
   (C) colossal
   (D) fantastic
   (E) reputable

3. **HORDE**
   (A) refuge
   (B) crowd
   (C) portrait
   (D) shade
   (E) hostility

4. **HOSPITABLE**
   (A) awesome
   (B) exhilarating
   (C) cordial
   (D) open
   (E) famine

5. **HOSTILE**
   (A) antagonistic
   (B) elusive
   (C) splendid
   (D) constant
   (E) brief

6. **HUE**
   (A) color
   (B) frivolity
   (C) mural
   (D) freight
   (E) cargo

7. **HUMBLE**
   (A) stern
   (B) unanimous
   (C) modest
   (D) awesome
   (E) extraordinary

8. **HURL**
   (A) envelop
   (B) diminish
   (C) substitute
   (D) fling
   (E) boycott

9. **HYPNOTIC**
   (A) unique
   (B) outmoded
   (C) discreet
   (D) complicated
   (E) spellbinding

10. **HYPOCRITICAL**
    (A) elated
    (B) deceitful
    (C) continuous
    (D) leisurely
    (E) tentative

Check-up 6-4

Each of the following questions consists of one word followed by five words or phrases. You are to select the one word or phrase whose meaning is closest to the word in capital letters.

1. ILLUMINATE
(A) brighten
(B) wonder
(C) assemble
(D) disguise
(E) intimidate

2. ILLUSTRIOUS
(A) reckless
(B) renowned
(C) defective
(D) squalid
(E) pathetic

3. IMPASSIVE
(A) brisk
(B) ravenous
(C) callous
(D) indolent
(E) relentless

4. IMPECCABLE
(A) resolute
(B) flawless
(C) controversial
(D) tranquil
(E) insolent

5. IMPETUOUS
(A) bankrupt
(B) invaluable
(C) rigorous
(D) insolvent
(E) impulsive

6. IMPLIED
(A) earnest
(B) superb
(C) rural
(D) implicit
(E) sinister

7. IMPROVISE
(A) extemporize
(B) originate
(C) relocate
(D) beget
(E) exasperate

8. IMPULSE
(A) remedy
(B) expansion
(C) impetus
(D) riot
(E) blizzard

9. INADEQUATE
(A) deficient
(B) placid
(C) ecstatic
(D) genuine
(E) realistic

10. INADVERTENT
(A) intended
(B) solitary
(C) unwitting
(D) fruitful
(E) futile

Check-up 6-5

Directions   Each of the following questions consists of one word followed by five words or phrases. You are to select the one word or phrase whose meaning is closest to the word in capital letters.

1. INANE
- (A) silly
- (B) efficient
- (C) fragrant
- (D) arrogant
- (E) stern

2. INCENTIVE
- (A) dictator
- (B) disaster
- (C) inducement
- (D) concept
- (E) upbringing

3. INCIDENT
- (A) affliction
- (B) fume
- (C) lumber
- (D) event
- (E) rebel

4. INCOGNITO
- (A) lethal
- (B) effective
- (C) acrid
- (D) muddled
- (E) anonymous

5. INDOMITABLE
- (A) futile
- (B) invincible
- (C) treacherous
- (D) hectic
- (E) distinct

6. INDUSTRIOUS
- (A) mortal
- (B) aghast
- (C) alleged
- (D) diligent
- (E) blatant

7. INEPT
- (A) unskilled
- (B) adept
- (C) apathetic
- (D) deft
- (E) alternative

8. INITIATE
- (A) commence
- (B) infest
- (C) declare
- (D) bluster
- (E) emerge

9. INQUIRE
- (A) posture
- (B) restraint
- (C) breach
- (D) ask
- (E) transport

10. INSANITY
- (A) sage
- (B) lunacy
- (C) procrastination
- (D) filibuster
- (E) veto

113

301	inspect	306	inundate
302	inspire	307	invade
303	integrate	308	invert
304	intellectual	309	irrelevant
305	intense	310	jabber

"If there is no struggle, there is no progress."

- Frederick Douglass

SSATKOREA.com

inspect
[in-**spekt**]

v. to look carefully at or over

점검하다, 조사하다

He inspected every detail, looking at every part of it carefully.

syn. examine, check, scrutinize

inspire
[in-**spahy***uhr*]

v. to fill with an amazing, quickening, or exalting influence

격려하다, 고무하다

His performance inspired the young boy to do something new or unusual.

syn. stimulate, encourage, influence

integrate
[**in**-ti-greyt]

v. to bring together or incorporate into a whole

통합시키다, 합치다

The wanderers integrated into a social group and became a major part of this society.

syn. combine, amalgamate, merge

intellectual
[in-tl-**ek**-choo-*uhl*]

adj. appealing to or engaging the intellect

지적인, 높은 지능과 지식을 가진

Companies should protect their intellectual property with patents and trademarks.

syn. mental, cerebral, cognitive

Intense
[in-**tens**]

adj. occurring in a high or extreme degree

극심한, 강렬한

The principal is under intense pressure to resign.

syn. acute, forceful, severe

inundate
[**in**-*uh*n-deyt]

v. to fill completely, usually with water

범람하다, 침수시키다

Flood waters typically inundate farmland, making the land unworkable.

syn. flood, deluge, overrun, overwhelm

invade
[in-**veyd**]

v. to enter forcefully as an enemy
침입하다, 침략하다

I don't want to invade your private life unnecessarily.

syn. intrude, raid, occupy

invert
[in-**vurt**]

v. to turn upside down
(아래 위를) 뒤집다

Place a plate over the pancake and invert it.

syn. reverse, upturn, transpose

irrelevant
[ih-**rel**-uh-v*uh*nt]

adj. having no connection with the subject
무관한, 상관없는

She considered politics irrelevant to her life.

syn. immaterial, impertinent, inappropriate

jabber
[**jab**-er]

v. to talk rapidly, indistinctively or nonsensically
(흥분해서 알아듣기 힘들게) 지껄이다

The kids were jabbering very quickly, and I could not understand them.

syn. prattle, babble, chatter

Sentence Completion 7-1

Directions : Fill in the blanks to complete the sentences.

1. Spencer started to _____; he talks on and on about this or that in an incoherent way.

2. I _____ a cake pan, turning it upside down on a plate in order to remove the cake.

3. As you read books, you can be a friend with one of most brilliant _____ of human history like Plato, Albert Einstein, and Richard Feynman.

4. When you're buying a used car, you should _____ it inside and out.

5. A pinch of salt can make _____ sweetness of the sugar in a pineapple.

6. The military might _____ a neighboring country to gain more land.

7. One of the results of the Civil Rights Movement was the decision to _____ the schools of the American South.

Answers

1 jabber
2 invert
3 intellectual
4 inspect
5 intense
6 invade
7 integrate

311 jostle	316 lapse
312 jubilant	317 literal
313 jumble	318 litigate
314 juvenile	319 lore
315 labyrinth	320 magnanimous

"We become what we think about."

- Earl Nightingale

SSATKOREA.com

jostle
[**jos**-*uhl*]

v. to bump, push, or elbow roughly or rudely

(많은 사람들 사이에서) 거칠게 밀치다

People were jostling in a crowd, and they were trying to get past me.

syn. shove, bump, nudge

jubilant
[**joo**-buh-l*uh*nt]

adj. showing great joy, satisfaction, or triumph

승리감에 넘치는, 득의 만면한, 의기양양한

She was jubilant after making an impressive comeback.

syn. overjoyed, exultant, triumphant

jumble
[**juhm**-*buhl*]

v. to mix in a confused mass

뒤섞다

Toys, books, and blocks were jumbled together on the floor.

syn. muddle, disorganize, clutter

juvenile
[**joo**-vuh-nl]

adj. of, pertaining to, characteristics of, or suitable or intended for young persons

청소년의

A juvenile delinquent is a young person who is guilty of committing crimes.

syn. young, childish, immature, puerile

labyrinth
[**lab**-uh-rinth]

n. an intricate combination of paths or passages in which it is difficult to find one's way or to reach the exit

미로

The labyrinth was made up of a complicated series of paths or passages.

syn. maze, warren, tangle, web

lapse
[laps]

n. a slip or error, often of a trivial sort

실수, 과실

A momentary lapse of concentration in the final round cost her the match.

syn. mistake, blunder, blooper

literal
[lit-er-*uhl*]

adj. in accordance with, involving, or being the primary or strict meaning of the word

문자 그대로의

Doesn't it feel like a literal translation?

syn.   exact, factual, word for word

litigate
[**lit**-i-geyt]

v. to make the subject of a lawsuit

소송하다, 고소하다

The majority of lawsuits can be very complicated to litigate.

syn.   prosecute, sue, appeal, contest

lore
[lawr]

n. traditional wisdom

민간 전승, 전해 내려오는 이야기

According to local lore, this hot spring has healing properties.

syn.   information, knowledge, wisdom

magnanimous
[mag-**nan**-uh-m*uhs*]

adj. generous in forgiving an insult or injury

관대한, 마음이 넓은

The magnanimous ruler behaved generously towards his enemy.

syn.   altruistic, charitable, considerate

Sentence Completion 7-2

Directions : Fill in the blanks to complete the sentences.

1. Getting a doctoral degree with raising four children seems a veritable _____ of wrong turns and false hope.

2. Katharine's room is overflowing with clothes in its _____ sense.

3. The Captain's decision to ignore the safety warnings shows a remarkable _____ of judgment.

4. You'd better have a lawyer is you decide to _____.

5. When John had two consecutive holes-in-one, he was _____.

6. Laurence is _____ to forgive others easily.

7. _____ delinquency is the act of participating in unlawful behavior as minors.

Answers

1 labyrinth	
2 literal	5 jubilant
3 lapse	6 magnanimous
4 litigate	7 Juvenile

321 malleable   326 medley

322 massive   327 mend

323 mayhem   328 migrate

324 meager   329 miraculous

325 meandering   330 miserable

"Life is what happens to us while we are making other plans."

- Allen Saunders

SSATKOREA.com

malleable
[**mal**-ee-uh-b*uhl*]

adj. easily influenced, trained, or controlled

영향을 잘 받는, 잘 변하는

Malleable materials can be formed cold using stamping or pressing.

syn. pliable, flexible, amenable

massive
[**mas**-iv]

adj. consisting of or forming a large mass

거대한, 엄청나게 큰

Eight massive stone pillars supported the roof.

syn. huge, enormous, tremendous

mayhem
[**mey**-hem]

n. the crime of willfully inflicting a bodily injury

신체 상해, 파괴 행위, 대혼란

Their arrival caused mayhem as crowds of fans rushed towards them.

syn. violence, chaos, destruction

meager
[**mee**-ger]

adj. deficient in quantity or quality

메마른, 빈약한, 결핍된

His meager wage is not enough to support his family.

syn. inadequate, scanty, scant

meandering
[mee-**an**-dering]

adj. winding or indirect

구불구불한

Meandering paths lead into a small town.

syn. rambling, roaming, winding

medley
[**med**-lee]

n. a mixture of different things, especially tunes put together

여러 가지 뒤섞인 것

The jazz band played a medley of Beatles songs.

syn. assortment, miscellany, mixture

mend
[mend]

v. to make whole, sound, or usable by repairing

수리하다, 고치다

Never try to mend a broken machine without disconnecting it from the electricity supply.

syn.   alter, fix, amend

migrate
[**mahy**-greyt]

v. to travel to another place

(새나 동물이) 계절에 따라 이동하다

These birds migrate to Europe in the summer season.

syn.   move, emigrate, travel

miraculous
[mi-**rak**-yuh-l*uh*s]

adj. surprisingly wonderful

기적적인

She made a miraculous recovery from her fatal injuries.

syn.   incredible, supernatural, amazing

miserable
[**miz**-er-uh-b*uh*l]

adj. wretchedly unhappy

비참한, 우울한

Why do you make yourself miserable by taking on too much work?

syn.   wretched, gloomy, depressed

Sentence Completion 7-3

Directions : **Fill in the blanks to complete the sentences.**

1. When Carry was caught in the pouring rain and miss the last train, she felt _____.

2. Morgan only has a _____ amount of money, and he has a hard time making rent.

3. Some birds _____ north in summer and south in winter.

4. A _____ is the most common form of overture for musical theater productions.

5. If you do not want to sit in the dark, _____ your broken lamp.

6. With 30 kids in a classroom and only one teacher to supervise, it was complete _____.

7. It's easier to learn to play golf when you're young and _____.

Answers

1   miserable
2   meager
3   migrate
4   medley
5   mend
6   mayhem
7   malleable

331	mislead	336	motive
332	moderate	337	multitude
333	modify	338	mumble
334	mollify	339	murky
335	motif	340	mutiny

"The way to get started is to quit talking and begin doing."

- Walt Disney

SSATKOREA.com

mislead
[mis-**leed**]

v. to lead someone in the wrong direction

속이다, 잘못된 방향으로 이끌다

It is prohibited to provide false information to mislead consumers.

syn.   deceive, defraud, misinform

moderate
[**mod**-er-it]

adj. keeping within reasonable or proper limits

보통의, 중간의

He was an easygoing man of very moderate views.

syn.   mild, temperate, average

modify
[**mod**-uh-fahy]

v. to change somewhat the form or qualities of

수정하다, 바꾸다

Established habits are difficult to modify.

syn.   alter, change, adjust

mollify
[**mol**-uh-fahy]

v. to soften in feeling or temper

(사람을) 달래다, 진정시키다

Please say something to mollify his anger.

syn.   appease, placate, pacify

motif
[moh-**teef**]

n. a recurring subject, theme, or idea

(문학이나 음악 작품 속에서 반복되는) 주제, 모티프

The theme of creation is a recurrent motif in Celtic mythology.

syn.   design, theme, idea

motive
[**moh**-tiv]

n. something that causes a person to act in a certain way

동기, 이유

There seemed to be no clear motive for the attack.

syn.   reason, purpose, aim

multitude
[**muhl**-ti-tood]

n. a great number
아주 많은 수, 다수, 대중

Success covers a multitude of blunders.

syn. horde, legion, myriad

mumble
[**muhm**-buhl]

v. to speak in a low indistinct manner
웅얼거리듯 말하다, 중얼거리다

I wish you wouldn't mumble; I can't hear you clearly.

syn. mutter, murmur

murky
[**mur**-kee]

adj. dark, gloomy, obscure with mist
(연기나 안개 등으로 불쾌하게) 어두컴컴한, 흐린

The light was too murky to continue playing.

syn. gloomy, obscure, dark

mutiny
[**myoot**-n-ee]

n. rebellion against any authority
반역, 반란

Mark led a military mutiny against the commanders.

syn. revolt, riot, uprising

Sentence Completion 7-4

Directions : Fill in the blanks to complete the sentences.

1.   The detective won't understand the crime until he understands the _____ of crime.

2.   In the trailers of some popular horror movies, you can see a _____ of zombies is approaching.

3.   Robert looked up the gloomy and _____ sky with an apprehensive look.

4.   The crews in a ship led a _____ against the captain.

5.   A _____ voter is not quite left or right, but somewhere in the middle.

6.   The criminals deliberately _____ the police, give them false information or obstruct them.

7.   The restaurant manger's main job was to _____ angry customers.

Answers

1 motive
2 multitude
3 murky
4 mutiny
5 moderate
6 mislead
7 mollify

MIDDLE LEVEL Lesson 7-5

341 nimble   346 objection

342 nomad   347 objective

343 novel   348 obscure

344 novice   349 obvious

345 nudge   350 offend

*"Either you run the day,
or the day runs you."*

- Jim Rohn

SSATKOREA.com

nimble
[**nim**-b*uh*l]

adj. quick and light in movement
(동작이) 빠른, 날렵한

*Her **nimble** fingers undid the knot
in seconds.*

syn.   agile, quick, lively

nomad
[**noh**-mad]

n. a person or tribe that has no adj. of a
new and unusual kind
유목민

*He is a **nomad** moving from place to
place to find pasture and food.*

syn.   itinerant, traveler, migrant

novel
[**nov**-uhl]

adj. of a new and unusual kind
새로운, 독창적인

*Rachel has suggested a **novel**
approach to the problem.*

syn.   original, new, innovative

novice
[**nov**-is]

n. a person who is new to the
circumstances
초보자

*I'm a **novice** at these things,
but you're the professional.*

syn.   beginner, tyro, newcomer

nudge
[nuhj]

v. to push slightly or gently
(팔꿈치로 살짝) 쿡 찌르다

*She **nudged** gently in my ribs to
tell me to shut up.*

syn.   poke, elbow, push

objection
[*uh*b-**jek**-sh*uh*n]

n. a reason or argument offered in
disagreement
이의, 반대

*The Congress overrode the President's
objection and passed the law.*

syn.   protest, protestation, demur

objective
[*uh*b-**jek**-tiv]

n. something that one's efforts or actions are intended to attain

목적, 목표

Winning is not the prime objective in this sport.

syn.   goal, target, aim

obscure
[*uh*b-**skyoor**]

adj. not clear or plain

잘 알려져 있지 않는, 불명확한

Her poetry is full of obscure literary allusions.

syn.   unclear, ambiguous, nebulous

obvious
[**ob**-vee-*uh*s]

adj. easily seen, recognized, or understood

분명한, 확실한

Lack of qualifications is an obvious disadvantage.

syn.   clear, plain, evident, apparent

offend
[uh-**fend**]

v. to affect disagreeably

기분 상하게 하다, 불쾌하게 하다

I didn't mean to offend you.

syn.   affront, displease, upset, distress

Sentence Completion 7-5

Directions : Fill in the blanks to complete the sentences.

1. Daniel is a _____ photographer, just learning how to take beautiful pictures.

2. My _____ in learning a new language is to improve the understanding of the world.

3. The painted lines on the roads can be _____ in heavy rain.

4. Dustin is a _____ who would rather wander from place to place than set down roots.

5. It was _____ that he was so bored because I saw him roll his eyes.

6. The acrobat is so _____ that she can move quickly and with ease.

7. At that time, handheld computers are _____ devices.

Answers

1 novice
2 objective
3 obscure
4 nomad
5 obvious
6 nimble
7 novel

Analogy 7. Kinds of

종류와 그 중 하나를 연결짓는 관계입니다. 다른 곳에서 보기 힘든 다양한 명사가 등장하니 이 유형의 잘 나오는 어휘들은 꼭 기억해두세요.

hammock : bed
그물침대, 해먹 : 침대

stool : chair
등받이 없는 의자, 스툴 : 의자

coal : mineral
석탄 : 광물

gold : metal
금 : 금속

cave : dwelling
동굴 : 거주지

cactus : plant
선인장 : 식물

elm : tree
느릅나무 : 나무

tendril : vine
덩굴손 : 덩굴식물

violin : string
바이올린 : 현악기

flute : woodwind
플루트 : 목관악기

cymbals : percussion
심벌즈 : 타악기

trombone : brass
트롬본 : 금관악기

ebony : wood
흑단 : 목재

sable : fur
흑담비 : 모피

gauntlet : glove
갑옷용 장갑 : 장갑

beret : hat
베레모 : 모자

moccasin : shoes
모카신 : 신발

pullover : sweater
풀오버 : 스웨터

POP QUIZ

1. Cello is to string as
- (A) flute is to woodwind
- (B) cymbals is to brass
- (C) grand is to piano
- (D) conductor is to orchestra
- (E) trombone is to percussion

2. Hammock is to bed as
- (A) painter is to exhibit
- (B) recital is to musician
- (C) fleet is to ships
- (D) tent is to house
- (E) cave is to dwelling

Check-up 7-1

Directions   Each of the following questions consists of one word followed by five words or phrases. You are to select the one word or phrase whose meaning is closest to the word in capital letters.

1. INSPECT
(A) examine
(B) hatch
(C) interpret
(D) moor
(E) baffle

2. INSPIRE
(A) stimulate
(B) sear
(C) loom
(D) hoax
(E) complicate

3. INTEGRATE
(A) contaminate
(B) merge
(C) shroud
(D) pierce
(E) analyze

4. INTELLECTUAL
(A) lethargic
(B) cerebral
(C) pretentious
(D) momentous
(E) scanty

5. INTENSE
(A) unbiased
(B) esteemed
(C) acute
(D) indifferent
(E) buoyant

6. INUNDATE
(A) suspend
(B) cultivate
(C) overwhelm
(D) expel
(E) preserve

7. INVADE
(A) topple
(B) accommodate
(C) assume
(D) abdicate
(E) raid

8. INVERT
(A) betray
(B) cultivate
(C) lean
(D) reverse
(E) excavate

9. IRRELEVANT
(A) immaterial
(B) sacred
(C) legendary
(D) inevitable
(E) lucrative

10. JABBER
(A) accelerate
(B) babble
(C) hop
(D) narrate
(E) demolish

125

Check-up 7-2

DirectionsEach of the following questions consists of one word followed by five words or phrases. You are to select the one word or phrase whose meaning is closest to the word in capital letters.

1. JOSTLE
- (A) betray
- (B) cultivate
- (C) decline
- (D) bump
- (E) excavate

2. JUBILANT
- (A) rustic
- (B) parochial
- (C) proficient
- (D) sleek
- (E) triumphant

3. JUMBLE
- (A) dictate
- (B) employ
- (C) muddle
- (D) burden
- (E) provoke

4. JUVENILE
- (A) privileged
- (B) wary
- (C) unwitting
- (D) trifling
- (E) young

5. LABYRINTH
- (A) sermon
- (B) maze
- (C) fragment
- (D) amulet
- (E) priority

6. LAPSE
- (A) mistake
- (B) charm
- (C) lullaby
- (D) pause
- (E) companion

7. LITERAL
- (A) robust
- (B) far-fetched
- (C) factual
- (D) impractical
- (E) receptive

8. LITIGATE
- (A) allege
- (B) negotiate
- (C) annihilate
- (D) fascinate
- (E) sue

9. LORE
- (A) distinction
- (B) era
- (C) abyss
- (D) information
- (E) apathy

10. MAGNANIMOUS
- (A) ruthless
- (B) charitable
- (C) scrupulous
- (D) tedious
- (E) ungainly

Answer 1.D 2.E 3.C 4.E 5.B 6.A 7.C 8.E 9.D 10.B

Check-up 7-3

1. MALLEABLE

(A) urgent
(B) toxic
(C) amenable
(D) wrathful
(E) climactic

2. MASSIVE

(A) vigilant
(B) subtle
(C) tiny
(D) bounty
(E) tremendous

3. MAYHEM

(A) theme
(B) violence
(C) climax
(D) casualty
(E) authority

4. MEAGER

(A) unscathed
(B) stringent
(C) ponderous
(D) scanty
(E) vulnerable

5. MEANDERING

(A) staunch
(B) obnoxious
(C) plausible
(D) strenuous
(E) winding

6. MEDLEY

(A) mixture
(B) citrus
(C) abode
(D) bigot
(E) authority

7. MEND

(A) alter
(B) comply
(C) teem
(D) oppose
(E) consist

8. MIGRATE

(A) concur
(B) resemble
(C) travel
(D) antagonize
(E) petrify

9. MIRACULOUS

(A) nomadic
(B) ominous
(C) incredible
(D) murky
(E) personable

10. MISERABLE

(A) permanent
(B) wretched
(C) precise
(D) negligent
(E) naive

Check-up 7-4

Each of the following questions consists of one word followed by five words or phrases. You are to select the one word or phrase whose meaning is closest to the word in capital letters.

1. MISLEAD
(A) suspend
(B) topple
(C) deceive
(D) present
(E) idle

2. MODERATE
(A) fanciful
(B) average
(C) humid
(D) supreme
(E) hardy

3. MODIFY
(A) resume
(B) change
(C) retain
(D) retire
(E) preserve

4. MOLLIFY
(A) sever
(B) afflict
(C) pacify
(D) aggravate
(E) terminate

5. MOTIF
(A) quarry
(B) victim
(C) theme
(D) symptom
(E) hail

6. MOTIVE
(A) century
(B) capital
(C) grace
(D) purpose
(E) talon

7. MULTITUDE
(A) myriad
(B) peer
(C) livelihood
(D) portion
(E) vision

8. MUMBLE
(A) assume
(B) murmur
(C) reign
(D) expel
(E) suspend

9. MURKY
(A) gloomy
(B) progress
(C) outrage
(D) practice
(E) threat

10. MUTINY
(A) rabble
(B) altercation
(C) retrospection
(D) novelty
(E) revolt

Check-up 7-5

Directions   Each of the following questions consists of one word followed by five words or phrases. You are to select the one word or phrase whose meaning is closest to the word in capital letters.

1. NIMBLE
(A) preliminary
(B) agile
(C) casual
(D) extravagant
(E) versatile

2. NOMAD
(A) maestro
(B) surrogate
(C) itinerant
(D) contributor
(E) deputy

3. NOVEL
(A) frugal
(B) convenient
(C) brisk
(D) original
(E) apprehensive

4. NOVICE
(A) scoundrel
(B) authority
(C) veteran
(D) connoisseur
(E) tyro

5. NUDGE
(A) coincide
(B) poke
(C) exist
(D) fuse
(E) esteem

6. OBJECTION
(A) priority
(B) siege
(C) woe
(D) protest
(E) elation

7. OBJECTIVE
(A) onset
(B) controversy
(C) goal
(D) peril
(E) rigor

8. OBSCURE
(A) cheerful
(B) monotonous
(C) mediocre
(D) prominent
(E) unclear

9. OBVIOUS
(A) clear
(B) appropriate
(C) inept
(D) mobile
(E) oblivious

10. OFFEND
(A) exclude
(B) compete
(C) affront
(D) corrode
(E) rejoice

Answer 1.B 2.C 3.D 4.E 5.B 6.D 7.C 8.E 9.A 10.C

351	opponent	356	overwhelm
352	option	357	pamper
353	organize	358	paragon
354	original	359	partial
355	overlap	360	perceive

"Limitations live only in our minds."

- Jamie Paolinetti

━━━━━━━━━━ SSATKOREA.com

opponent
[uh-**poh**-n*uh*nt]

n. a person who is on an opposing side in a game

경쟁 상대, 적수

In a debate, she was a formidable opponent.

syn. adversary, foe, antagonist

option
[op-sh*uh*n]

n. the power or right of choosing

선택, 선택권, 선택사항

She had no option but to ask him to leave.

syn. choice, alternative, recourse

organize
[**awr**-guh-nahyz]

v. to form into a coherent unity

조직하다, 정리하다

We rely heavily on computers to organize our work.

syn. systemize, arrange, integrate

original
[uh-**rij**-uh-nl]

adj. created, undertaken, or presented for the first time

독창적인

He has a highly original mind.

syn. creative, inventive, fresh, novel

overlap
[oh-ver-**lap**]

v. to cover and extend beyond

겹치다, 포개지다

Overlap the slices carefully, so there are no gaps.

syn. flap, overlie, imbricate

overwhelm
[oh-ver-**hwelm**]

v. to overcome completely in mind or feeling

(격한 감정이) 휩싸다, 압도하다

Napoleon's army was strong enough to overwhelm nearly any potential enemy.

syn. flood, crush, inundate

pamper
[**pam**-per]

v. to treat or gratify with extreme indulgence, kindness, or care

소중히 보살피다, 애지중지하다

Why not pamper yourself after a hard day with a hot bath with aroma oils?

syn. indulge, coddle, whim

paragon
[**par**-uh-gon]

n. a model or pattern of excellence

좋은 예, 귀감, 모범

The professor is a paragon of virtue and learning.

syn. exemplar, outstanding example, epitome

partial
[**pahr**-sh*uhl*]

adj. biased or prejudiced in favor of a person or side

편파적인, 편견을 가진

The information we have is somewhat partial and biased.

syn. biased, prejudiced, unfair

perceive
[per-**seev**]

v. to become aware of, know, or identify by means of the senses

감지하다, 인지하다

Voters perceive him as a decisive and resolute international leader.

syn. discern, recognize, distinguish

Sentence Completion 8-1

Directions : **Fill in the blanks to complete the sentences.**

1. One of the great things about being a scientist is the close _____ between job and personal interests.

2. The best _____ would be to cancel the trip altogether.

3. The reporting in the papers is entirely _____ and makes no attempt to be objective.

4. Is this an _____ Van Gogh?

5. He is a perfect _____ of excellence.

6. Do you _____ yourself as a good student?

7. My coaches tell me never to underestimate my _____.

Answers

1 overlap
2 option
3 partial
4 original
5 paragon
6 perceive
7 opponent

361	permanent	366	pertinent
362	perpetual	367	pester
363	persevere	368	phenomenal
364	persistent	369	piquant
365	perspective	370	placate

"Ask, and it shall be given you;
seek, and you shall find."
- the Bible

SSATKOREA.com

permanent
[**pur**-muh-n*uh*nt]

adj. long-lasting or nonfading
영원한, 영구적인

Heavy drinking can cause permanent damage to the brain.

syn. perpetual, constant, lasting

perpetual
[per-**pech**-oo-*uh*l]

adj. continuing or enduring forever
(오래 동안) 끊임없이 계속되는

A contented mind is a perpetual feast.

syn. everlasting, eternal, permanent

persevere
[pur-suh-**veer**]

v. to persist in anything undertaken
인내하며 계속하다

You'll need to persevere if you want to succeed.

syn. persist, continue

persistent
[per-**sis**-t*uh*nt]

adj. persisting, especially in spite of opposition, obstacles, discouragement
끈질긴, 집요한

They were removed from the school for persistent bad behavior.

syn. chronic, tenacious, unrelenting

perspective
[per-**spek**-tiv]

n. a mental view or prospect
관점, 시각

His experience abroad provides a wider perspective.

syn. view, outlook, aspect

pertinent
[**pur**-tn-*uh*nt]

adj. relating directly and significantly to the matter
(특정한 상황에) 적절한, 관련 있는

Please keep your comments pertinent to the topic under discussion.

syn. relevant, apposite, appropriate

pester
[**pes**-ter]

v. to bother persistently

괴롭히다

She used to pester her father until she got exactly what she wanted.

syn. bother, annoy, badger

phenomenal
[**fi**-nom-uh-nl]

adj. highly extraordinary or exceptional

놀랄만한, 보통이 아닌, 엄청난

The space shuttle travels at phenomenal speed.

syn. exceptional, extraordinary, prodigious

piquant
[**pee**-*kuh*nt]

adj. agreeably pungent or sharp in taste

톡 쏘는 듯한, 짜릿한

Bland vegetables are often served with a piquant sauce.

syn. spicy, intriguing, stimulating

placate
[**pley**-keyt]

v. to appease or pacify

달래다, 진정시키다

She smiled, trying to placate me.

syn. pacify, calm, appease

Sentence Completion 8-2

Directions : Fill in the blanks to complete the sentences.

1. A story that's filled with _____ details has plenty of juicy, provocative points.

2. Air drying is the most common way to _____ flowers.

3. The _____ coach refused to give up.

4. When a horde of tourists asks Julia same thing over and over again, she felt _____.

5. K-pop cultures are growing at a _____ rate.

6. A _____ software license authorizes an individual to use a program indefinitely.

7. Think twice about writing in _____ marker- it is very hard to erase.

💬 **Answers**

1 piquant
2 persevere
3 persistent
4 pester
5 phenomenal
6 perpetual
7 permanent

371	plead	376	portion
372	plight	377	possess
373	pluck	378	precipitate
374	poise	379	predominant
375	ponderous	380	prestige

"I have not failed. I've just found 10,000 ways that won't work."

- Thomas A. Edison

SSATKOREA.com

plead
[pleed]

v. to appeal or entreat earnestly

애원하다

He had a good lawyer to plead his case.

syn. beg, implore, entreat

plight
[plahyt]

n. an unfavorable condition

역경, 곤경

The plight of the refugees arouses our compassion.

syn. predicament, quandary, trouble

pluck
[pluhk]

v. to pull off or out from the place of growth

(털을) 뽑다

The falcons pluck the feathers and strip the flesh off their bird prey.

syn. calmness, aplomb, self-composure

poise
[poiz]

n. a state of balance or equilibrium

침착, 균형, 평형

The queen's poise expressed both dignity and grace.

syn. calmness, aplomb, self-composure

ponderous
[**pon**-der-*uh*s]

adj. of great weight, awkward or unwieldy

육중한, 크고 무거워 움직임이 둔한

His steps were heavy and ponderous.

syn. heavy, bulky, awkward, clumsy

portion
[**pawr**-sh*uh*n]

n. a part of any whole

부분, 일부, 1인분

She only eats a small portion of food.

syn. part, piece, share, slice

possess
[**puh**-zes]

v. to own or have

가지다, 소유하다

Mercury was believed to possess magical properties.

syn. have, own, acquire

precipitate
[pri-**sip**-i-teyt]

v. to hasten the occurrence of

(나쁜 일을) 빨리 일어나게 하다, 진척시키다

An invasion would certainly precipitate a political crisis.

syn. hurry, speed, accelerate

predominant
[pri-**dom**-uh-n*uh*nt]

adj. most common or frequent

두드러진, 뚜렷한

Which country is the predominant member of the alliance?

syn. common, prevalent, main

prestige
[pre-**steezh**]

n. reputation arising from success, achievement, or rank

위신, 명망, 명성

As the king's prestige continues to fall, people consider him a liability.

syn. status, stature, reputation

Sentence Completion 8-3

Directions : Fill in the blanks to complete the sentences.

1. Denzel was shocked by the _____ of sea birds after an oil spill.

2. The university has gained international _____.

3. The king looked embarrassed for a moment, then quickly regained his _____.

4. Because so many people like dance music it is the _____ music heard at a school dance.

5. The menacing environment turned a bulky and _____ creature into a fearsome predator.

6. A large _____ of the company's profit goes straight back into new projects.

7. I _____ with you-- never, ever give up on hope.

Answers

1 plight
2 prestige
3 poise
4 predominant
5 ponderous
6 portion
7 plead

381 presume	386 provisional
382 prodigal	387 prowl
383 proficient	388 purge
384 profound	389 pursue
385 proponent	390 quest

"Spread love everywhere you go."

- Mother Teresa

■ SSATKOREA.com

presume
[pri-**zoom**]

v. to suppose or assume something

추정하다, 추측하다

I presume that an agreement will eventually be reached.

syn. believe, assume, guess

prodigal
[**prod**-i-g*uh*l]

adj. wastefully extravagant, giving profusely

낭비하는, 돈을 펑펑 쓰는

A miserly father makes a prodigal son.

syn. wasteful, extravagant, profligate

proficient
[pruh-**fish**-*uh*nt]

adj. well-advanced or competent in any art, science, or subject

능숙한, 솜씨 좋은

With practice, you should become proficient within a year.

syn. skilled, skillful, expert

profound
[pruh-**found**]

adj. penetrating deeply into subjects of thought

매우 깊은, 심오한

Meditation made a profound man.

syn. deep, intense, thoughtful

proponent
[pruh-**poh**-n*uh*nt]

n. a person who puts forward a proposition or proposal

지지자, 옹호자

She is a proponent of alternative medicine that uses a holistic approach.

syn. advocate, champion, supporter

provisional
[pruh-**vizh**-uh-nl]

adj. providing or serving for the time being only

임시의, 일시적인

We accept provisional bookings by phone.

syn. interim, tentative, conditional

prowl
[proul]

v. to rove over in search of what may be found

(동물이) 돌아다니다, 어슬렁대다

Several wolves prowled earlier.

syn. lurk, stroll, roam

purge
[purj]

v. to rid of whatever is impure or undesirable

나쁜 것을 몰아내다, 정화하다

His first act as leader was to purge the party of extremists.

syn. cleanse, clear, purify

pursue
[per-soo]

v. to follow in order to overtake, to strive to gain

추구하다, 밀고 나가다

If you are passionate about something, pursue it.

syn. follow, strive, chase

quest
[kwest]

n. a search or pursuit made in order to find or obtain something

탐구, 탐색, 탐험

Nothing will stop them in their quest for truth.

syn. search, exploration

Sentence Completion 8-4

Directions : Fill in the blanks to complete the sentences.

1. His _____ son is reckless wasteful.

2. The renowned philosopher made many _____ pronouncements.

3. Students might be a _____ of more extended vacations, but parents might be different.

4. After all those hours playing many different games, Anthony became _____ at them.

5. You have the right to cast a _____ ballot if your name is not listed on the voting rolls.

6. The paparazzi _____ a famous actress as a hungry tiger pursues a zebra.

7. Jack traveled the world in a _____ for diamonds.

 Answers

1 prodigal
2 profound
3 proponent
4 proficient
5 provisional
6 pursue
7 quest

391	quote	396	reasonable
392	radiant	397	rebellion
393	rambling	398	rebuff
394	rash	399	recede
395	ratio	400	redundant

"When you reach the end of your rope, tie a knot in it and hang on."

- Franklin D. Roosevelt

SSATKOREA.com

quote
[kwoht]

v. to use a brief excerpt from
인용하다, (남의 말을 그대로) 전달하다

I can quote you several instances of her being deliberately rude.

syn. cite, repeat, recall

radiant
[**rey**-dee-*uh*nt]

adj. emitting rays of light, bright with joy
(행복감이나 건강 등으로) 빛나는, 환한

She was radiant with joy at her wedding.

syn. shinning, bright, illuminated

rambling
[**ram**-bling]

adj. straying from one subject to another
횡설수설하는, 장황하고 두서 없는

Be not careless in deeds, nor confused in words, nor rambling in thought.

syn. straggling, desultory, digressive

rash
[rash]

adj. acting or tending to act too hastily
무분별한, 무모한

He made a rash decision, and now he is suffering for it.

syn. reckless, impulsive, impetuous

ratio
[**rey**-shoh]

n. proportional relation or rate
비율, 비례

The ratio of boys to girls was two to one.

syn. percentage, proportion, quota

reasonable
[**ree**-zuh-nuh-b*uh*l]

adj. agreeable to reason or sound judgement
타당한, 논리적인, 이치에 맞는

The reasonable man adapts himself to the world.

syn. sensible, rational, logical

rebellion
[ri-**bel**-y*uh*n]

n. resistance to one's government or ruler

반란, 모반

Oppression provoked the people to start the rebellion.

syn.   uprising, revolt, defiance

rebuff
[ri-**buhf**]

n. a blunt or abrupt rejection

퇴짜, 거절

He avoided speaking to her, expecting a rebuff.

syn.   rejection, snub, repulse, refusal

recede
[ri-**seed**]

v. to go or move away

(서서히) 물러나다, 약해지다

The flood waters finally began to recede in September.

syn.   retreat, withdraw, diminish

redundant
[ri-**duhn**-d*uh*nt]

adj. relating to unnecessary repetition in expressing ideas

(글이나 말에서) 불필요하게 반복되는

Your writing has too much redundant detail.

syn.   repetitive, unnecessary, superfluous

Sentence Completion 8-5

Directions : **Fill in the blanks to complete the sentences.**

1. Floodwaters _____, as do glaciers.

2. The _____ of teachers to students in this school is one to eight.

3. In your essay, the repeated parts are _____.

4. The _____ man shows sound judgments.

5. Sean realized he blurts out something inappropriate and asked the journalist not to _____ him on that.

6. Jeff regrets his _____ decision - he didn't think about the costs involved.

7. The government has mercilessly crushed the _____.

Analogy 8. Shells

물체와 그 외피를 연결시키는 문제도 자주 출제됩니다.

A는 B의 껍질

corn : husk 옥수수 : 옥수수 껍질	tree : bark 나무 : 나무 껍질
potato : skin 감자 : 감자 껍질	apple : peel 사과 : 사과 껍질
grapefruit : rind 자몽 : 두꺼운 껍질	oyster : shell 굴 : 굴 껍질
engine : housing 엔진 : 엔진 커버	watch : case 시계 : 시계 프레임
horse : hide 말 : 말 가죽	bird : plumage 새 : 깃털
goose : down 거위: 거위털	sheep : wool 양 : 양털
head : scalp 머리 : 두피	body : skin 몸 : 피부
rabbit : angora 토끼 : 토끼털	bread : crust 빵 : 빵 껍질

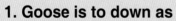

1. Goose is to down as
- (A) bird is to wing
- (B) horse is to mane
- (C) potato is to peel
- (D) sheep is to wool
- (E) flax is to linen

2. Scalp is to head as
- (A) cherry is to pit
- (B) housing is to engine
- (C) grapefruit is to skin
- (D) rind is to orange
- (E) apple is to crate

Check-up 8-1

Directions   Each of the following questions consists of one word followed by five words or phrases.
You are to select the one word or phrase whose meaning is closest to the word in capital letters.

1. OPPONENT
(A) adversary
(B) velocity
(C) exploit
(D) stench
(E) loom

2. OPTION
(A) splendor
(B) choice
(C) sanctuary
(D) tyrant
(E) leeway

3. ORGANIZE
(A) elaborate
(B) scoff
(C) arrange
(D) hover
(E) contribute

4. ORIGINAL
(A) creative
(B) err
(C) wend
(D) inflate
(E) exhibit

5. OVERLAP
(A) exhaust
(B) conserve
(C) flap
(D) exterminate
(E) abbreviate

6. OVERWHELM
(A) sheathe
(B) inhabit
(C) inhibit
(D) flood
(E) dissent

7. PAMPER
(A) inscribe
(B) quench
(C) swivel
(D) retrieve
(E) indulge

8. PARAGON
(A) trace
(B) victor
(C) awe
(D) majority
(E) exemplar

9. PARTIAL
(A) grudging
(B) drastic
(C) paltry
(D) biased
(E) skeptical

10. PERCEIVE
(A) segregate
(B) discern
(C) ooze
(D) swarm
(E) jeopardize

Check-up 8-2

1. PERMANENT

(A) rash
(B) abundant
(C) perpetual
(D) conspicuous
(E) skeptical

2. PERPETUAL

(A) marvelous
(B) eternal
(C) innate
(D) arid
(E) vital

3. PERSEVERE

(A) fathom
(B) evict
(C) persist
(D) foster
(E) enroll

4. PERSISTENT

(A) nimble
(B) ultimate
(C) tenacious
(D) principal
(E) naive

5. PERSPECTIVE

(A) complement
(B) authority
(C) makeshift
(D) view
(E) counterpart

6. PERTINENT

(A) impartial
(B) bashful
(C) aboveboard
(D) sheepish
(E) relevant

7. PESTER

(A) badger
(B) assent
(C) dwindle
(D) bestow
(E) loathe

8. PHENOMENAL

(A) ultimate
(B) extraordinary
(C) mediocre
(D) absolute
(E) cursory

9. PIQUANT

(A) detrimental
(B) impromptu
(C) stimulating
(D) mythical
(E) predatory

10. PLACATE

(A) aspire
(B) beseech
(C) dumbfound
(D) enlighten
(E) appease

Check-up 8-3

Directions Each of the following questions consists of one word followed by five words or phrases. You are to select the one word or phrase whose meaning is closest to the word in capital letters.

1. PLEAD
(A) ebb
(B) implore
(C) abduct
(D) wax
(E) acclaim

2. PLIGHT
(A) figment
(B) garrison
(C) homage
(D) agent
(E) predicament

3. PLUCK
(A) pull out
(B) take in
(C) get over
(D) push down
(E) let out

4. POISE
(A) acquisition
(B) debut
(C) calmness
(D) garland
(E) bias

5. PONDEROUS
(A) illiterate
(B) lush
(C) mottled
(D) bulky
(E) inanimate

6. PORTION
(A) maneuver
(B) revelry
(C) share
(D) obsession
(E) nomad

7. POSSESS
(A) own
(B) delude
(C) compel
(D) wane
(E) administer

8. PRECIPITATE
(A) devour
(B) emphasize
(C) accelerate
(D) gobble
(E) emit

9. PREDOMINANT
(A) exotic
(B) incredulous
(C) devoid
(D) prevalent
(E) indifferent

10. PRESTIGE
(A) status
(B) hovel
(C) omen
(D) mentor
(E) plight

Answer 1.B 2.E 3.A 4.C 5.D 6.C 7.A 8.C 9.D 10.A

Check-up 8-4

Directions Each of the following questions consists of one word followed by five words or phrases. You are to select the one word or phrase whose meaning is closest to the word in capital letters.

1. PRESUME
- (A) detach
- (B) forage
- (C) insulate
- (D) assume
- (E) haggle

2. PRODIGAL
- (A) capricious
- (B) distraught
- (C) formidable
- (D) haughty
- (E) extravagant

3. PROFICIENT
- (A) atypical
- (B) skilled
- (C) congested
- (D) headlong
- (E) dismal

4. PROFOUND
- (A) docile
- (B) uneasy
- (C) deep
- (D) vain
- (E) widespread

5. PROPONENT
- (A) anchor
- (B) bliss
- (C) benefit
- (D) advocate
- (E) ordeal

6. PROVISIONAL
- (A) suitable
- (B) threadbare
- (C) transparent
- (D) valiant
- (E) interim

7. PROWL
- (A) inundate
- (B) stroll
- (C) devastate
- (D) smolder
- (E) adopt

8. PURGE
- (A) dissuade
- (B) endure
- (C) cleanse
- (D) flourish
- (E) kindle

9. PURSUE
- (A) monitor
- (B) sustain
- (C) oblige
- (D) chase
- (E) perturb

10. QUEST
- (A) search
- (B) replenish
- (C) ponder
- (D) outcome
- (E) dispatch

Check-up 8-5

Directions   Each of the following questions consists of one word followed by five words or phrases. You are to select the one word or phrase whose meaning is closest to the word in capital letters.

1. QUOTE
(A) cite
(B) scavenge
(C) adopt
(D) affect
(E) ban

2. RADIANT
(A) impetuous
(B) illuminated
(C) heedful
(D) grievous
(E) dumbfounded

3. RAMBLING
(A) exceptional
(B) finicky
(C) digressive
(D) fragile
(E) humble

4. RASH
(A) intelligent
(B) keen
(C) marine
(D) reckless
(E) precious

5. RATIO
(A) brig
(B) mutiny
(C) talent
(D) proportion
(E) source

6. REASONABLE
(A) recent
(B) petty
(C) novel
(D) mature
(E) sensible

7. REBELLION
(A) token
(B) spine
(C) uprising
(D) bough
(E) terror

8. REBUFF
(A) mope
(B) snub
(C) persist
(D) ensure
(E) mystify

9. RECEDE
(A) flutter
(B) exclaim
(C) intrude
(D) retreat
(E) hibernate

10. REDUNDANT
(A) severe
(B) sullen
(C) spacious
(D) temporary
(E) repetitive

145

401	refined	406	remedy
402	regulate	407	rendezvous
403	reject	408	reside
404	relieve	409	resolute
405	reluctant	410	resource

"You will face many defeats in life, but never let yourself be defeated."

- Maya Angelou

SSATKOREA.com

refined
[ri-**fahynd**]

adj. showing well-bred feeling or taste
교양 있는, 세련된, 고상한

*He was a boy of a **refined** nature, an avid reader and an eager student.*

syn. cultured, civilized, cultivated

regulate
[**reg**-yuh-leyt]

v. to control by a rule or principle
규제하다, 조절하다

*This system can **regulate** the temperature of the room automatically.*

syn. manage, organize, adjust

reject
[ri-**jekt**]

v. to refuse to have or take
거절하다, 거부하다

*Never **reject** an idea, dream or goal because it will be hard work.*

syn. rebuff, dismiss, snub

relieve
[ri-**leev**]

v. to ease or alleviate
(고통을) 없애 주다, 덜어 주다

*His jokes helped to **relieve** the tension.*

syn. alleviate, mitigate, assuage

reluctant
[ri-**luhk**-t*uh*nt]

adj. disinclined to become involved
꺼리는, 마지못한

*People are very **reluctant** to talk about their private lives.*

syn. unwilling, grudging, disinclined

remedy
[**rem**-i-dee]

n. something that cures a disease
치료약, 처리방안, 해결책

*Danger itself is the best **remedy** for danger.*

syn. cure, solution, antidote

rendezvous
[**rahn**-duh-voo]

n. an agreement between two or
more persons to meet

만남, 만날 약속

*I have a rendezvous with Ben
at a restaurant.*

syn. meeting, appointment, assignation

reside
[ri-**zahyd**]

v. to dwell permanently

(특정한 곳에) 살다

*Happiness does not reside in
strength or money.*

syn. live, dwell, occupy, inhabit

resolute
[**rez**-uh-loot]

adj. firmly resolved or determined

단호한, 확고한

*Employees' resolute opposition to the
new system was difficult to overcome.*

syn. determined, persistent, adamant

resource
[**ree**-sawrs]

n. a source of supply, support, or aid

(목적을 이루는 데 도움이 되는) 재료, 재원

*The company's greatest resource
is the dedication of its workers.*

syn. supply, ability, property

Sentence Completion 9-1

Directions : Fill in the blanks to
complete the sentences.

1. Jenny and Sidney met at a
secret _____ in the park.

2. Adapt what is useful,
_____ what is useless,
and add what is specifically your
own.

3. Charles is a _____
man who has good manners and
good taste.

4. Aloe is an excellent
_____ for sunburn.

5. An ice pack can
_____ pain in your wrist.

6. His dad felt _____ to
talk openly with his children.

7. Peter was _____ in
his refusal to apologize.

Answers

1. rendezvous
2. reject   3. refined   4. remedy
5. relieve   6. reluctant   7. resolute

---

411 retain	416 sacrifice
412 reverse	417 sanitary
413 revise	418 savage
414 rigid	419 scarce
415 rummage	420 scheme

"Life is either a daring adventure or nothing at all."

- Helen Keller

SSATKOREA.com

retain
[ri-**teyn**]

v. to keep possession of

(계속) 유지하다

She retains a clear memory of those days.

syn.   hold, contain, possess

reverse
[ri-**vurs**]

v. to turn something the other way around or up or inside out.

(정반대로) 뒤바꾸다, 뒤집다

Can anything be done to reverse this trend?

syn.   overturn, shift, invert

revise
[ri-**vahyz**]

v. to rewrite or reorganize something

(책을) 개정하다, 변경하다

You must revise your first draft.

syn.   correct, alter, amend

rigid
[**rij**-id]

adj. stiff or strict

(규칙이나 방법 등이) 엄격한, 융통성 없는

He grew even more rigid and uncompromising as he got older and older.

syn.   rigorous, rigid, strict

rummage
[**ruhm**-ij]

v. to search thoroughly

뒤지다

He rummaged through piles of second-hand clothes for something that fits.

syn.   search, hunt, explore

sacrifice
[**sak**-ruh-fahys]

n. the offering of animal, plant, or human life to a deity

희생, 희생물

Success is no accident. It is hard work, perseverance, learning, studying, sacrifice and most of all, love of what you are doing.

syn.   victim, scapegoat, offering

sanitary
[**san**-i-ter-ee]

adj. relating to health, especially reference to cleanliness

위생적인, 깨끗한

Diseases were spread through poor sanitary conditions.

syn. hygienic, clean, antiseptic

savage
[**sav**-ij]

adj. fierce, violent, or hostile

야만적인, 잔인한

The article was a savage attack on her past actions.

syn. fierce, ruthless, brutal

scarce
[skairs]

adj. insufficient to satisfy the need

부족한, 드문

Food was often scarce in the winter.

syn. scanty, meager, rare, sparse

scheme
[skeem]

n. a plan, design, or program of action to be followed

계획, 책략, 제도

The scheme was criticized as too idealistic and impracticable.

syn. plot, project, strategy

Sentence Completion 9-2

Directions : Fill in the blanks to complete the sentences.

1. As Clint was such a great assistant, his boss wanted to _____ him for as long as he can.

2. You can _____ a car by putting it in gear called "R."

3. These _____ icicles look stiff and not very flexible.

4. Sally's kitchen was impressively _____ and pristine.

5. If you met a hungry grizzly bear in its native environment, it would seem more _____.

6. Fresh vegetables were _____ during the drought.

7. There's a new _____ in our town for recycling plastic cups.

Answers

1 retain
2 reverse
3 rigid
4 sanitary
5 savage
6 scarce
7 scheme

421	secure	426	shorten
422	seize	427	shove
423	sensitivity	428	significant
424	sentiment	429	simulate
425	serene	430	sink

*"Three can keep a secret,
if two of them are dead."*

- Benjamin Franklin

SSATKOREA.com

secure
[si-**kyoor**]

adj. free from or not exposed to danger or harm

안심하는, 안전한

She doesn't feel secure when she is alone in the house.

syn.   safe, protected, defended

seize
[seez]

v. to take hold of suddenly

꽉 붙잡다, 움켜잡다

Seize the opportunity when it comes up.

syn.   grab, grasp, clutch

sensitivity
[sen-si-**tiv**-i-tee]

n. the state or quality of being sensitive

세심함, 예술적 감성

Migrating birds show extreme sensitivity to air currents.

syn.   responsiveness, sensitiveness, consideration

sentiment
[**sen**-tuh-m*uh*nt]

n. an attitude toward something, a mental feeling

정서, 감정

His speech was encouraging nationalistic sentiment.

syn.   feeling, attitude, sentimentality

serene
[suh-**reen**]

adj. calm, peaceful, or tranquil

고요한, 평화로운, 조용한

She looked as calm and serene as she always did.

syn.   calm, composed, tranquil

shorten
[**shawr**-tn]

v. to make short or shorter

짧게 하다, 단축하다

When the days shorten in winter, some people suffer depression.

syn.   abbreviate, abridge, condense

shove
[shuhv]

v. to move along by force from behind
(거칠게) 밀치다

Help me shove this furniture aside.

syn.   push, thrust, propel

significant
[sig-**nif**-i-k*uh*nt]

adj. expressing a meaning
중요한, 의미 있는

His most significant achievement was the abolition of slavery.

syn.   notable, noteworthy, remarkable

simulate
[**sim**-yuh-leyt]

v. to imitate the appearance or condition
…한 척하다, 가장하다

Computer software can be used to simulate conditions.

syn.   pretend, imitate, affect

sink
[singk]

v. to go beneath the surface of a liquid
(물에) 가라앉다

The boat started to sink into the sea.

syn.   founder, go under, capsize

Sentence Completion 9-3

Directions : Fill in the blanks to complete the sentences.

1. This novel is full of characters who remain _____ no matter how terrible the news.

2. It's better to _____ the rope by a few inches.

3. Now, your money is _____ in a bank.

4. As his little boat has a leak, it might _____ to the bottom of the lake.

5. Lucy's motto is Carpe Diem meaning "_____ the day."

6. A _____ result in a scientific study is a result large enough to matter.

7. Gene has a _____ to pollen that he's sneezing any time it's in the air.

Answers

1 serene
2 shorten
3 secure
4 sink
5 seize
6 significant
7 sensitivity

---

431 skeptical	436 splendor
432 slothful	437 sporadic
433 sociable	438 spotless
434 specific	439 sprinkle
435 spirited	440 steady

"Life isn't about finding yourself.
Life is about creating yourself."

- George Bernard Shaw

SSATKOREA.com

skeptical
[**skep**-ti-k*uh*l]

adj. doubtful about a particular thing
의심 많은, 회의적인

*He is skeptical about how much will
be accomplished by legislation.*

syn. dubious, doubtful, suspicious

slothful
[**slawth**-f*uh*l]

adj. disinclined to work or exertion
나태한, 게으른

Fatigue had made him slothful.

syn. lazy, idle, inactive

sociable
[**soh**-shuh-b*uh*l]

adj. inclined to associate with others
사람들과 어울리기 좋아하는, 사교적인

*Dogs show a very sociable
disposition.*

syn. friendly, affable, gregarious

specific
[spi-**sif**-ik]

adj. stated explicitly or in detail
구체적인, 명확한, 분명한

*Massage may help to increase blood
flow to specific areas of the body.*

syn. particular, specified, detailed

spirited
[**spir**-i-tid]

adj. having courage, vigor, liveliness, etc.
명랑한, 활발한

She was by nature a spirited little girl.

syn. lively, vivacious, vibrant

splendor
[**splen**-der]

n. a brilliant or gorgeous appearance
화려함, 웅장함

*All the splendor in the world is not
worth a good friend.*

syn. magnificence, radiance, grandeur

sporadic
[spuh-**rad**-ik]

adj. happening at irregular intervals in time

산발적인, 이따금 발생하는

*There was rioting and **sporadic** fighting in the city, as rival gangs clashed.*

syn. intermittent, occasional, infrequent

spotless
[**spot**-lis]

adj. immaculately clean

티끌 하나 없는

*This player has a **spotless** record so far.*

syn. perfect, impeccable, flawless

sprinkle
[**spring**-k*uh*l]

v. to scatter in drops of particles

뿌리다, 간간히 섞다

***Sprinkle** chocolate on top of the ice cream.*

syn. splash, scatter, trickle

steady
[**sted**-ee]

adj. stable in position or equilibrium

꾸준한, 변함없는

*Watching **steady** swings of the pendulum relieves some stress.*

syn. stable, constant, regular

Sentence Completion 9-4

Directions : Fill in the blanks to complete the sentences.

1. At a party, it's a good idea to be _____ and make new friends.

2. _____ employees could get fired because they don't feel like doing much of anything.

3. _____ protests look to continue into the night.

4. A _____ person looks at the world with doubt.

5. Ben was astonished by the _____ of the view at the Grand Canyon.

6. His _____ white sneakers have any single smudge on it.

7. Please be more _____. We need more detailed and exact information.

441 steer	446 strive
442 stifle	447 subdue
443 stout	448 subside
444 strategy	449 substantial
445 strenuous	450 substitute

"Never let the fear of striking out keep you from playing the game"
- Babe Ruth

SSATKOREA.com

steer
[steer]

v. to guide the course of by a rudder
(보트나 배 등을) 조종하다, 몰다

Try to steer the lifeboat towards the big ship so that we can pick it up.

syn. guide, direct, maneuver

stifle
[**stahy**-f*uh*l]

v. to quell, crush, or end by force
(감정 등을) 억누르다, 억압하다, 숨막히게 하다

How can the government stifle debate on such a crucial issue?

syn. suffocate, suppress, constrain

stout
[stout]

adj. bulky in figure
통통한, 튼튼한

He was a tall, stout man with black hair.

syn. rotund, corpulent, burly

strategy
[**strat**-i-jee]

n. a careful plan for achieving a goal
전략, 계획

Tactics win battles; strategy wins wars.

syn. plan of action, scheme, method

strenuous
[**stren**-yoo-*uh*s]

adj. characterized by vigorous exertion
힘이 많이 드는, 몹시 힘든, 격렬한

The doctor advised Jay to avoid strenuous exercise.

syn. arduous, herculean, onerous

strive
[strahyv]

v. to exert oneself vigorously
분투하다, 힘들게 노력하다

Two dogs strive for a bone, the third runs away with it.

syn. endeavor, attempt, struggle

subdue
[suhb-**doo**]

v. to overpower by superior force

진압하다, 억누르다

The police subdued the protest.

syn.   quell, repress, suppress

subside
[suhb-**sahyd**]

v. to become quiet or less active

가라앉다, 진정되다

King's rage was beginning to subside.

syn.   abate, decrease, ebb, diminish

substantial
[suhb-**stan**-shuhl]

adj. of considerable amount, quantity, size, etc.

(양이나 가치, 중요성 등이) 상당한

The findings show a substantial difference between the two parties.

syn.   significant, material, consequential

substitute
[suhb-sti-toot]

n. someone or something that takes the place of another for a period of time

대리인, 대체물

Butter can be a substitute for olive oil in this recipe.

syn.   backup, surrogate, replacement

Sentence Completion 9-5

Directions : Fill in the blanks to complete the sentences.

1. A little teapot was short and
_____.

2. His dad spent a
_____amount of money
without any concerns.

3. A _____ work
requires all the effort and strength.

4. People _____for self-
improvement, a better world, or
success in general.

5. You have brains in your head.
You have feet in your shoes. You
can _____ yourself any
direction you choose.

6. The nation's strategy for world
domination relied on its naval
superiority.

7. The troops tried to _____
the rebel forces.

Answers

1 stout
2 substantial
3 strenuous
4 strive
5 steer
6 strategy
7 subdue

SSAT MIDDLE LEVEL   **155**

Analogy 9. Unit & Measure

여러가지 기본 단위, 재는 도구와 대상을 연결짓는 관계입니다. 특히 아래 수학 단위 세 가지는 가장 기본이니 꼭 알아두어야 합니다.

MATH UNIT
Distance : 1 yard = 3 feet = 36 inches
Volume : 1 gallon = 4 quarts = 8 pints = 16 cups
Weight : 1 pound = 16 ounces

A는 B의 단위	
carat : diamond 캐럿 : 다이아몬드	fathom : depth 패덤 (물의 깊이 측정 단위, 6피트) : 깊이
acre : farmland 에이커 : 농지	decibel : sound 데시벨 : 소리
foot : distance 피트 : 거리	calorie : heat 칼로리 : 열량

A는 B를 재는 도구	
altimeter : height 고도계 : 높이	speedometer : velocity 속도계 : 속도
odometer : mileage 주행기록계 : 주행거리, 마일 수	thermometer : temperature 온도계 : 온도
scale : weight 저울 : 무게	compass : direction 나침반 : 방향

POP QUIZ

1. Odometer is to mileage as
- (A) thermometer is to height
- (B) altimeter is to population
- (C) pedometer is to circumference
- (D) thermometer is to temperature
- (E) compass is to distance

2. Diamond is to carat as
- (A) farmland is to acre
- (B) yard is to foot
- (C) pint is to quart
- (D) milk is to inch
- (E) dozen is to egg

Check-up 9-1

Directions Each of the following questions consists of one word followed by five words or phrases. You are to select the one word or phrase whose meaning is closest to the word in capital letters.

1. REFINED
(A) scarce
(B) cultured
(C) uneasy
(D) parallel
(E) opposite

2. REGULATE
(A) afford
(B) coax
(C) manage
(D) banish
(E) cease

3. REJECT
(A) blend
(B) appall
(C) bustle
(D) snub
(E) contain

4. RELIEVE
(A) confirm
(B) deprive
(C) forbid
(D) embrace
(E) alleviate

5. RELUCTANT
(A) unwilling
(B) petty
(C) stout
(D) responsible
(E) positive

6. REMEDY
(A) pessimist
(B) phase
(C) antidote
(D) scoundrel
(E) depth

7. RENDEZVOUS
(A) endeavor
(B) meeting
(C) climate
(D) dusk
(E) merit

8. RESIDE
(A) examine
(B) extinguish
(C) equip
(D) dwell
(E) descend

9. RESOLUTE
(A) severe
(B) threadbare
(C) persistent
(D) quaint
(E) sentimental

10. RESOURCE
(A) supply
(B) contrast
(C) contempt
(D) misgiving
(E) impact

Check-up 9-2

Each of the following questions consists of one word followed by five words or phrases. You are to select the one word or phrase whose meaning is closest to the word in capital letters.

1. RETAIN
(A) intrude
(B) invade
(C) jeer
(D) hold
(E) isolate

2. REVERSE
(A) mystify
(B) invert
(C) launch
(D) limp
(E) memorize

3. REVISE
(A) locate
(B) master
(C) starve
(D) torch
(E) correct

4. RIGID
(A) furious
(B) rigorous
(C) active
(D) dreary
(E) exceptional

5. RUMMAGE
(A) migrate
(B) waft
(C) yield
(D) hunt
(E) mock

6. SACRIFICE
(A) source
(B) orchard
(C) meadow
(D) foliage
(E) scapegoat

7. SANITARY
(A) additional
(B) hygienic
(C) bold
(D) capable
(E) drab

8. SAVAGE
(A) crafty
(B) amiable
(C) fierce
(D) drowsy
(E) feeble

9. SCARCE
(A) external
(B) familiar
(C) hearty
(D) scanty
(E) excessive

10. SCHEME
(A) plot
(B) breadth
(C) surface
(D) peasant
(E) grove

Check-up 9-3

Directions   Each of the following questions consists of one word followed by five words or phrases. You are to select the one word or phrase whose meaning is closest to the word in capital letters.

1. SECURE
(A) individual
(B) gradual
(C) forlorn
(D) protected
(E) mammoth

2. SEIZE
(A) dissolve
(B) reinforce
(C) plummet
(D) grasp
(E) improvise

3. SENSITIVITY
(A) channel
(B) lack
(C) responsiveness
(D) interval
(E) jet

4. SENTIMENT
(A) hue
(B) feeling
(C) shelter
(D) hamlet
(E) chamber

5. SERENE
(A) tranquil
(B) instant
(C) parallel
(D) recent
(E) quaint

6. SHORTEN
(A) abbreviate
(B) glare
(C) domesticate
(D) evolve
(E) vanquish

7. SHOVE
(A) restrain
(B) thrust
(C) abandon
(D) persevere
(E) captivate

8. SIGNIFICANT
(A) sensitive
(B) doleful
(C) notable
(D) restless
(E) reckless

9. SIMULATE
(A) glimpse
(B) hone
(C) exaggerate
(D) pretend
(E) swarm

10. SINK
(A) gripe
(B) possess
(C) extend
(D) originate
(E) founder

159

Check-up 9-4

1. SKEPTICAL
(A) dubious
(B) merciful
(C) conciliatory
(D) allaying
(E) vengeful

2. SLOTHFUL
(A) rash
(B) grateful
(C) weary
(D) insightful
(E) lazy

3. SOCIABLE
(A) cunning
(B) euphonious
(C) gregarious
(D) unforgiving
(E) querulous

4. SPECIFIC
(A) contemptuous
(B) detailed
(C) aspirant
(D) redoubtable
(E) grandiose

5. SPIRITED
(A) accumulated
(B) relevant
(C) brutal
(D) lively
(E) rancorous

6. SPLENDOR
(A) albino
(B) radiance
(C) garment
(D) oblivion
(E) miniature

7. SPORADIC
(A) intermittent
(B) favored
(C) adaptable
(D) limited
(E) praised

8. SPOTLESS
(A) abandoned
(B) impeccable
(C) permanent
(D) wholesome
(E) boring

9. SPRINKLE
(A) shed
(B) linger
(C) recount
(D) scatter
(E) persecute

10. STEADY
(A) restive
(B) admirable
(C) remorseful
(D) frail
(E) stable

Check-up 9-5

Directions   Each of the following questions consists of one word followed by five words or phrases.
You are to select the one word or phrase whose meaning is closest to the word in capital letters.

1. STEER
- (A) direct
- (B) imprison
- (C) stare
- (D) reign
- (E) emancipate

2. STIFLE
- (A) veto
- (B) suffocate
- (C) determine
- (D) enfranchise
- (E) detect

3. STOUT
- (A) refined
- (B) prodigal
- (C) rotund
- (D) incognito
- (E) emaciated

4. STRATEGY
- (A) caliber
- (B) scheme
- (C) depth
- (D) nobility
- (E) etiquette

5. STRENUOUS
- (A) arduous
- (B) barbarian
- (C) cultivated
- (D) haggard
- (E) smug

6. STRIVE
- (A) torture
- (B) transform
- (C) coerce
- (D) endeavor
- (E) summit

7. SUBDUE
- (A) splice
- (B) capsize
- (C) vanquish
- (D) sink
- (E) repress

8. SUBSIDE
- (A) convert
- (B) fling
- (C) wax
- (D) diminish
- (E) alter

9. SUBSTANTIAL
- (A) lackluster
- (B) scintillating
- (C) drab
- (D) material
- (E) sizeable

10. SUBSTITUTE
- (A) glut
- (B) term
- (C) investigation
- (D) entourage
- (E) surrogate

Answer 1.A 2.B 3.C 4.B 5.A 6.D 7.E 8.D 9.D 10.E

451	suffering	456	suspend
452	summon	457	sustain
453	suppress	458	sympathy
454	supreme	459	systematic
455	surrender	460	tangle

"Imagination is more important than knowledge."

- Albert Einstein

SSATKOREA.com

suffering
[**suhf**-er-ing]

n. feelings of mental or physical pain

고통, 괴로움

The famine caused great suffering of the people.

syn.   agony, pain, distress

summon
[**suhm**-*uh*n]

v. to call upon to do something specified

소환하다, 호출하다, 부르다

The event summoned up old memories.

syn.   ask, recall, assemble

suppress
[suh-**pres**]

v. to keep down by unjust use of one's authority

진압하다, 억누르다

She tried to suppress a smile but felt the corner of her mouth twitch.

syn.   restrain, hold in check, abolish

supreme
[suh-**preem**]

adj. highest in rank or authority

(계급이나 위치 면에서) 최고의

The Pope is the supreme leader of the Roman Catholic Church.

syn.   absolute, foremost, perfect

surrender
[suh-**ren**-der]

v. to give up one's power or possessions

항복하다, 굴복하다, 투항하다

The terrorists were given ten minutes to surrender.

syn.   give up, resign, abandon

suspend
[suh-**spend**]

v. to hold or keep undetermined

(결정을) 미루다, 유예하다

The government has decided to suspend production at the country's biggest plant.

syn.   delay, hold off, adjourn

sustain
[suh-**steyn**]

v. to support, hold, or bear up from below

(힘, 생명 등을) 버티다, 지속하다

*These four pillars **sustain** the entire structure.*

syn. maintain, keep up, endure

sympathy
[**sim**-puh-thee]

n. harmony of or agreement in feeling

동정, 연민

*His remorse is just an artifice to gain **sympathy**.*

syn. compassion, affinity, rapport

systematic
[sis-tuh-**mat**-ik]

adj. having a system, method, or plan

체계적인, 조직적인

*Science is the **systematic** classification of experience.*

syn. orderly, methodical, organized

tangle
[**tang**-g*uh*l]

v. to bring together into a mass of confusedly interlaced threads

헝클어뜨리다, 헝클어지다

*The broom somehow got **tangled** up in my long skirt.*

syn. entangle, snarl, entwine

Sentence Completion 10-1

Directions : **Fill in the blanks to complete the sentences.**

1. The ability to feel _____ for others is a great asset as a human.

2. Leonardo was _____ commander of the allied troops.

3. He would rather die than _____ to the invaders.

4. Martha is so _____ about packing for a long trip.

5. Pandemics cause widespread human _____.

6. Russel seems to find it difficult to _____ relationships with colleagues.

7. There is a _____ of cords behind the computer.

Answers

1 sympathy
2 supreme
3 surrender
4 systematic
5 suffering
6 sustain
7 tangle

461	tedious	466	terminate
462	temperate	467	timid
463	tempo	468	tolerant
464	temporary	469	torment
465	tender	470	torture

*"You must be the change
you wish to see in the world."*

- Mahatma Ghandi

SSATKOREA.com

tedious
[**tee**-dee-*uhs*]

adj. marked by monotony or tedium

지루한, 싫증나는

*He was bored by the speaker's
tedious talk.*

syn. boring, dull, monotonous

temperate
[**tem**-per-it]

adj. moderate or self-restrained

온화한

*Please be more temperate in your
language.*

syn. mild, clement, moderate

tempo
[**tem**-poh]

n. characteristic rate, rhythm,
or pattern of work or activity

(음악 작품의) 박자, 템포

This tune has a fast tempo.

syn. speed, pace, rate

temporary
[**tem**-puh-rer-ee]

adj. lasting for a limited amount of time

일시적인, 잠깐 동안의

*Never make a permanent decision for
your temporary emotion.*

syn. brief, interim, fleeting

tender
[**ten**-der]

adj. soft or delicate in substance

상냥한, 다정한, 애정 어린

The steak was tender and juicy.

syn. delicate, fragile, kindhearted

terminate
[**tur**-muh-neyt]

v. to bring to an end

끝나다, 종료되다

*He had no right to terminate the
contract.*

syn. end, abort, finish

timid
[**tim**-id]

adj. lacking in self-assurance, courage, or bravery

소심한, 용기가 없는, 자신감이 없는

She was a rather timid and meek child.

syn. apprehensive, fearful, timorous

tolerant
[**tol**-er-*uh*nt]

adj. inclined or disposed to tolerate

관대한, 아량 있는

People need to be tolerant of different points of view.

syn. open-minded, forbearing, liberal

torment
[tawr-**ment**]

v. to afflict with great bodily or mental suffering

고통, 고민거리

He was tormented by feelings of insecurity.

syn. torture, distress, anguish

torture
[**tawr**-cher]

n. the act of inflicting excruciating pain

고문

Half of the prisoners died after torture and starvation.

syn. torment, persecution, suffering

Sentence Completion 10-2

Directions : **Fill in the blanks to complete the sentences.**

1. Humphrey likes to live in a warm, sunny, and _____ climate.

2. Those who are _____ often worry that things will go wrong.

3. Even the best lecture will seem _____ on this great sunny day.

4. I wish this fantastic party would never _____.

5. Waiting for the result of the admission was sheer _____.

6. She is a _____ person that she says nothing about his awful play.

7. Abandoned puppies need some _____ loving cares.

Answers

1 temperate
2 timid
3 tedious
4 terminate
5 torment
6 tolerant
7 tender

471	toxic	476	ungainly
472	trickery	477	unique
473	trim	478	unwavering
474	ultimate	479	urge
475	uncouth	480	valiant

"If the wind will not serve,
take to the oars."

- Latin Proverb

SSATKOREA.com

toxic
[**tok**-sik]

adj. of, pertaining to, affected with or caused by a toxin or poison

독이 있는, 유독성의

These factories are releasing toxic gases into the atmosphere.

syn. poisonous, virulent, noxious

trickery
[**trik**-uh-ree]

n. the use or practice of tricks

사기, 속임수

The impostor resorted to trickery to get what he wanted.

syn. deception, deceit, artifice

trim
[trim]

v. to put into a neat by clipping, to remove by cutting

다듬다, 손질하다

We should trim off the unnecessary parts of our spending.

syn. cut, crop, shorten

ultimate
[**uhl**-tuh-mit]

adj. last or ending a process or series

궁극적인, 최후의

The ultimate decision lies with the parents.

syn. final, eventual, last

uncouth
[uhn-**kooth**]

adj. strange and ungraceful in appearance

무례한, 상스러운

He may embarrass you with his uncouth behavior.

syn. vulgar, crude, uncivilized

ungainly
[uhn-**geyn**-lee]

adj. not graceful

어색한, 솜씨없는

On land the turtle is ungainly, but in the water, it is very agile.

syn. awkward, clumsy, ungraceful

unique
[yoo-**neek**]

adj. existing as the only one
유일한, 하나만 존재하는

Each person's genetic code is unique except in the case of identical twins.

syn. singular, distinctive, remarkable

unwavering
[un-**wey**-ver-ing]

adj. marked by firm determination
변함없는, 확고한

She has been encouraged by the unwavering support of her family.

syn. steady, fixed, resolute

urge
[urj]

v. to push or force along
충고하다, 설득하려 하다

She urged to shout at him.

syn. encourage, exhort, spur

valiant
[**val**-y*uh*nt]

adj. boldly courageous
용맹한, 용감한

The prince was handsome and valiant like all princes in stories.

syn. brave, courageous, valorous

Sentence Completion 10-3

Directions : Fill in the blanks to complete the sentences.

1. George's _____ goal is to be President of this country.

2. The little boy admired a _____ and determined hero in a comic book.

3. He appeared _____ first and then surprised his coaches with great athletic ability.

4. The boor is an _____, vulgar, and ill-mannered person.

5. The swindler resorted to all sorts of _____ to take over the company as a whole.

6. Each person's genetic code is _____.

7. That was a firm, unshakable and _____ decision.

Answers
1 ultimate
2 valiant
3 ungainly
4 uncouth
5 trickery
6 unique
7 unwavering

481	vanish	486	vigor
482	verdict	487	virtuous
483	verge	488	vital
484	veto	489	vogue
485	vibrant	490	voracious

*"There is no friend
as loyal as a book."*

- Ernest Hemingway

SSATKOREA.com

vanish
[**van**-ish]

v. to disappear from sight

(갑자기 불가사의하게) 사라지다

*The building **vanished** as the fire
swiftly moved through it.*

syn.   disappear, fade, die out

verdict
[**vur**-dikt]

n. the decision reached by a judge
or jury

(배심원단의) 평결, (숙고 뒤 내린) 결정

*The jury reached a unanimous
verdict of 'not guilty.'*

syn.   judgment, adjudication, decision

verge
[vurj]

n. the edge, rim, or margin of something

가장자리, 끝부분

*This treaty brought the country to the
verge of economic collapse.*

syn.   edge, border, threshold

veto
[**vee**-toh]

n. the power vested in one branch of a
government to cancel or postpone the
decisions

거부권, 금지

*The President has the **veto** over new
legislation.*

syn.   ban, embargo, prohibition

vibrant
[**vahy**-bruhnt]

adj. pulsating with vigor and energy

활기찬

*Seoul is a **vibrant**, dynamic and
fascinating city.*

syn.   spirited, vivid, lively

vigor
[**vig**-er]

n. good health

생기, 활력

*A brief rest restored the traveler's
vigor.*

syn.   vitality, liveliness, energy

virtuous
[**vur**-choo-*uhs*]

adj. showing goodness

도덕적인, 고결한

*I cleaned the flat, which left me feeling **virtuous**.*

syn. righteous, good, pure

vital
[**vahyt**-l]

adj. so important that it is required

필수적인, (생명 유지에) 꼭 필요한

*Police have found a **vital** clue to solve the mystery.*

syn. essential, indispensable, crucial

vogue
[vohg]

n. something in fashion, as at a particular time

유행

*Long hairstyles were the **vogue** in the twenties.*

syn. mode, fad, fashion

voracious
[vaw-rey-sh*uhs*]

adj. having a desire to eat large amounts of food

게걸스러운, 탐욕스러운

*He was a **voracious** antique collector.*

syn. greedy, gluttonous, insatiable

Sentence Completion 10-4

Directions : Fill in the blanks to complete the sentences.

1. A patient's _____ signs show they are still alive or not.

2. The _____ man swallows and devours food in a ravenous manner.

3. Congress overrode a _____ issued by the president.

4. Her first novel had a great _____ ten years ago.

5. _____ people are bright and full of personality.

6. A jury in the courtroom made a _____.

7. My puppy is full of _____: he runs all over the house all the time.

491	vulgar	496	whet
492	wander	497	whimsical
493	wane	498	wicked
494	watchful	499	willing
495	wax	500	withdrawn

*"It is never too late to be
what you might have been."*

- George Eliot

SSATKOREA.com

vulgar
[**vuhl**-ger]

adj. lacking good manners or taste
저속한, 천박한

*I think that is the most **vulgar** and
tasteless remark I ever heard in my life.*

syn.   rude, indecent, indelicate

wander
[**won**-der]

v. to ramble without a definite purpose
거닐다, 돌아다니다, 헤매다

*The cattle are allowed to **wander**
freely.*

syn.   stroll, stray, depart

wane
[weyn]

v. to decrease in strength
약해지다, 줄어들다

*The leaders' influence had begun
to **wane** by this time.*

syn.   decline, diminish, decrease

watchful
[**woch**-*fuhl*]

adj. vigilant or alert
지켜보는, 경계하는

*My dad was both a **watchful** parent
and an affectionate friend.*

syn.   observant, alert, vigilant

wax
[waks]

v. to increase in extent, quantity,
intensity or power
점점 커지다

*The moon **waxes** and wanes; it first
increases and then decreases.*

syn.   augment, increase, enlarge

whet
[hwet]

v. to make keen or eager
(욕구나 흥미를) 돋우다

*The book will **whet** your appetite
for more of her work.*

syn.   sharpen, stimulate, excite

whimsical
[**whim**-si-cal]

adj. erratic or unpredictable

엉뚱한, 기발한, 변덕스러운

She has a whimsical sense of humor.

syn. fickle, capricious, fanciful

wicked
[**wik**-id]

adj. very mean or evil

못된, 사악한

The wicked fairy bewitched the princess and made her fall into a long sleep.

syn. vicious, sinful, immoral

willing
[wil-ing]

adj. disposed or consenting

~을 하려 하는, ~에 반대하지 않는

Nothing is impossible to a willing mind.

syn. ready, prepared, disposed

withdrawn
[with-**drawn**]

adj. shy or reticent

내성적인, 내향적인

She became withdrawn and pensive, hardly speaking to anyone.

syn. introverted, reserved, inhibited

Sentence Completion 10-5

Directions : Fill in the blanks to complete the sentences.

1. A _____ is an extremely solitary and withdrawn person for a long time.

2. Write down your goal; otherwise, you could _____ and drift aimlessly.

3. Henry was a _____ participant who is happy to join our project.

4. Ralph serves guests light appetizers to _____ everyone's appetite for dinner.

5. Christoph was so _____ that he decided at the last minute to fly to Europe.

6. He has a _____ sense of criticism, aiming sharply at its victims.

7. Max was a _____ dog keeping an eye on the sidewalk in front of my house all afternoon.

Answers

1 withdrawn
2 wander
3 willing
4 whet
5 whimsical
6 wicked
7 watchful

Analogy 10. Animals

동물 관련 Analogy는 언제나 사랑받는 유형이죠. 특히 Middle Level을 준비하는 학생이라면 더욱 꼼꼼하게 봐야합니다. 흔히 외웠던 단어들이 아닌 고유명사와 명칭이 많으니 따로 꼭 기억해주세요.

동물 : 형용사

beaver : rodent
비버 : 설치류의

kangaroo : marsupial
캥거루 : 주머니과의

암컷 : 수컷

ewe : ram
암양 : 숫양

doe : stag
암사슴 : 수사슴

동물 : 사는 곳 (사람이 만든 곳)

bee : apiary
벌 : 양봉장

bird : aviary
새 : 새장

동물 : 동물 새끼

cow : calf
소 : 송아지

kangaroo : joey
캥거루 : 아기캥거루

동물 : 무리

lion : pride
사자 : 사자 떼

wolf : pack
늑대 : 늑대 떼

동물 : 내는 소리

owl : hoot
올빼미 : 올빼미가 우는 소리

snake : hiss
뱀 : 뱀이 쉿하고 내는 소리

1. Snake is to hiss as
- (A) bellow is to bird
- (B) chirp is to donkey
- (C) bray is to raven
- (D) crow is to tiger
- (E) owl is to hoot

2. Horse is to foal as
- (A) bear is to eaglet
- (B) eagle is to calf
- (C) dog is to kitten
- (D) elephant is to herd
- (E) kangaroo is to joey

Check-up 10-1

Directions   Each of the following questions consists of one word followed by five words or phrases.
You are to select the one word or phrase whose meaning is closest to the word in capital letters.

1. SUFFERING
(A) unanimity
(B) friendliness
(C) agony
(D) impartiality
(E) bias

2. SUMMON
(A) ask
(B) prefer
(C) evacuate
(D) ascertain
(E) coerce

3. SUPPRESS
(A) extenuate
(B) restrain
(C) fabricate
(D) debunk
(E) linger

4. SUPREME
(A) absolute
(B) feasible
(C) dubious
(D) equitable
(E) facile

5. SURRENDER
(A) inscribe
(B) loom
(C) extol
(D) resign
(E) baffle

6. SUSPEND
(A) founder
(B) imitate
(C) delay
(D) loathe
(E) sway

7. SUSTAIN
(A) break in
(B) keep up
(C) catch up
(D) fall out
(E) come apart

8. SYMPATHY
(A) impediment
(B) hyperbole
(C) homage
(D) implement
(E) compassion

9. SYSTEMATIC
(A) beaming
(B) lax
(C) radiant
(D) tardy
(E) methodical

10. TANGLE
(A) lament
(B) entangle
(C) inhabit
(D) moan
(E) inhibit

173

Check-up 10-2

1. TEDIOUS
(A) evanescent
(B) radical
(C) monotonous
(D) downtrodden
(E) gradual

2. TEMPERATE
(A) ignoble
(B) famished
(C) moderate
(D) haughty
(E) reverent

3. TEMPO
(A) pace
(B) abode
(C) fair
(D) domicile
(E) era

4. TEMPORARY
(A) eternal
(B) naïve
(C) cunning
(D) fleeting
(E) erratic

5. TENDER
(A) rash
(B) fragile
(C) vacant
(D) indefatigable
(E) indispensable

6. TERMINATE
(A) initiate
(B) hinder
(C) commence
(D) finish
(E) deter

7. TIMID
(A) ghastly
(B) soiled
(C) fierce
(D) sacred
(E) timorous

8. TOLERANT
(A) forbearing
(B) grievous
(C) herbivorous
(D) hostile
(E) omnipotent

9. TORMENT
(A) insinuation
(B) filament
(C) distress
(D) itinerary
(E) neophyte

10. TORTURE
(A) malice
(B) liaison
(C) replica
(D) lexicon
(E) torment

Check-up 10-3

Directions Each of the following questions consists of one word followed by five words or phrases. You are to select the one word or phrase whose meaning is closest to the word in capital letters.

1. TOXIC
(A) poisonous
(B) innocuous
(C) indolent
(D) meritorious
(E) misconstrued

2. TRICKERY
(A) deception
(B) jubilee
(C) kiln
(D) satire
(E) epic

3. TRIM
(A) grieve
(B) shorten
(C) contrive
(D) devise
(E) narrate

4. ULTIMATE
(A) nonchalant
(B) diurnal
(C) eventual
(D) invidious
(E) jovial

5. UNCOUTH
(A) sophisticated
(B) indifferent
(C) uncivilized
(D) kinetic
(E) leery

6. UNGAINLY
(A) nocturnal
(B) nosy
(C) obvious
(D) clumsy
(E) meddlesome

7. UNIQUE
(A) paltry
(B) xenophobic
(C) officious
(D) singular
(E) ostentatious

8. UNWAVERING
(A) onerous
(B) steady
(C) sumptuous
(D) pliable
(E) opinionated

9. URGE
(A) quell
(B) mollify
(C) appease
(D) raze
(E) spur

10. VALIANT
(A) prejudiced
(B) presumptuous
(C) valorous
(D) opulent
(E) proficient

175

Check-up 10-4

Each of the following questions consists of one word followed by five words or phrases. You are to select the one word or phrase whose meaning is closest to the word in capital letters.

1. VANISH
(A) procure
(B) inquire
(C) aspire
(D) stoop
(E) disappear

2. VERDICT
(A) judgement
(B) loom
(C) pier
(D) synopsis
(E) knack

3. VERGE
(A) edge
(B) residual
(C) litigant
(D) marquee
(E) reminiscence

4. VETO
(A) ruse
(B) ban
(C) patron
(D) sequence
(E) pinnacle

5. VIBRANT
(A) penitent
(B) insolvent
(C) spirited
(D) prominent
(E) reclusive

6. VIGOR
(A) ovation
(B) portal
(C) plight
(D) liveliness
(E) predicament

7. VIRTUOUS
(A) posthumous
(B) righteous
(C) precipitous
(D) eminent
(E) puny

8. VITAL
(A) refractory
(B) superfluous
(C) reputable
(D) refutable
(E) essential

9. VOGUE
(A) compassion
(B) grit
(C) advocate
(D) dissertation
(E) mode

10. VORACIOUS
(A) insatiable
(B) skeptical
(C) acute
(D) obtuse
(E) sluggish

Check-up 10-5

Directions Each of the following questions consists of one word followed by five words or phrases.
You are to select the one word or phrase whose meaning is closest to the word in capital letters.

1. VULGAR
(A) serene
(B) subservient
(C) rude
(D) tacit
(E) disenchanted

2. WANDER
(A) repudiate
(B) stroll
(C) purify
(D) agitate
(E) relinquish

3. WANE
(A) diminish
(B) rectify
(C) siege
(D) petrify
(E) sojourn

4. WATCHFUL
(A) uniform
(B) toxic
(C) succinct
(D) observant
(E) solitary

5. WAX
(A) lunge
(B) increase
(C) smite
(D) thwart
(E) writhe

6. WHET
(A) transgress
(B) sully
(C) wily
(D) sharpen
(E) terminate

7. WHIMSICAL
(A) smeared
(B) tenacious
(C) capricious
(D) unscrupulous
(E) sullen

8. WICKED
(A) lengthy
(B) verbose
(C) untimely
(D) vicious
(E) therapeutic

9. WILLING
(A) prepared
(B) wordy
(C) competent
(D) tenuous
(E) vivacious

10. WITHDRAWN
(A) gregarious
(B) woeful
(C) reserved
(D) doleful
(E) wanton

UPPER

한세희의 SSAT HIT VOCABULARY

LEVEL

1 abbreviate   6 acclaim

2 abdicate   7 accost

3 abscond   8 acquiesce

4 abstain   9 acquit

5 accentuate   10 adamant

School Motto

"Aspirando et Perseverando"

(Aspiring and Persevering)

- Avon Old Farms School

SSATKOREA.com

abbreviate
[uh-**bree**-vee-eyt]

v. to shorten a word or phrase

축약하다, 줄여서 쓰다

You can abbreviate the word, "page" to "p."

syn. shorten, abridge, reduce

abdicate
[**ab**-di-keyt]

v. to give up or renounce authority, duties or an office

(왕위나 권리를) 포기하다, 버리다

Edward VIII abdicated the British throne to marry the woman he loved.

syn. resign, repudiate, quit

abscond
[ab-**skond**]

v. to depart secretly

몰래 도주하다, 무단 이탈하다

Detained patients absconded from the hospital.

syn. run away, disappear, depart secretly

abstain
[ab-**steyn**]

v. to hold oneself back voluntarily from an action

자제하다, 삼가다

After reading the article on the effect of meat on blood pressure, she decided to abstain from eating meat.

syn. refrain, hold back

accentuate
[ak-**sen**-choo-eyt]

v. to put stress on

강조하다, 두드러지게 하다

Delete the negative; accentuate the positive!

syn. underline, underscore, emphasize

acclaim
[uh-**kleym**]

v. to announce with great approval

칭송하다, 환호를 보내다

She was acclaimed as Sportscaster of the Year in 1978.

syn. applaud, laud, praise

accost
[uh-**kost**]

v. to speak to someone

다가가 말 걸다

He accosted me with excessive kindness, for he had been drinking much.

syn. address, come up to, approach

acquiesce
[ak-wee-**es**]

v. to comply silently without protest

마지못해 조용히 따르다, 순순히 따르다

Alex acquiesced to his brother's request to join the party.

syn. comply, consent, agree

acquit
[uh-**kwit**]

v. declare not guilty

무죄를 선고하다

The jury acquitted John, but he still thinks he's guilty.

syn. exonerate, absolve, vindicate

adamant
[**ad**-uh-m*uh*nt]

adj. stubbornly refusing to change one's mind

요지부동의, 단호한

Ellen was adamant that she would not go.

syn. unyielding, determined, insistent

Sentence Completion 1-1

Directions : Fill in the blanks to complete the sentences.

1. Luke is an _____ man who stubbornly refuses to change his mind.

2. The broker helped prisoners _____ last night.

3. Collins reluctantly decided to_____ to plans.

4. Jacqueline likes to _____ her name to "Jackie."

5. Christian tends to _____ certain words in his monologue to emphasize his anger.

6. The king had to _____ his authority when he married a divorcee.

7. The attorney has never failed to _____ a client charged with murder.

8. The paparazzi's job is to _____ celebrities and snap their candid photos.

Answers

1. adamant
2. abscond
3. acquiesce
4. abbreviate
5. accentuate
6. abdicate
7. acquit
8. accost

11 adhere	16 advocate
12 admonish	17 aesthetic
13 adroit	18 affected
14 adversary	19 affiliate
15 adversity	20 affinity

School Motto

"Amat Victoria Curam"

(Victory Loves Care)

- Baylor School

SSATKOREA.com

adhere
[ad-**heer**]

v. to stick fast

달라붙다, 지지하다

Her wet clothes adhere to the skin.

syn. stick, cling, attach

admonish
[ad-**mon**-ish]

v. to caution, advise, or counsel

부드럽게 타이르다, 훈계하다

The teacher admonished the students not to forget the homework.

syn. advise, warn, censure

adroit
[uh-**droit**]

adj. expert or nimble in the use of the hands or body

솜씨 좋은, 노련한

The adroit basketball player scored forty points and twenty assists.

syn. nimble, dexterous, skillful

adversary
[**ad**-ver-ser-ee]

n. someone who fights against

적, 적대자

He will take vengeance on his adversaries.

syn. foe, enemy, opponent

adversity
[ad-**vur**-si-tee]

n. adverse fortune or fate

역경, 고난

By facing adversity, people learn how to handle difficult situations.

syn. hardship, mishap, trouble

advocate
[**ad**-vuh-keyt]

n. a supporter

지지자, 옹호자

Nancy got a powerful advocate to defend her.

syn. backer, proponent, supporter

aesthetic
[es-**thet**-ik]

adj. having a sense of beauty

아름다움의, 심미적인, 미적인

*The colors she uses in her paintings create a lively **aesthetic** sense.*

syn. beautiful, artistic, esthetic

affected
[uh-**fek**-tid]

adj. assumed artificially or pretending

~ 한 척하는, 가장된, 꾸민

*Her **affected** laugh shows her indifference.*

syn. assumed, feigned, unnatural

affiliate
[uh-**fil**-ee-eyt]

v. to associate with a larger organization

제휴하다, 연계하다

*The research center is **affiliated** with the university.*

syn. ally, associate, incorporate

affinity
[uh-**fin**-i-tee]

n. a natural liking for or attraction to a person, thing, or idea

친밀감

*Henry has always had an **affinity** and a passion for cars.*

syn. affection, liking, fondness

Sentence Completion 1-2

Directions : **Fill in the blanks to complete the sentences.**

1. Jessy's smile is _____ and pretentious.

2. The teachers _____ me for running in a hallway.

3. Meryl is an undefeated chess champion; there was no _____ who was able to beat her.

4. Refugees from troubled regions encounter terrible _____.

5. Josh is surprisingly _____ in the kitchen.

6. Yeri's little purse has an _____ value; it looks like a work of art.

7. Teenagers tend to _____ themselves with those from a similar background.

8. A dry surface helps the tiles _____ to the wall.

 Answers

1. affected	
2. admonish	
3. adversary	
4. adversity	
5. adroit	
6. aesthetic	
7. affiliate	
8. adhere	

21 aftermath   26 altercation

22 akin   27 ambivalent

23 allege   28 amend

24 allot   29 amicable

25 aloof   30 amorphous

School Motto

"Pro Vita Non Pro Schola Discimus"

(Learning - Not just for School, but for Life)

- Berkshire School

SSATKOREA.com

aftermath
[**af**-ter-math]

n. the consequences of an event

결과, 여파, 후유증

The United Nations was founded in the aftermath of World War II.

syn.   consequence, result, chain reaction

akin
[uh-**kin**]

adj. related by blood

비슷한, 관련 있는

This game is closely akin to football.

syn.   related, connected, blood-related

allege
[uh-**lej**]

v. to assert without proof

혐의를 제기하다, 주장하다

The police allege that the man was murdered, but they have given no proof.

syn.   assert, claim, charge

allot
[uh-**lot**]

v. to administer or bestow, as in small portions

나누어 주다, 할당하다

How much time has been allotted to this work?

syn.   assign, give portion, allocate

aloof
[uh-**loof**]

adj. remote in manner

냉담한, 무관심한

They always stood aloof from their classmates.

syn.   remote, detached, phlegmatic

altercation
[awl-ter-**key**-sh*uh*n]

n. a heated or angry dispute

심한 논쟁, 언쟁, 말싸움

He became involved in an altercation with a police officer over a parking ticket.

syn.   verbal fight, argument, brawl

ambivalent

[am-**biv**-uh-l*uh*nt]

adj. having mixed feelings about someone or something

반대 감정이 공존하는

*She felt **ambivalent** about her new school.*

syn.   conflicting, contradictory, mixed

amend

[uh-**mend**]

v. to make better

고치다, 더 좋게 바꾸다

*Congress has the right to **amend** the Constitution.*

syn.   change, alter, mend

amicable

[**am**-i-kuh-b*uh*l]

adj. showing goodwill

우호적인, 원만한

*The **amicable** relations between the two countries helped them quickly agree to reduce the tariff.*

syn.   friendly, amiable, affable

amorphous

[uh-**mawr**-f*uh*s]

adj. without definite shape

확실한 형태가 없는, 무정형의

*The idea of "the cloud" is still **amorphous** to most people.*

syn.   formless, shapeless

Sentence Completion 1-3

Directions : Fill in the blanks to complete the sentences.

1. The _____ of a car crash has changed Carry into a whole new person.

2. This lovely restaurant is a bit tucked away in the town center, but it has an _____ atmosphere.

3. Diane is the _____ murderer; she's been accused but not convicted.

4. Mario felt _____ about his lunch options between a tomato pasta and cream pasta.

5. James seems _____ , distant and reserved, but he is warm-hearted.

6. The _____ between his parents makes Marilyn scared, sad, and upset.

7. Hundreds of _____ jellyfish were drifting on the surface of the ocean.

8. Football is _____ to the sport of rugby.

Answers

1. aftermath	5. aloof
2. amicable	6. altercation
3. alleged	7. amorphous
4. ambivalent	8. akin

31	analogous	36	anonymous
32	anguish	37	anthology
33	animosity	38	antithesis
34	annihilate	39	apathy
35	annotation	40	aplomb

School Motto

"Venite, Studete, Discite"

(Come, Study, Learn)

- Blair Academy

SSATKOREA.com

analogous
[uh-**nal**-uh-g*uh*s]

adj. corresponding in some particular

유사한, 비슷한

The director is analogous to the conductor of a symphony orchestra.

syn.   agreeing, similar, corresponding

anguish
[**ang**-gwish]

n. severe suffering or pain

고통, 괴로움, 고민

He felt not the physical pain but mental anguish.

syn.   agony, suffering, pain

animosity
[an-uh-**mos**-i-tee]

n. a feeling of strong dislike

적대감, 적개심

Life appears to me too short to be spent in nursing animosity.

syn.   hatred, hostility, antipathy

annihilate
[uh-**nahy**-uh-leyt]

v. to destroy utterly

전멸시키다, 완패시키다

The massive attack almost annihilated the city.

syn.   pulverize, demolish, decimate

annotation
[an-uh-**tey**-sh*uh*n]

n. a critical or explanatory note

주석, 낱말이나 문장의 뜻을 쉽게 풀이하는 설명

You can provide instant feedback from anywhere, adding an annotation.

syn.   footnote, comment, note

anonymous
[uh-**non**-uh-m*uh*s]

adj. without any name acknowledged

익명으로, 존재를 알리지 않고

Coincidence is God's way of remaining anonymous.

syn.   nameless, unknown, unidentified

anthology
[an-**thol**-uh-jee]

adj. a collection of selected writings

시 선집, 문집, 작품 모음집

A well-chosen anthology is a medicine for the mental distress.

syn. collection, compilation, selection

antithesis
[an-**tith**-uh-sis]

n. opposition or contrast

정반대

The writer's life has been the antithesis of his famous book.

syn. opposite, reverse, contrast

apathy
[**ap**-uh-thee]

n. absence of passion or emotion

냉담, 무관심

Hate is not the opposite of love; apathy is.

syn. indifference, aloofness, detachment

aplomb
[uh-**plom**]

n. great calmness and composure

침착함, 태연함

The manager could handle angry customers with aplomb.

syn. poise, assurance, calmness

Sentence Completion 1-4

Directions : Fill in the blanks to complete the sentences.

1. Grace's _____ shows great restraint under even the most stressful circumstances.

2. The wings of a bird are _____ to the wings of an airplane.

3. In the golden ages of the Hippie Movement, voters elected Richard Nixon, the _____ of a hippie.

4. The next king ordered his subjects to _____ any traces of the previous sovereign.

5. As Ruth humiliated him in front of a crowd, their friendship turned into _____.

6. An _____ donor gave a lot of donations to a museum.

7. The teacher was so angry at Alec that she treated him with _____ instead of yelling at him.

8. A trip to a dentist causes Jeff _____.

Answers

1. aplomb
2. analogous
3. antithesis
4. annihilate
5. animosity
6. anonymous
7. apathy
8. anguish

41 apprehensive	46 assess
42 archaic	47 assiduous
43 ardent	48 assimilate
44 articulate	49 atone
45 ascertain	50 audacious

School Motto

"Victuri te Salutamus"

(we greet thee, we, about to live)

- Brooks School

SSATKOREA.com

apprehensive
[ap-ri-**hen**-siv]

adj. uneasy or fearful about something that might happen

걱정되는, 두려워하는, 불안한

He was apprehensive about telling anyone he really liked her.

syn. anxious, fearful, afraid

archaic
[ahr-**key**-ik]

adj. primitive or old

오래된, 구식의, 고대의

You can see a wonderful archaic Greek marble object in this museum.

syn. ancient, antiquated, obsolete

ardent
[**ahr**-dnt]

adj. eager or enthusiastic

열렬한, 열정적인

James is an ardent supporter of the national soccer team.

syn. passionate, zealous, eager

articulate
[ahr-**tik**-yuh-lit]

v. to express and pronounce clearly

또박또박 말하다, 분명히 표현하다

Good business leaders create a vision and articulate the vision.

syn. clarify, explain, explicate

ascertain
[as-er-**teyn**]

v. to find out

알아내다, 확인하다

The police are trying to ascertain what happened.

syn. determine, certify, conclude

assess
[uh-**ses**]

v. to estimate officially the value

평가하다, 측정하다

The government needs to assess the value of your home before they set the property tax.

syn. appraise, estimate, measure

assiduous

[uh-**sij**-oo-*uh*s]

adj. working diligently at a task

근면한, 성실한

She was assiduous in her attendance at church.

syn. industrious, laborious, diligent

assimilate

[uh-**sim**-uh-leyt]

v. to become similar

동화되다, 비슷해지다

Immigrants want to assimilate quickly.

syn. absorb, adapt, adjust

atone

[uh-**tohn**]

v. to make up for

뉘우치다, 회개하다, 속죄하다

How can I atone for hurting your feelings?

syn. recompense, compensate

audacious

[aw-**dey**-sh*uh*s]

adj. extremely bold or daring

대담한, 뻔뻔한

Fortune favors the audacious.

syn. bold, daring, brazen

Sentence Completion 1-5

Directions : Fill in the blanks to complete the sentences.

1. When Matilda tries to cross a busy intersection with no stop signs, she is a bit _____.

2. Joan was _____ to undertake a new venture and take risks.

3. Many _____ fans buy every single item relating to the pop star.

4. A highly _____ person can express thoughts and feelings quickly and clearly.

5. The detective has been unable to _____ the cause of the explosion.

6. Good detectives are _____ ; they care a lot and make a persistent effort.

7. Before Henry tried to sell his car, he asked an expert to _____ its value.

8. Many immigrants could not _____ into an alien culture immediately.

MIDDLE 1 2 3 4 5 6 7 8 9 10

UPPER 1 2 3 4 5 6 7 8 9 10

Analogy 11. Group : Member

전체와 그 구성원을 연결하는 문제 입니다. 매번 빠지지 않고 등장하는 출제 빈도가 높은 유형이죠.

A는 B로 구성되어 있는 것

constellation : star
별자리: 별

archipelago : island
군도 : 섬

faculty : teacher
강사진 : 선생님

jury : juror
배심원단 : 배심원

orchestra : instrumentalist
오케스트라 : 연주자

choir : singer
합창단 : 가수

mosaic : tile
모자이크 : 타일

bouquet : flower
꽃다발 : 꽃

team : player
팀 : 선수

congregation : worshipper
(예배보러 모인) 신도들 : 신도

mob : insurgent
군중 : 반역자

regiment : soldier
(군대의) 연대 : 군인

city : precinct
도시 : 구역

company : division
회사 : 부서

paragraph : sentence
문단 : 문장

sentence : word
문장 : 단어

poem : stanza
시 : 연

book : chapter
책 : 장

play : act
연극 : 막

symphony : movement
교향곡 : 악장

POP QUIZ

1. Mob is to insurgent as
- (A) sentence is to paragraph
- (B) regiment is to soldier
- (C) city is to municipal
- (D) line is to stanza
- (E) faculty is to caliber

2. Movement is to symphony as
- (A) play is to act
- (B) flower is to bouquet
- (C) chapter is to book
- (D) aria is to singer
- (E) company is to division

Check-up 1-1

Directions   Each of the following questions consists of one word followed by five words or phrases.
You are to select the one word or phrase whose meaning is closest to the word in capital letters.

1. ABBREVIATE
(A) retire
(B) forsake
(C) shorten
(D) mimic
(E) liberate

2. ABDICATE
(A) captivate
(B) imbibe
(C) prohibit
(D) resign
(E) illuminate

3. ABSCOND
(A) depart secretly
(B) listen secretly
(C) watch secretly
(D) save secretly
(E) tell secretly

4. ABSTAIN
(A) obtain
(B) refrain
(C) pertain
(D) attain
(E) sustain

5. ACCENTUATE
(A) recount
(B) abate
(C) perplex
(D) emphasize
(E) beckon

6. ACCLAIM
(A) confer
(B) abridge
(C) counsel
(D) edify
(E) applaud

7. ACCOST
(A) inquire
(B) obtain
(C) address
(D) insinuate
(E) praise

8. ACQUIESCE
(A) comply
(B) inspire
(C) yearn
(D) dwindle
(E) associate

9. ACQUIT
(A) extend
(B) confine
(C) acquire
(D) summon
(E) exonerate

10. ADAMANT
(A) aesthetic
(B) unyielding
(C) bewildered
(D) insane
(E) adjoining

Answer 1.C 2.D 3.A 4.B 5.D 6.E 7.C 8.A 9.E 10.B

Check-up 1-2

Each of the following questions consists of one word followed by five words or phrases.
You are to select the one word or phrase whose meaning is closest to the word in capital letters.

1. ADHERE
(A) stick
(B) detach
(C) contact
(D) retain
(E) adjust

2. ADMONISH
(A) amuse
(B) warn
(C) predict
(D) activate
(E) require

3. ADROIT
(A) remote
(B) placid
(C) lofty
(D) treacherous
(E) dexterous

4. ADVERSARY
(A) wilderness
(B) taunt
(C) foe
(D) debris
(E) mischief

5. ADVERSITY
(A) corrosion
(B) hoist
(C) mishap
(D) tremor
(E) route

6. ADVOCATE
(A) miniature
(B) backer
(C) scale
(D) expedition
(E) affliction

7. AESTHETIC
(A) artistic
(B) solitary
(C) immense
(D) meddlesome
(E) vital

8. AFFECTED
(A) feigned
(B) splendid
(C) natural
(D) dreadful
(E) apprehensive

9. AFFILIATE
(A) dwell
(B) associate
(C) shroud
(D) esteem
(E) soothe

10. AFFINITY
(A) originality
(B) embarrassment
(C) affection
(D) consequence
(E) affectation

Check-up 1-3

Directions Each of the following questions consists of one word followed by five words or phrases. You are to select the one word or phrase whose meaning is closest to the word in capital letters.

1. AFTERMATH
(A) consequence
(B) replica
(C) prejudice
(D) fusion
(E) recipient

2. AKIN
(A) related
(B) prominent
(C) unattainable
(D) humid
(E) distant

3. ALLEGE
(A) furnish
(B) shake
(C) hoard
(D) ooze
(E) assert

4. ALLOT
(A) scoff
(B) lessen
(C) require
(D) assign
(E) diminish

5. ALOOF
(A) approximate
(B) detached
(C) archaic
(D) obsolete
(E) vulnerable

6. ALTERCATION
(A) competition
(B) trauma
(C) brawl
(D) volition
(E) tome

7. AMBIVALENT
(A) conflicting
(B) sumptuous
(C) blended
(D) astute
(E) succinct

8. AMEND
(A) supersede
(B) transfer
(C) shed
(D) repel
(E) alter

9. AMICABLE
(A) peculiar
(B) beneficial
(C) affable
(D) stupendous
(E) querulous

10. AMORPHOUS
(A) formless
(B) eccentric
(C) raucous
(D) posthumous
(E) visible

193

Check-up 1-4

Directions   Each of the following questions consists of one word followed by five words or phrases. You are to select the one word or phrase whose meaning is closest to the word in capital letters.

1. ANALOGOUS
(A) severe
(B) similar
(C) exacting
(D) versatile
(E) resourceful

2. ANGUISH
(A) jubilee
(B) voyage
(C) rash
(D) agony
(E) fatigue

3. ANIMOSITY
(A) brawl
(B) prelude
(C) supplement
(D) fracture
(E) hatred

4. ANNIHILATE
(A) investigate
(B) pulverize
(C) abolish
(D) afflict
(E) smite

5. ANNOTATION
(A) harbinger
(B) outskirts
(C) rodent
(D) perseverance
(E) footnote

6. ANONYMOUS
(A) prodigious
(B) compassionate
(C) titular
(D) nameless
(E) mere

7. ANTHOLOGY
(A) motive
(B) plight
(C) precedent
(D) collection
(E) hazard

8. ANTITHESIS
(A) fad
(B) nomad
(C) labyrinth
(D) pedestal
(E) opposite

9. APATHY
(A) skirmish
(B) indifference
(C) controversy
(D) objective
(E) likeness

10. APLOMB
(A) anxiety
(B) poise
(C) novelty
(D) atlas
(E) bondage

Check-up 1-5

Directions Each of the following questions consists of one word followed by five words or phrases. You are to select the one word or phrase whose meaning is closest to the word in capital letters.

1. APPREHENSIVE
(A) unwieldy
(B) bold
(C) vertical
(D) anxious
(E) numerous

2. ARCHAIC
(A) subsequent
(B) fanciful
(C) innate
(D) minute
(E) ancient

3. ARDENT
(A) zealous
(B) aloft
(C) sinister
(D) exhilarating
(E) nostalgic

4. ARTICULATE
(A) pursue
(B) revive
(C) decelerate
(D) clarify
(E) accelerate

5. ASCERTAIN
(A) slither
(B) determine
(C) accustom
(D) translate
(E) segregate

6. ASSESS
(A) estimate
(B) inscribe
(C) envelop
(D) diminish
(E) possess

7. ASSIDUOUS
(A) industrious
(B) fruitful
(C) monotonous
(D) auspicious
(E) inattentive

8. ASSIMILATE
(A) absorb
(B) avoid
(C) assent
(D) avow
(E) avert

9. ATONE
(A) detain
(B) terminate
(C) insist
(D) glare
(E) recompense

10. AUDACIOUS
(A) fair
(B) brazen
(C) indifferent
(D) laudable
(E) deficient

51	augment	56	banal
52	auspicious	57	belittle
53	austere	58	belligerent
54	avert	59	benediction
55	badger	60	benevolent

School Motto

"Servons"

(Let Us Serve)

- Cate School

SSATKOREA.com

augment
[awg-**ment**]

v. to add to

증가시키다, 늘리다

She wants to find work to augment her income.

syn.   amplify, enlarge, expand

auspicious
[aw-**spish**-uhs]

adj. favored by fortune

상서로운, 길조의

Getting an A on your first quiz is an auspicious way to start the semester.

syn.   favorable, fortunate, prosperous

austere
[aw-**steer**]

adj. severe in manner or appearance

꾸밈없는, 엄격한

The courtroom was a large dark chamber, an austere place.

syn.   harsh, severe, strict

avert
[uh-**vurt**]

v. to turn away or aside

외면하다, 피하다

We averted getting stuck in traffic by leaving early in the morning.

syn.   prevent, avoid, preclude

badger
[**baj**-er]

v. to harass or urge persistently

귀찮게 하다, 괴롭히다

The boys badgered their mother for candy.

syn.   annoy, pester, vex

banal
[buh-**nal**]

adj. devoid of freshness or originality

진부한, 평범한

It was just another banal gossip.

syn.   hackneyed, trite, insipid

belittle
[bih-**lit**-l]

v. to regard or portray as less impressive or important
우습게 알다, 하찮게 여기다

She felt her boss belittled her achievements.

syn. depreciate, disparage, put down

belligerent
[buh-**lij**-er-uhnt]

adj. combative, pugnacious, aggressive
호전적인, 적대적인

The belligerent student was always starting fights.

syn. aggressive, hostile, bellicose

benediction
[ben-i-**dik**-shuhn]

n. an utterance of good wishes
축복, 축복의 기도

The pastor pronounced a benediction before the big football game.

syn. blessing, prayer

benevolent
[buh-**nev**-uh-luhnt]

adj. expressing goodwill or kindly feelings
친절한, 자애로운

Donating her bone marrow to her cousin was a benevolent act.

syn. good, kind, humane

Sentence Completion 2-1

Directions : Fill in the blanks to complete the sentences.

1. Jeffrey's poetry is full of _____ and repeated phrases.

2. Lilian won her first match of the season 7–1 which was an _____ start.

3. Dustin had _____ parents because of financial difficulties.

4. The landlords relentlessly _____ the families about rent.

5. The teacher collects Vivien's homework with a _____ smile.

6. Don't _____ yourself – you did well.

7. When their team lost, angry hockey fans tended to be _____.

8. Put some salt on an icy sidewalk to _____ accidents.

 **Answers**

1. banal
2. auspicious
3. austere
4. badger
5. benevolent
6. belittle
7. belligerent
8. avert

61 berate	66 bulge
62 bias	67 bulwark
63 blemish	68 caliber
64 blend	69 callous
65 bondage	70 candid

School Motto

"Fidelitas et Integritas"

(Fidelity and Integrity)

- Choate Rosemary Hall

SSATKOREA.com

berate
[bih-**reyt**]

v. to scold

질책하다, 심하게 꾸짖다

John's mother berated him for not studying more for the test.

syn. reproach, rebuke, reprimand

bias
[**bahy**-uhs]

n. a particular tendency or inclination

편견

Some institutions still have a strong bias against women.

syn. prejudice, partiality, predilection

blemish
[**blem**-ish]

n. a defect or flaw

티, 흠, 오점, 잘못

A round chicken-pox scar was the only blemish on his face.

syn. defect, stain, flaw

blend
[blend]

v. to mix smoothly and inseparably together

섞다, 혼합하다

To make a milkshake, blend ice cream and milk.

syn. combine, compound, unite

bondage
[**bon**-dij]

n. slavery or involuntary servitude

노예제, 구속, 속박

Abraham Lincoln freed the slaves from their bondage.

syn. slavery, subjugation, enslavement

bulge
[b*uh*lj]

v. to swell or bend outward

가득 차다, 불룩하다, 툭 튀어 나오다

His stomach bulged after the huge meal.

syn. swell, protrude, bloat

bulwark
[**bool**-werk]

n. a wall of earth or other material protection for defense

방어물, 성채, 요새

The king ordered the construction of defensive bulwarks around the castle.

syn.   fort, fortress, citadel

caliber
[**kal**-uh-ber]

n. degree of capacity or competence

도량, 재간, 능력

She needs a lawyer of high caliber to ensure she doesn't go to jail.

syn.   ability, quality, capability

callous
[**kal**-uhs]

adj. insensitive or emotionally hardened

냉담한, 감정이 없는

The tyrant showed a callous indifference to human suffering.

syn.   insensitive, indifferent, apathetic

candid
[**kan**-did]

adj. open and sincere

솔직한, 숨김 없는

Let me be quite candid with you.

syn.   frank, open, ingenuous

Sentence Completion 2-2

Directions : Fill in the blanks to complete the sentences.

1. Yul's parents always trust their _____ son.

2. The slaves were kept in _____ until their death.

3. The president has accused the media of _____.

4. If you _____ red and yellow, you get orange.

5. The angry customer started to _____ Rachel, calling her names in front of the whole store.

6. John has become an insensitive or _____ person after his wife died.

7. When Olivia found the tiniest _____ on her new bike, she made a fuss.

8. A leak in the roof made the ceiling _____.

Answers

1. candid
2. bondage
3. bias
4. blend
5. berate
6. callous
7. blemish
8. bulge

---

71 capricious   76 chagrin

72 catastrophe   77 chide

73 cease   78 chronic

74 celestial   79 circumvent

75 censure   80 cite

School Motto

"Aim High"

- Cranbrook Schools

SSATKOREA.com

cease
[sees]

v. to stop or end
중단되다, 그치다

All chattering ceases every time my gym teacher blows her whistle.

syn. discontinue, quit, stop, halt

celestial
[suh-**les**-ch*uh*l]

adj. pertaining to the sky or visible heaven
하늘의, 천상의, 천체의

Planets, stars, and comets are all celestial objects.

syn. heavenly, ethereal, divine

capricious
[kuh-**prish**-uhs]

adj. impulsive and unpredictable
변덕스러운, 잘 변하는

The capricious spring weather is unpredictable.

syn. fickle, whimsical, erratic

censure
[**sen**-sher]

v. to criticize or reproach in a harsh or vehement manner
비난, 질책하다

The teacher censured Luke for talking in class.

syn. blame, chide, reprove

catastrophe
[kuh-**tas**-truh-fee]

n. a sudden and widespread disaster
대참사, 대재앙

The expansion of the business was a catastrophe for the firm.

syn. calamity, disaster, misfortune

chagrin
[shuh-**grin**]

n. a feeling of vexation, disappointment or humiliation
원통함, 분함

The severe racism was a source of chagrin for Tiara.

syn. disappointment, humiliation

chide

[chahyd]

v. to express disapproval of

꾸짖다, 야단치다

*Tania's mother **chided** her for not eating her vegetables.*

syn. reprimand, scold, reprove

chronic

[**kron**-ik]

adj. continuing over a long period

만성적인, 고질적인

*Ray's **chronic** lateness frustrated his teacher.*

syn. persistent, stubborn, constant

circumvent

[sur-kuhm-**vent**]

v. to avoid fulfilling, answering, or performing

피하다

*The fugitive **circumvented** capture by anticipating the movements of the police.*

syn. avoid, bypass, evade

cite

[sahyt]

v. to quote a passage, book, author

이유나 예를 들다, 인용하다

*An effective essay will **cite** several authorities' sources.*

syn. mention, quote, indicate

Sentence Completion 2-3

Directions : Fill in the blanks to complete the sentences.

1. Every time my gym teacher blows her whistle, students _____ chattering.

2. Jennifer's wedding reception was a _____ with a fistfight between the groom and his friend.

3. Judy's back pain is not occasional but _____.

4. The Sun is a _____ body.

5. Tim could not help but _____ his son for making the same mistakes again and again.

6. Although Ian is a famous musician, his children have never shown an interest in music, much to his _____.

7. They chose to _____ the problem by using a different program.

8. If you take your dad's car without telling him, he might _____ you severely.

Answers

1. cease
2. catastrophe
3. chronic
4. celestial
5. chide
6. chagrin
7. circumvent
8. censure

UPPER LEVEL **Lesson 2-4**

81	clamor	86	cogent
82	clandestine	87	coherent
83	clot	88	commend
84	clutch	89	compassion
85	coerce	90	compel

School Motto

"Amor Caritas"

(love charity)

- Dana Hall School

SSATKOREA.com

clamor
[**klam**-er]

n. a loud uproar, as from a crowd of people

아우성, 소란, 외침, 떠들썩함

The students rushed out of the school to and the source of the clamor.

syn. commotion, tumult, uproar

clandestine
[klan-**des**-tin]

adj. done in or executed with secrecy or concealment

은밀한, 남몰래 하는

Romeo and Juliet had to arrange clandestine meetings.

syn. stealthy, surreptitious, furtive

clot
[klot]

n. a solid lump or mass

피가 응고된 덩어리

Some clots that occur inside blood vessels can be harmful.

syn. blood clot, lump, clump

clutch
[kluhch]

v. to seize with or as with the hands or claws, snatch

꽉 움켜잡다

The little girl clutched the money her mother gave her to buy bread.

syn. clench, grasp, grip

coerce
[koh-**urs**]

v. to compel by force, intimidation, or authority

강요하다, 강제로 시키다

Linda was coerced into signing the contract.

syn. force, compel, impel

cogent
[**koh**-juhnt]

adj. powerfully persuasive

설득력 있는

The teacher praised Jane for the cogent arguments in her essay.

syn. convincing, telling, influential

coherent

[koh-**heer**-uhnt]

adj. logically connected

조리 있는, 논리 정연한

Students should try to construct coherent points in their paragraphs.

syn. logical, rational, consistent

commend

[kuh-**mend**]

v. to express a good opinion of

칭찬하다

We should commend his good deeds.

syn. praise, recommend, applaud

compassion

[kuhm-**pash**-uhn]

n. a feeling of deep sympathy and sorrow for another

동정심, 연민

I was hoping she might show a little compassion.

syn. sympathy, commiseration, empathy

compel

[kuhm-**pel**]

v. to force or drive, especially to a course of action

강제하다, 억지로 시키다

Do you think you can compel obedience from me?

syn. constrain, force, necessitate

Sentence Completion 2-4

Directions : Fill in the blanks to complete the sentences.

1. The _____ of sirens in the night awakes Marlene.

2. After a hurricane hits, others will feel _____ for the victims.

3. A _____ that forms inside one of your blood vessels can be harmful.

4. Even though Jay felt chilly, school continued to _____ him to wear shorts.

5. Cloy made a clear, persuasive, and _____ argument.

6. Daniel persisted to _____ the safety bar on the roller coaster for dear life.

7. When Jodie calmed down, she was more _____ and logical.

8. The _____ attempts to usurp the throne failed.

Answers

1. clamor
2. compassion
3. clot
4. compel
5. cogent
6. clutch
7. coherent
8. clandestine

91 compensate   96 confer

92 complacent   97 conscientious

93 conceited   98 consensus

94 conciliatory   99 contention

95 condone   100 contiguous

School Motto

"Worthy of Your Heritage"

- Deerfield Academy

━━━ SSATKOREA.com

conceited
[khun-**see**-tid]

adj. having an exaggerated sense of self-importance

자만하는, 거만한, 잘난 척하는

I thought him conceited and arrogant.

syn. pompous, smug, pretentious

conciliatory
[kuhn-**sil**-ee-uh-tawr-ee]

adj. making or willing to make concessions

달래는, 회유하는

If you want to end the fight with your friends, you should make a conciliatory gesture.

syn. pacifying, appeasing, mollifying

compensate
[**kom**-puhn-seyt]

v. give (someone) something, typically money, in recognition of loss, suffering, or injury

보상하다, 보상금을 주다

The food company gave her a hundred dollars to compensate her for her trouble.

syn. reimburse, pay, recompense

condone
[kuhn-**dohn**]

v. to pardon or forgive

용납하다, 봐주다

We cannot condone violence of any sort.

syn. excuse, forgive, pardon

complacent
[kuhm-**pley**-suhnt]

adj. satisfied with oneself

현실에 안주하는, 자기 만족적인

If a student becomes complacent about his studies, his grades might drop.

syn. content, contented, self-satisfied

confer
[kuhn-**fur**]

v. to consult together

상의하다, 협의하다

I must confer with my lawyer before I decide.

syn. consult, deliberate, parley

conscientious
[kon-shee-**en**-shuhs]

adj. characterized by extreme care and great effort

양심적인, 성실한

He was a conscientious doctor who did everything possible to help a patient.

syn. moral, principled, fastidious

consensus
[kuhn-**sen**-suhs]

n. majority of opinion

의견 일치, 합의

The two parties have reached a consensus.

syn. agreement, accord, consensus

contention
[kuhn-**ten**-shuhn]

n. the disagreement that results from opposing arguments

논쟁, 언쟁, 주장

Contention arose about how to take care of their ill mother.

syn. competition, argument, dispute

contiguous
[kuhn-**tig**-yoo-uhs]

adj. in close proximity without actually touching

인접한, 근접한

France is contiguous with Spain.

syn. bordering, neighboring, tangential

Sentence Completion 2-5

Directions : Fill in the blanks to complete the sentences.

1. The interviewee tried to _____ for his poor grades with great passion.

2. Julia is not _____ with the status quo.

3. The _____ flutist talks incessantly about his accomplishments.

4. Lauren needs some time to _____ with her parents.

5. Some tolerant teachers _____ chewing gum, but Martha is not that kind.

6. Whenever there's disagreement, there's no _____.

7. Quality management has long been a bone of _____.

8. Rita is a diligent, industrious, and _____ student.

Analogy 12. Without

[A는 B가 없는] 것의 without 관계 문제는 B 부분이 형용사 adjective 일수도 있고, 명사 noun 형태로 나올 수도 있습니다. 매우 자주 출제되는 유형 중 하나이니 관계를 확실히 이해 해두는 것이 필요합니다.

A는 B가 없는

slack : tension
느슨한 : 긴장

brash : discretion
경솔한 : 신중함

impeccable : flaw
흠 없는 : 결점

frivolous : solemnness
경박한 : 진지함

numb : sensation
마비된 : 감각

unrehearsed : rehearsal
리허설을 하지 않은 : 리허설(예행 연습)

brazen : tact
뻔뻔한 : 재치, 요령

Impromptu : plan
즉흥적인 : 계획

Ignorant : knowledge
무식한 : 지식

inattentive : attention
주의를 기울이지 않는 : 집중

dehydration : water
탈수 : 물

starvation : food
기근 : 식량

Insomnia : sleep
불면증 : 잠

amnesia : memory
기억상실 : 기억

POP QUIZ

1. Brazen is to tact as

(A) impromptu is to impetus
(B) famine is to water
(C) dehydrated is to food
(D) ignorant is to knowledge
(E) inattentive is to ambition

2. Insomnia is to sleep as

(A) disillusion is to vision
(B) disenchantment is to coma
(C) amnesia is to memory
(D) souvenir is to keepsake
(E) numbness is to anesthesia

Check-up 2-1

Each of the following questions consists of one word followed by five words or phrases. You are to select the one word or phrase whose meaning is closest to the word in capital letters.

1. AUGMENT
(A) amplify
(B) betray
(C) debunk
(D) concur
(E) reassure

2. AUSPICIOUS
(A) terse
(B) hardy
(C) tranquil
(D) favorable
(E) earnest

3. AUSTERE
(A) stout
(B) dormant
(C) foolhardy
(D) diligent
(E) harsh

4. AVERT
(A) manipulate
(B) avoid
(C) abdicate
(D) convert
(E) swivel

5. BADGER
(A) concord
(B) annoy
(C) unveil
(D) violate
(E) interpret

6. BANAL
(A) mobile
(B) aloft
(C) hackneyed
(D) elegant
(E) gigantic

7. BELITTLE
(A) depreciate
(B) encounter
(C) petrify
(D) improve
(E) corrode

8. BELLIGERENT
(A) perpetual
(B) brittle
(C) vital
(D) paltry
(E) aggressive

9. BENEDICTION
(A) colony
(B) majority
(C) blessing
(D) predicament
(E) fee

10. BENEVOLENT
(A) apprehensive
(B) woeful
(C) scalding
(D) kind
(E) heroic

Check-up 2-2

Each of the following questions consists of one word followed by five words or phrases. You are to select the one word or phrase whose meaning is closest to the word in capital letters.

1. BERATE
(A) reproach
(B) stall
(C) distress
(D) evade
(E) budge

2. BIAS
(A) campaign
(B) hue
(C) prejudice
(D) restraint
(E) abode

3. BLEMISH
(A) compliment
(B) budget
(C) defect
(D) dictator
(E) extortionist

4. BLEND
(A) fume
(B) shed
(C) detect
(D) rejoice
(E) combine

5. BONDAGE
(A) blizzard
(B) avalanche
(C) task
(D) poverty
(E) slavery

6. BULGE
(A) admonish
(B) swell
(C) resign
(D) taper
(E) dwell

7. BULWARK
(A) oblivion
(B) revenge
(C) crusade
(D) fort
(E) lineage

8. CALIBER
(A) ability
(B) option
(C) prairie
(D) pension
(E) scabbard

9. CALLOUS
(A) conspicuous
(B) abashed
(C) insensitive
(D) numerous
(E) arrogant

10. CANDID
(A) unanimous
(B) brittle
(C) slovenly
(D) frank
(E) confident

Check-up 2-3

Directions   Each of the following questions consists of one word followed by five words or phrases.
You are to select the one word or phrase whose meaning is closest to the word in capital letters.

1. CAPRICIOUS
(A) cumbersome
(B) fickle
(C) edible
(D) substantial
(E) engrossing

2. CATASTROPHE
(A) breach
(B) calamity
(C) quest
(D) tremor
(E) refuge

3. CEASE
(A) yearn
(B) vow
(C) discontinue
(D) attain
(E) collide

4. CELESTIAL
(A) brief
(B) apt
(C) cordial
(D) peculiar
(E) heavenly

5. CENSURE
(A) blame
(B) establish
(C) soar
(D) plunge
(E) applaud

6. CHAGRIN
(A) immigrant
(B) eclipse
(C) marvel
(D) disappointment
(E) famine

7. CHIDE
(A) shove
(B) nudge
(C) reprimand
(D) blunder
(E) accustom

8. CHRONIC
(A) flimsy
(B) ridiculous
(C) previous
(D) ingenious
(E) persistent

9. CIRCUMVENT
(A) assign
(B) negotiate
(C) revive
(D) analyze
(E) avoid

10. CITE
(A) quote
(B) challenge
(C) boast
(D) provoke
(E) beseech

Check-up 2-4

1. CLAMOR

(A) outskirts
(B) mob
(C) commotion
(D) pedestal
(E) stem

2. CLANDESTINE

(A) stealthy
(B) puny
(C) distinct
(D) remote
(E) prominent

3. CLOT

(A) game
(B) lump
(C) domicile
(D) motion
(E) haven

4. CLUTCH

(A) accelerate
(B) burden
(C) oppose
(D) clench
(E) abandon

5. COERCE

(A) allude
(B) meddle
(C) compel
(D) clasp
(E) grasp

6. COGENT

(A) versatile
(B) evident
(C) ferocious
(D) overdue
(E) convincing

7. COHERENT

(A) indignant
(B) exacting
(C) frugal
(D) logical
(E) severe

8. COMMEND

(A) translate
(B) deteriorate
(C) command
(D) praise
(E) mimic

9. COMPASSION

(A) oblivion
(B) sympathy
(C) keepsake
(D) priority
(E) skirmish

10. COMPEL

(A) excavate
(B) compensate
(C) constrain
(D) wander
(E) repel

Check-up 2-5

Directions Each of the following questions consists of one word followed by five words or phrases.
You are to select the one word or phrase whose meaning is closest to the word in capital letters.

1. COMPENSATE
(A) reimburse
(B) deprive
(C) withdraw
(D) equivocate
(E) broach

2. COMPLACENT
(A) awesome
(B) evident
(C) obedient
(D) desperate
(E) contented

3. CONCEITED
(A) innate
(B) marvelous
(C) sparse
(D) exhilarating
(E) pompous

4. CONCILIATORY
(A) sonic
(B) methodical
(C) ambulatory
(D) mollifying
(E) egregious

5. CONDONE
(A) retain
(B) excuse
(C) attain
(D) coincide
(E) employ

6. CONFER
(A) consult
(B) baffle
(C) erode
(D) investigate
(E) stroll

7. CONSCIENTIOUS
(A) treacherous
(B) placid
(C) esteemed
(D) delicate
(E) moral

8. CONSENSUS
(A) tact
(B) acquaintance
(C) agreement
(D) indictment
(E) propaganda

9. CONTENTION
(A) revenge
(B) loom
(C) territory
(D) argument
(E) property

10. CONTIGUOUS
(A) ludicrous
(B) aboveboard
(C) neighboring
(D) reluctant
(E) inept

211

101 contradict	106 correlate
102 convalesce	107 cosmopolitan
103 cope	108 credulous
104 copious	109 criterion
105 corpulent	110 crude

School Motto

"Gaudet Patientia Duris"

(Patience Rejoices in Adversity)

- Emma Willard School

SSATKOREA.com

contradict
[kon-truh-**dikt**]

v. to assert the contrary of

부정하다, 반박하다, 모순되다

She loves to quote Albert Einstein because nobody dares to contradict her.

syn. belie, contravene, counter

convalesce
[kon-vuh-**les**]

v. to recover health and strength after illness

요양하다, 건강을 회복하다

He fell in love with the nurse while he was convalescing in a hospital.

syn. recover, recuperate

cope
[kohp]

v. to face and deal with problems

대항하다, 맞서다, 대처하다

The way you cope with life is what makes the difference.

syn. manage, contend, confront

copious
[**koh**-pee-uh-s]

adj. large in quantity or number

많은, 풍부한, 풍요로운

He drank copious amounts of wine.

syn. abundant, affluent, ample

corpulent
[**kawr**-pyuh-luh-nt]

adj. large or bulky of body

뚱뚱한, 과체중의

A "fat" man can be politely described as "corpulent" gentleman.

syn. fat, obese, stout

correlate
[**kawr**-uh-leyt]

v. to have a mutual or reciprocal relation

연관성이 있다, 상관관계가 있다

Red is such an interesting color to correlate with emotion.

syn. equate, compare, correspond

cosmopolitan

[koz-muh-**pol**-i-tn]

adj. free from local, provincial, or national ideas

전세계적인, 국제적인

Paris is a very cosmopolitan city, with people and ideas from all over the world.

syn. global, international, universal

credulous

[**krej**-uh-luhs]

adj. willing to believe or trust too readily

잘 믿는, 잘 속는

Credulous people are easily misled by false advertisements.

syn. naive, gullible

criterion

[krahy-**teer**-ee-uhn]

n. standard of judgment or criticism

표준, 기준

Only a man's character is the real criterion of worth.

syn. standard, yardstick

crude

[krood]

adj. in a raw or unprepared state

대충의, 대강의, 다듬어지지 않은

They were fighting with crude weapons like catapults and slingshots.

syn. rough, undeveloped, unrefined

Sentence Completion 3-1

Directions : Fill in the blanks to complete the sentences.

1. Santa Claus seems like a _____ man with a jolly grin.

2. Timothy is so _____ that he believes everything on Youtube.

3. Recent evidence (has) turned out to _____ established theories.

4. Shirley drank _____ amounts of wine.

5. Clark, a native New Yorker, is wealthy, sophisticated, and _____.

6. You will learn to _____ with stress at work.

7. In this competition, the number one _____ is speed.

8. The experimental data will hopefully _____ positively with the actual data.

Answers

1. corpulent
2. credulous
3. contradict
4. copious
5. cosmopolitan
6. Cope
7. criterion
8. correlate

111	cull	116	debilitated
112	culpable	117	decimate
113	cursory	118	decree
114	curtail	119	defer
115	cynical	120	deference

School Motto

"Fortiter, fideliter, feliciter"

(Strongly, faithfully, joyfully)

- Episcopal High School

━━━━━━━━━━━━━━━━━ SSATKOREA.com

cull
[k*uh*l]

v. to remove something that has been rejected

골라내다, 추리다

Mary culled some of the nicest flowers in the garden for her bouquet.

syn.　choose, select, pick

culpable
[**k*uh*l**-puh-b*uh*l]

adj. responsible for action

과실이 있는, 비난 받을 만한

She thought him culpable because he was the only one at the crime scene.

syn.　guilty, blameworthy

cursory
[**kur**-suh-ree]

adj. going rapidly over something, without noticing details

피상적인, 대충하는, 건성의

He signed with only a cursory glance at the report.

syn.　superficial, hasty, perfunctory

curtail
[ker-**teyl**]

v. to cut short

짧게 줄이다, 축소하다

We must try to curtail our spending.

syn.　shorten, abridge, reduce

cynical
[**sin**-i-k*uh*l]

adj. distrusting or disparaging the motives of others

빈정대는, 냉소적인

His cynical belief was that everyone was motivated by selfish interests.

syn.　sardonic, satirical, scornful

debilitated
[dih-**bil**-i-tey-tid]

adj. weak or feeble

쇠약해진, 약해진

Jonah was debilitated by severe migraine headaches.

syn.　infirm, enfeebled, enervated

decimate

[**des**-uh-meyt]

v. to destroy a great number or proportion of

대량으로 죽이다, 학살하다

The oil spill in the Caribbean Sea decimated the wildlife along the coast.

syn. annihilate, slaughter, exterminate

decree

[dih-**kree**]

n. a formal and authoritative order

법령, 판결

By decree of the king, all foreign visitors to the city must wear a red badge.

syn. command, mandate, order

defer

[dih-**fur**]

v. to put off action or consideration to a future time

미루다, 보류하다

The decision has been deferred by the admission committee until next week.

syn. suspend, table, procrastinate

deference

[**def**-er-uhns]

n. respectful submission

존경, 경의

They treat her with such deference.

syn. respect, submission, compliance

Sentence Completion 3-2

Directions : Fill in the blanks to complete the sentences.

1. You can see the massive difference with just a _____ examination.

2. With all the snow, the boss had to ___ our work hours.

3. The final _____ is the final judgment issued by a court after legal proceedings.

4. First, _____ the best photos and then arrange them.

5. The director thought all team members were _____ of the outcome.

6. The servant bowed his head in _____ to his master.

7. Buster asked the bank to _____ his loan.

8. Judi has a pretty _____ view of men.

121	deficient	126	despondent
122	dehydrated	127	detain
123	delectable	128	deter
124	deplore	129	detour
125	despicable	130	devastate

School Motto

"mens sana in corpore sano"
(A healthy mind in a healthy body)
- Foxcroft School

SSATKOREA.com

deficient
[dih-**fish**-uhnt]

adj. lacking some element or characteristic
부족한, 결핍된

Jenna's essay was deficient in quality citations.

syn. defective, inadequate, wanting

dehydrated
[dee-**hahy**-drey-tid]

adj. free from moisture for preservation
건조된, 마른, 탈수된

They brought dehydrated fruit on the hike.

syn. dried, parched, arid

delectable
[dih-**lek**-tuh-b*uh*l]

adj. extremely delicious or appealing
매우 맛있는, 맛있어 보이는

Delectable smells rose from the kitchen.

syn. delicious, savory, tasty

deplore
[dih-**plawr**]

v. to regret deeply or strongly
몹시 슬퍼하다, 한탄하다

My father deplores the fact that my sister and I spend so much time texting.

syn. lament, mourn, sorrow

despicable
[**des**-pi-kuh-b*uh*l]

adj. deserving to be despised, contemptible
비열한, 야비한, 못된

Posting mean rumors about her on Facebook was a despicable act.

syn. abhorrent, contemptible, detestable

despondent
[dih-**spon**-duhnt]

adj. feeling profound hopelessness
기가 죽은, 의기소침한

Victor was despondent after he received a D on the test.

syn. depressed, discouraged, dejected

detain

[dih-**teyn**]

v. to keep under restraint or in custody

가두다, 억류하다

He was detained by the police.

syn. hold, keep back, confine

deter

[dih-**tur**]

v. to discourage or restrain from acting or proceeding

그만두게 하다, 단념시키다

One goal of law is to deter bad behavior.

syn. obstruct, discourage, dissuade

detour

[**dee**-toor]

n. a longer, less direct or roundabout way to get

우회로, 돌아가는 길

A traffic accident means you have to take a detour.

syn. deviation, diversion, indirect course

devastate

[**dev**-uh-steyt]

v. to lay waste or destroy

완전히 파괴하다

The storm devastated his town.

syn. demolish, ruin, ravage

Sentence Completion 3-3

Directions : Fill in the blanks to complete the sentences.

1. Deborah was _____ in caffeine that day.

2. Fever resulted from becoming _____.

3. Emma was pleased to see an array of _____ desserts and pastries.

4. Catherine and her siblings _____ the inhumane treatment of animals.

5. Dave's misdeed is beyond mean. It's _____ — a vile and harmful act.

6. Tarah felt _____ about the deforestation of the Amazon.

7. The police should _____ Michael for questioning.

8. The risk of being expelled shall _____ kids from cheating in school.

Answers

1. deficient
2. dehydrated
3. delectable
4. deplore
5. despicable
6. despondent
7. detain
8. deter

131	deviation	136	dilapidated
132	devour	137	diminutive
133	diction	138	diplomatic
134	diffuse	139	discard
135	digress	140	discerning

School Motto

"Men for Others"

- Georgetown Preparatory School

SSATKOREA.com

deviation
[dee-vee-**ey**-shuhn]

n. anything that varies from the accepted standard

일탈, 탈선, 기준에서 벗어남, 변이

When something causes a creature's DNA to change, it creates a deviation.

syn. aberration, anomaly, alteration

devour
[dih-**vou**-uhr]

v. to swallow or eat up hungrily, voraciously, or ravenously

걸신들린 듯 먹다

The boys devour a meal like ravenous cowhands.

syn. swallow, consume, gobble

diction
[**dik**-shuhn]

n. style of speaking or writing

말씨, 말투

Be sure to use formal diction when writing an essay.

syn. word, articulation, enunciation

diffuse
[dih-**fyooz**]

v. to spread

널리 퍼지다

Buddhism diffused from India throughout Asia.

syn. disperse, distribute, scatter

digress
[dih-**gres**]

v. to deviate from the main topic

주제에서 벗어나다

Do you mind if I digress for a moment?

syn. drift, stray, wander

dilapidated
[dih-**lap**-i-dey-tid]

adj. fallen into partial ruin or decay as from age or neglect

다 허물어져 가는

The dilapidated building is going to need a lot of fixing up.

syn. decrepit, run-down, battered

diminutive
[dih-**min**-yuh-tiv]

adj. very small

아주 작은

*Despite its **diminutive** size, the car is quite comfortable.*

syn. tiny, minute, infinitesimal

diplomatic
[dip-luh-**mat**-ik]

adj. skilled in dealing with sensitive matters or people

외교적 수완이 있는, 능수능란한

*Politicians are usually very **diplomatic**.*

syn. astute, clever, tactful

discard
[dih-**skahrd**]

v. to get rid of

버리다, 폐기하다

*Let's **discard** some of these old magazines.*

syn. abandon, dispose of, eliminate

discerning
[dih-**sur**-ning]

adj. having keen insight and good judgment

안목이 있는, 통찰력이 있는

*A **discerning** person is good at distinguishing the good from the bad.*

syn. discriminating, insightful, astute

Sentence Completion 3-4

Directions : Fill in the blanks to complete the sentences.

1. The _____ peacemaker can make both sides happy.

2. When Susan goes all day without eating anything, she will _____ her dinner.

3. Why don't you _____ some of your old-fashioned clothes?

4. If you don't take care of your farmhouse, it can become _____.

5. We were already late, and there was no time to let you _____.

6. Kelly has a _____ fashion sense; her choices are perfect.

7. Companies often use SNS to _____ ideas from person to person.

8. It is helpful for a stage performer to have excellent _____.

  Answers

1. diplomatic
2. devour
3. discard
4. dilapidated
5. digress
6. discerning
7. diffuse
8. diction

---

141 discreet   146 dissect

142 disdain   147 disseminate

143 dismantle   148 dissent

144 disparage   149 distinctive

145 dispel   150 diverge

School Motto

"Cui servire est regnare"

(To serve is to rule)

- Groton school

SSATKOREA.com

discreet
[dih-**skreet**]

adj. appropriately quiet, prudent, and restrained

신중한, 조심스러운

He was wearing a discreet gray suit, so nobody noticed him.

syn. cautious, sensible, prudent

disdain
[dis-**deyn**]

n. haughty contempt

경멸, 모멸, 오만

The arrogant wrestler showed disdain for his opponents.

syn. contempt, scorn, derision

dismantle
[dis-**man**-tl]

v. to take apart

분해하다, 해체하다

The country will dismantle its nuclear program.

syn. disassemble, take apart, tear down

disparage
[dih-**spar**-ij]

v. to belittle or degrade a person or idea

얕보다, 무시하다

To pursue science is not to disparage the things of the spirit.

syn. depreciate, belittle, degrade

dispel
[dih-**spel**]

v. to drive off in various directions

떨쳐버리다, 쫓아버리다

John wants to dispel the rumor that his parents got divorced.

syn. disperse, dissipate, scatter

dissect
[dih-**sekt**]

v. to methodically cut up a body, part, or plant in order to study its internal parts

해부하다

Christine dissected a frog during biology class.

syn. anatomize, analyze, explore

disseminate
[dih-**sem**-uh-neyt]

v. to scatter or spread widely

퍼뜨리다, 유포하다

It is important to disseminate helpful information.

syn. disperse, distribute, spread

dissent
[dih-**sent**]

n. disagreement or difference

반대, 반대 의견

These voices of dissent grew louder and louder.

syn. disagreement, disapproval

distinctive
[dih-**stingk**-tiv]

adj. serving to distinguish

독특한, 다른 것과 구별되게 하는

Her black eyes and plump lips are distinctive features.

syn. different, unique, distinguishing

diverge
[dih-**vurj**]

v. to go in different directions

갈라지다, 나뉘지다

Friends' lives often diverge after they start college.

syn. branch, separate, split

Sentence Completion 3-5

Directions : Fill in the blanks to complete the sentences.

1. The _____ secretary is appropriately quiet, prudent, and restrained.

2. Jeff had no other choice but to _____ the computer to see what the problem was.

3. Two roads _____ in the woods.

4. The actress is about to _____ a few rumors that have been spreading recently.

5. The boss decided to _____ Ben's unscrupulous attitude.

6. The Internet has been and will _____ new ideas all over the world.

7. These kinds of dolphins have a _____ call.

8. Still now, there are one or two voices of _____ or disagreement.

Analogy 13. Synonyms Vs. Antonym

Analogy의 유형중 동의어와 반의어를 찾는 유형도 자주 등장합니다. 그런데 관계가 쉽고 예측이 가능한 만큼 이 유형에 나오는 단어들의 난이도가 높다는 것이 포인트 이죠. 전체 문제 중 앞 쪽에 나오는 경우는 문제 유형은 반의어가 더 많고, 뒤 쪽에 나오는 경우는 동의어처럼 보이지만 Degree 인 경우가 많다는 것도 기억할 만한 점입니다.

A와 B는 Synonyms 관계

endeavor : struggle
노력, 시도 : 투쟁, 고투

debacle : catastrophe
대실패 : 파국

peril : danger
유해함 : 위험

bedlam : chaos
난리, 법석 : 혼돈, 혼란

gregarious : sociable
남과 어울리기 좋아하는 : 사교적인

hang : suspend
매달다 : 걸다

passionate : fervent
열정적인 : 열렬한

malicious : spiteful
악의적인 : 앙심을 품은

mar : spoil
망치다 : 못쓰게 하다

omit : exclude
생략하다 : 제외하다

surmise : guess
추측하다 : 알아맞히다

mission : purpose
임무 : 목적

A와 B는 Antonyms 관계

originality : banality
독창성 : 진부함

benevolent : malevolent
선한, 자비로운 : 악한, 악의적인

gallantry : trepidation
용맹 : 겁, 두려움

philanthropy : greed
자선, 베품 : 탐욕, 욕심

sensitive : callous
민감한 : 둔한

listless : unflagging
무기력한 : 지칠 줄 모르는

glib : sincere
말만 잘하는 : 진실된

garrulous : reserved
수다스러운 : 과묵한

POP QUIZ

1. Thrive is to flourish as
  (A) vex is to appease
  (B) truncate is to lengthen
  (C) hoax is to pester
  (D) endorse is to disapprove
  (E) concur is to agree

2. Debacle is to catastrophe as
  (A) specter is to spectator
  (B) surmise is to thesis
  (C) jeopardy is to security
  (D) gallantry is to courage
  (E) bedlam is to composure

Check-up 3-1

Directions   Each of the following questions consists of one word followed by five words or phrases.
You are to select the one word or phrase whose meaning is closest to the word in capital letters.

1. CONTRADICT
(A) belie
(B) choose
(C) command
(D) suspend
(E) invent

2. CONVALESCE
(A) deceive
(B) preserve
(C) recover
(D) suggest
(E) separate

3. COPE
(A) prefer
(B) reproduce
(C) deceive
(D) manage
(E) replace

4. COPIOUS
(A) appropriate
(B) edible
(C) audible
(D) urbane
(E) ample

5. CORPULENT
(A) obese
(B) moral
(C) confident
(D) animated
(E) hilarious

6. CORRELATE
(A) suspend
(B) teem
(C) degrade
(D) correspond
(E) quench

7. COSMOPOLITAN
(A) vertical
(B) universal
(C) squalid
(D) elusive
(E) meager

8. CREDULOUS
(A) fascinating
(B) gullible
(C) mutual
(D) obsolete
(E) carnivorous

9. CRITERION
(A) bias
(B) council
(C) jeopardy
(D) terrain
(E) standard

10. CRUDE
(A) compatible
(B) somber
(C) parallel
(D) rough
(E) sinister

223

Check-up 3-2

Each of the following questions consists of one word followed by five words or phrases. You are to select the one word or phrase whose meaning is closest to the word in capital letters.

1. CULL
(A) blend
(B) lap
(C) chop
(D) join
(E) choose

2. CULPABLE
(A) delightful
(B) guilty
(C) exuberant
(D) ordinary
(E) furtive

3. CURSORY
(A) puzzled
(B) superficial
(C) arid
(D) barren
(E) nonchalant

4. CURTAIL
(A) shorten
(B) retort
(C) sustain
(D) feed
(E) pat

5. CYNICAL
(A) leisurely
(B) cyclical
(C) fantastic
(D) sardonic
(E) grim

6. DEBILITATED
(A) superb
(B) realistic
(C) astonished
(D) infirm
(E) ravenous

7. DECIMATE
(A) sob
(B) increase
(C) transport
(D) obtain
(E) annihilate

8. DECREE
(A) command
(B) awe
(C) fiber
(D) comrade
(E) occasion

9. DEFER
(A) guarantee
(B) collect
(C) conjecture
(D) suspend
(E) detach

10. DEFERENCE
(A) envy
(B) respect
(C) jealousy
(D) glee
(E) rage

Check-up 3-3

1. DEFICIENT
- (A) wanting
- (B) nostalgic
- (C) unbearable
- (D) supreme
- (E) hostile

2. DEHYDRATED
- (A) severe
- (B) rigid
- (C) stark
- (D) hearty
- (E) arid

3. DELECTABLE
- (A) enormous
- (B) disheartened
- (C) delicious
- (D) reflective
- (E) defective

4. DEPLORE
- (A) decline
- (B) batter
- (C) retain
- (D) lament
- (E) punctuate

5. DESPICABLE
- (A) outmoded
- (B) abhorrent
- (C) innate
- (D) mediocre
- (E) rippling

6. DESPONDENT
- (A) flimsy
- (B) prodigal
- (C) depressed
- (D) extensive
- (E) bracing

7. DETAIN
- (A) hold
- (B) advise
- (C) offend
- (D) coordinate
- (E) arrange

8. DETER
- (A) exult
- (B) crawl
- (C) inspire
- (D) obstruct
- (E) shed

9. DETOUR
- (A) idea
- (B) deviation
- (C) control
- (D) aftermath
- (E) discovery

10. DEVASTATE
- (A) gorge
- (B) harbor
- (C) insist
- (D) soothe
- (E) demolish

MIDDLE 1 2 3 4 5 6 7 8 9 10

UPPER 1 2 3 4 5 6 7 8 9 10

Check-up 3-4

Directions   Each of the following questions consists of one word followed by five words or phrases. You are to select the one word or phrase whose meaning is closest to the word in capital letters.

1. DEVIATION
(A) aberration
(B) poverty
(C) apparatus
(D) truce
(E) pact

2. DEVOUR
(A) share
(B) grasp
(C) leap
(D) wander
(E) consume

3. DICTION
(A) scale
(B) breach
(C) fad
(D) aroma
(E) articulation

4. DIFFUSE
(A) profuse
(B) disperse
(C) sever
(D) petrify
(E) invert

5. DIGRESS
(A) reign
(B) associate
(C) stray
(D) combine
(E) snarl

6. DILAPIDATED
(A) timid
(B) queer
(C) fierce
(D) dreadful
(E) battered

7. DIMINUTIVE
(A) deft
(B) sedentary
(C) frivolous
(D) tiny
(E) steadfast

8. DIPLOMATIC
(A) sparse
(B) tactful
(C) jocular
(D) resolute
(E) jocose

9. DISCARD
(A) dash
(B) relieve
(C) abandon
(D) repel
(E) conquer

10. DISCERNING
(A) meddlesome
(B) numerous
(C) discriminating
(D) engrossing
(E) instinctive

Check-up 3-5

Directions   Each of the following questions consists of one word followed by five words or phrases. You are to select the one word or phrase whose meaning is closest to the word in capital letters.

1. DISCREET
(A) fruitful
(B) cautious
(C) sensational
(D) accurate
(E) resolute

2. DISDAIN
(A) voyage
(B) contempt
(C) budget
(D) mischief
(E) cargo

3. DISMANTLE
(A) salvage
(B) extend
(C) disassemble
(D) reinforce
(E) gripe

4. DISPARAGE
(A) evaluate
(B) increase
(C) pursue
(D) depreciate
(E) waddle

5. DISPEL
(A) graze
(B) furnish
(C) shroud
(D) flail
(E) disperse

6. DISSECT
(A) swallow
(B) paralyze
(C) recall
(D) tremble
(E) anatomize

7. DISSEMINATE
(A) conserve
(B) bluster
(C) emerge
(D) disperse
(E) plummet

8. DISSENT
(A) disagreement
(B) acquittal
(C) euphemism
(D) connoisseur
(E) remedy

9. DISTINCTIVE
(A) convenient
(B) delicate
(C) different
(D) rigorous
(E) ecstatic

10. DIVERGE
(A) sear
(B) hatch
(C) esteem
(D) branch
(E) integrate

227

151	diversion	156	eccentric
152	divulge	157	ecumenical
153	dogmatic	158	edifice
154	dubious	159	effusive
155	eavesdrop	160	egregious

School Motto

"Whatsoever things are true"

- Hill School

SSATKOREA.com

diversion
[dih-**vur**-zhuh-n]

n. the act of diverting or turning aside

기분 전환

We made a short diversion to go and look at the castle.

syn. alteration, recreation, detour

divulge
[dih-**vuhlj**]

v. to make known

알려주다, 누설하다

Journalists do not divulge their sources.

syn. debunk, disclose, reveal

dogmatic
[dawg-**mat**-ik]

adj. asserting opinions in arrogant manner

독재적인

He was criticized by those around him for being dogmatic.

syn. opinionated, dictatorial, confident

dubious
[**doo**-bee-*uhs*]

adj. of doubtful quality or propriety

의심스러운

I am dubious about what he says.

syn. doubtful, suspicious, uncertain

eavesdrop
[**eevz**-drop]

v. to listen secretly to a private conversation

엿듣다

I caught him eavesdropping outside the window.

syn. spy, overhear, snoop

eccentric
[ik-**sen**-trik]

adj. deviating from the customary character or practice

별난, 기이한

Her father is a bit of an eccentric.

syn. bizarre, peculiar, odd

ecumenical

[ek-yoo-**men**-i-k*uhl*]

adj. general or universal

세계적인, 보편적인

They enlarge the system to more ecumenical form system and get some similar conclusion.

syn. universal, general, comprehensive

edifice

[**ed**-uh-fis]

n. a building, especially one of imposing appearance

크고 인상적인 건물

The Eiffel Tower is a great edifice of France.

syn. monument, huge construction, skyscraper

effusive

[ih-**fyoo**-siv]

adj. extravagantly demonstrative

야단스러운, 과장되게 표현하는

He made effusive remarks about his victory.

syn. profuse, gushing, talkative

egregious

[ih-**gree**-j*uhs*]

adj. extraordinary in some bad way

지독한, 엄청나게 나쁜

He must have had an egregious ailment.

syn. outrageous, notorious, atrocious

Sentence Completion 4-1

Directions : Fill in the blanks to complete the sentences.

1. This tabloid paper's job is to _____ which celebrities are secretly dating.

2. Burt made an _____ error that might not be forgivable.

3. An _____ council is where bishops and other Christian representatives from different regions convene.

4. A little Molly likes to _____ on her parents to find out what she's getting for Christmas.

5. Chuck was so _____ that he won't listen to anyone else.

6. Jessie's _____ behavior puzzled us.

7. Jackie played the piano for _____.

8. Sam's _____ mom holds nothing back, gushing about everything.

Answers

1. divulge
2. egregious
3. ecumenical
4. eavesdrop
5. dogmatic
6. eccentric
7. diversion
8. effusive

161 elated	166 embellish
162 eloquent	167 embezzle
163 elucidate	168 eminent
164 elusive	169 empathy
165 emancipate	170 emphatic

School Motto

"Virtus Scientia"

(Virtue through knowledge)

- Hockaday School

SSATKOREA.com

elucidate
[ih-**loo**-si-deyt]

v. to make lucid or explain clearly

명확히 해명하다, 명쾌하게 설명하다

Please elucidate the reasons for your decision.

syn. clear up, expound, illustrate

elusive
[ih-**loo**-siv]

adj. hard to express or define

규정하기 힘든, 찾기 힘든, 애매한

The answers to these questions remain as elusive as ever.

syn. evasive, mysterious, puzzling

elated
[ih-**ley**-tid]

adj. very happy or proud

기분 좋은, 신난, 행복한

It was like waking from a beautiful dream and feeling so elated.

syn. jubilant, delighted, excited

emancipate
[ih-**man**-suh-peyt]

v. to free from restraint, influence, or the like

풀어주다, 자유롭게 하다

That war preserved the Union and emancipated the slaves.

syn. set free, release, manumit

eloquent
[**el**-uh-kw*uh*nt]

adj. exercising the power of fluent speech

웅변을 잘하는, 말솜씨가 유창한

Ellen, in interviews, was eloquent, to the point, and assured.

syn. ardent, fluent, fervent

embellish
[em-**bel**-ish]

v. to beautify by or as if by ornamentation

장식하다, 아름답게 만들다

You can embellish the front of the door with Ivy leaves.

syn. decorate, adorn, deck

embezzle
[em-**bez**-*uhl*]

v. to appropriate fraudulently to one's own use.

횡령하다, 남의 재물을 불법으로 가지다

He embezzled thousands of dollars from the charity.

syn. misappropriate, loot, steal

eminent
[**em**-uh-n*uh*nt]

adj. high in station, rank, or repute

저명한, 유명한

She is eminent both as a writer and as a painter.

syn. famous, well-known, renowned

empathy
[**em**-puh-thee]

n. understanding and entering into another's feelings

공감, 감정이입

She had a lot of empathy for men, and the social pressures that they go through.

syn. understanding, insight, sympathy

emphatic
[em-**fat**-ik]

adj. forceful and definite in expression or action

단호한, 강조하는

His response was immediate and emphatic.

syn. insistent, unequivocal, assertive

Sentence Completion 4-2

Directions : Fill in the blanks to complete the sentences.

1. Matthew's father was _____ when he told Matthew not to drive late again.

2. He was _____ to hear he was admitted to his dream school.

3. The teacher will _____ the challenging notions for students.

4. President Abraham Lincoln issued the _____ Proclamation.

5. George couldn't resist but _____ the story of his accident.

6. One of the most _____ players in the history of basketball is Michael Jordan.

7. He displayed _____ with this famous quote, "I feel your pain."

8. Jane's memories are _____ and hard to remember.

Answers

1. emphatic
2. elated
3. elucidate
4. emancipate
5. embellish
6. eminent
7. empathy
8. elusive

171 endeavor	176 equilibrium
172 enigma	177 equitable
173 enrage	178 equivocal
174 entourage	179 evict
175 enunciate	180 exalt

School Motto

"Pro Deo et Genere Humano"

(For God and Humankind)

- Holderness School

SSATKOREA.com

endeavor
[en-**dev**-er]

v. to make an effort

노력하다, 애쓰다

We will always endeavor to offer you our most favorable things.

syn.   strive, effort, struggle

enigma
[uh-**nig**-muh]

n. a puzzling occurrence

수수께끼

Phoenix has always been an enigma to me.

syn.   mystery, puzzle, riddle

enrage
[en-**reyj**]

v. to make extremely angry

격분하다, 분노하다

Attempting to reason with enraged people may only enrage them more.

syn.   anger, madden, infuriate

entourage
[ahn-too-**rahzh**]

n. a group of attendants

(중요인물 주변의) 수행원들, 측근자들

The president visited China with his entourage.

syn.   attendants, associates, staff

enunciate
[ih-**nuhn**-see-eyt]

v. to pronounce words clearly

말하다, 발음하다

Speak out loud, and enunciate clearly.

syn.   articulate, speak clearly

equilibrium
[ee-kwuh-**lib**-ree-*uh*m]

n. a state of rest or balance

평형(균형) 상태

The body's state of equilibrium can be disturbed by stress.

syn.   balance, poise, stability

equitable
[**ek**-wi-tuh-b*uh*l]

adj. fair and impartial

공정한, 공평한

Are dental charges equitable and appropriate?

syn. impartial, decent, fair

equivocal
[ih-**kwiv**-uh-k*uh*l]

adj. allowing the possibility of several different meanings

모호한

Dad gave mom an equivocal answer.

syn. doubtful, uncertain, puzzling

evict
[ih-**vikt**]

v. to expel someone from a property

쫓아내다, 퇴거시키다

We haven't paid the rent, and the landlord may evict us.

syn. banish, oust, expel

exalt
[ig-**zawlt**]

v. to praise highly

대단히 칭송하다, 매우 칭찬하다.

The theater critics exalt the young actor.

syn. praise, glorify, promote

Sentence Completion 4-3

Directions : Fill in the blanks to complete the sentences.

1. We will always _____ to get your order shipped out as soon as possible.

2. Overly doting parents _____ their kids without any specific reasons.

3. The pop star's _____ includes managers, bodyguards, hairdressers, stylists, and trainers.

4. The group project team members want an _____ share of the credit.

5. Maggie was still an _____ to Hank.

6. Be polite to his parents or else you will _____ them.

7. Bettie needs to _____ her words more clearly.

8. Harry was deliberately _____, and he didn't say yes or no.

 Answers

1. endeavor	5. enigma
2. exalt	6. enrage
3. entourage	7. enunciate
4. equitable	8. equivocal

181 excruciating   186 extol

182 exculpate   187 extort

183 exhilarate   188 fabricate

184 exorbitant   189 fallow

185 explicate   190 fanatic

School Motto

"Whatsoever things are true"

- Lake Forest Academy

SSATKOREA.com

excruciating
[ik-**skroo**-shee-ey-ting]

adj. extremely painful
몹시 고통스러운, 극심한

The pain was so excruciating that talking was difficult for the man.

syn. torturous, painful, severe

exculpate
[**ek**-sk*uh*l-peyt]

v. to clear from a charge of guilt
무죄를 입증하다

He was exculpated by the testimony of several witnesses.

syn. excuse, justify, acquit

exhilarate
[ig-**zil**-uh-reyt]

v. to make someone feel very happy or elated
아주 기쁘게 만들다

Car racing had exhilarated him.

syn. cheer, delight, excite

exorbitant
[ig-**zawr**-bi-t*uh*nt]

adj. unreasonably high
과도한, 지나친

The price of bottled water has become exorbitant.

syn. extravagant, excessive, enormous

explicate
[**ek**-spli-keyt]

v. to make plain or clear
설명하다, 해석하다

The scientist did his best to explicate the complex theory of the universe.

syn. clarify, expand, untangle

extol
[ik-**stohl**]

v. to praise highly
극찬하다, 크게 칭찬하다

He was extolled as a hero.

syn. praise, celebrate, acclaim

extort
[ik-**stawrt**]

v. to obtain something by force or threats

갈취하다, 힘이나 나쁜 방법으로 뺏다

The gang extorted money from several local businesses.

syn. blackmail, cheat, wring

fabricate
[**fab**-ri-keyt]

v. to invent something typically with deceitful intent

조작하다, 위조하다

The evidence was totally fabricated.

syn. falsify, deceive, mislead

fallow
[**fal**-oh]

adj. left unsown for a period or unused

농지를 사용하지 않고 있는, 휴경지의

Farmers let their lands lie fallow.

syn. unused, resting, uncultivated

fanatic
[fuh-**nat**-ik]

n. a person with an extreme and uncritical enthusiasm

광적인 사람

You must be a fitness fanatic.

syn. devotee, zealot, maniac

Sentence Completion 4-4

Directions : Fill in the blanks to complete the sentences.

1. Jean thinks that riding a roller coaster will _____ him.

2. Patrick and his friends _____ the benefits of vegetarianism.

3. Sally cannot _____ the silly excuse on her assignments ever again.

4. The judge didn't _____ Ken from the robbery charge.

5. This theory should _____ the origin of the species.

6. The teacher failed to _____ a confession from the bully.

7. A _____ is someone who can't change his mind and won't change the subject.

8. Aiden was surprised at the _____ price for dinner.

Answers

1. exhilarate
2. extol
3. fabricate
4. exculpate
5. explicate
6. extort
7. fanatic
8. exorbitant

191	fatigue	196	finesse
192	feasible	197	flagrant
193	feign	198	foolhardy
194	fiasco	199	garrulous
195	fickle	200	glut

School Motto

"Virtus Semper Viridis"

(Virtue Always Green)

- Lawrenceville School

SSATKOREA.com

fatigue
[fuh-**teeg**]

n. weariness from bodily or mental exertion

피로, 피로감

A bar of chocolate relieved her fatigue.

syn. tiredness, exhaustion, lethargy

feasible
[**fee**-zuh-b*uh*l]

adj. capable of being done, effected, or accomplished

실현가능한

Do you think this project is feasible?

syn. possible, suitable, reasonable

feign
[feyn]

v. to represent fictitiously

가장하다, ~인 척하다

Some animals feign death when in danger.

syn. pretend, affect, fake

fiasco
[fee-**as**-koh]

n. a complete and ignominious failure

대 실패, 큰 실패

The enemy's plot ended in a fiasco.

syn. catastrophe, disaster, failure

fickle
[**fik**-*uhl*]

adj. likely to change

변덕스러운

The weather in this island is notoriously fickle.

syn. capricious, mercurial, whimsical

finesse
[fi-**ness**]

n. intricate and refined delicacy or skill

예리한 솜씨, 수완, 기교

He shows finesse in dealing with people.

syn. gimmick, maneuver, acumen

flagrant
[**fley**-gr*uh*nt]

adj. shockingly noticeable or evident

두드러지게 눈에 띄는, 명백한

He showed a flagrant disregard for anyone else's feelings.

syn. obvious, blatant, bold

foolhardy
[**fool**-hahr-dee]

adj. recklessly or thoughtlessly bold

무모한, 앞뒤를 가리지 않는

It would be foolhardy to sail in weather like this.

syn. impetuous, rash, bold, daring

garrulous
[**gar**-uh-l*uhs*]

adj. excessively talkative in a rambling manner

수다스러운, 말이 많은

The crowd grew garrulous before the speaker arrived.

syn. talkative, verbose, voluble

glut
[gluht]

n. an excessively abundant supply of something

과잉, 넘쳐나는 것

The potato glut is a real issue, and many farmers are dismayed.

syn. surplus, surfeit, excess, oversupply

Sentence Completion 4-5

Directions : Fill in the blanks to complete the sentences.

1. Mickey has _____, and she can handle difficult situations with diplomacy and tact.

2. Jessy's _____ auntie never stops talking.

3. Usually, a _____ is the result of human failure.

4. Jasmin is so _____ that she changes her mind so much.

5. That was a _____ abuse of the law.

6. Her _____ dad rushes into action without considering the consequence.

7. After Eva used her smartphone for a long time, she suffered from an eye _____.

8. Olivia had to _____ her interest in music because she knew how much Noah liked it.

💬 Answers

1. finesse
2. garrulous
3. fiasco
4. fickle
5. flagrant
6. foolhardy
7. fatigued
8. feign

Analogy 14. Action & Emotion

인간의 표정, 행동이 어떤 마음이나 감정을 표현하는지 매칭하는 문제 유형입니다.

A는 B를 표현하는 행동

grin : delight
싱긋 웃다 : 기쁨

frown : disgust
찡그리다 : 혐오

nod : assent
끄덕이다 : 동의

laughter : mirth
소리내어 웃다 : 즐거움

yawn : boredom
하품하다 : 지겨움

grumble : discontentment
투덜대다 : 불만

aplomb : confidence
침착함 : 자신감

cringe : fear
웅크리다 : 두려움

perspire : heat
땀 흘리다 : 더위

shiver : cold
떨다 : 추위

embrace : affection
껴안다 : 애정, 애착

sob : sorrow
흐느끼다, 울다 : 슬픔

salute : respect
경례하다 : 존경

jeer : contempt
비웃다 : 경멸

obeisance : submission
절. 고개 숙임 : 복종

retort : defiance
말대꾸하다 : 반항

POP QUIZ

1. Grin is to delight as
   (A) aplomb is to excitement
   (B) jeer is to condolence
   (C) grumble is to inquiry
   (D) frown is to disgust
   (E) nod is to disapproval

2. Cringe is to fear as
   (A) salute is to respect
   (B) kneel is to defiance
   (C) shiver is to hot
   (D) perspire is to cold
   (E) shrug is to assent

Check-up 4-1

Directions Each of the following questions consists of one word followed by five words or phrases. You are to select the one word or phrase whose meaning is closest to the word in capital letters.

1. DIVERSION
- (A) fulcrum
- (B) diffidence
- (C) recreation
- (D) starvation
- (E) guile

2. DIVULGE
- (A) abandon
- (B) burnish
- (C) plunder
- (D) debunk
- (E) occupy

3. DOGMATIC
- (A) luscious
- (B) fruitful
- (C) habitual
- (D) cunning
- (E) dictatorial

4. DUBIOUS
- (A) adept
- (B) capricious
- (C) fearless
- (D) suspicious
- (E) tractable

5. EAVESDROP
- (A) grumble
- (B) baffle
- (C) constrain
- (D) snoop
- (E) hail

6. ECCENTRIC
- (A) benign
- (B) peculiar
- (C) misleading
- (D) passionate
- (E) avid

7. ECUMENICAL
- (A) loaded
- (B) triumphant
- (C) universal
- (D) laden
- (E) perpetual

8. EDIFICE
- (A) huge construction
- (B) unusual idea
- (C) social
- (D) ancient form
- (E) talkative person

9. EFFUSIVE
- (A) gushing
- (B) practical
- (C) refined
- (D) universal
- (E) amiable

10. EGREGIOUS
- (A) harmful
- (B) erratic
- (C) productive
- (D) atrocious
- (E) guarded

Check-up 4-2

Each of the following questions consists of one word followed by five words or phrases. You are to select the one word or phrase whose meaning is closest to the word in capital letters.

1. ELATED
(A) jubilant
(B) derogatory
(C) genial
(D) pertinent
(E) twisted

2. ELOQUENT
(A) covetous
(B) fluent
(C) magnificent
(D) hackneyed
(E) untamed

3. ELUCIDATE
(A) hesitate
(B) irritate
(C) expound
(D) hasten
(E) isolate

4. ELUSIVE
(A) heterogeneous
(B) evasive
(C) dormant
(D) tranquil
(E) hedonistic

5. EMANCIPATE
(A) shun
(B) manumit
(C) endow
(D) jabber
(E) litigate

6. EMBELLISH
(A) invade
(B) loathe
(C) commove
(D) arouse
(E) deck

7. EMBEZZLE
(A) feign
(B) abhor
(C) hamper
(D) encroach
(E) misappropriate

8. EMINENT
(A) nimble
(B) inundated
(C) renowned
(D) intoxicating
(E) sobering

9. EMPATHY
(A) dilemma
(B) adversary
(C) neophyte
(D) understanding
(E) paradigm

10. EMPHATIC
(A) frivolous
(B) assertive
(C) hazardous
(D) agonizing
(E) furtive

Check-up 4-3

Directions   Each of the following questions consists of one word followed by five words or phrases.
You are to select the one word or phrase whose meaning is closest to the word in capital letters.

1. ENDEAVOR
(A) provoke
(B) strive
(C) consider
(D) afflict
(E) illuminate

2. ENIGMA
(A) agility
(B) sanction
(C) exemplar
(D) riddle
(E) epoch

3. ENRAGE
(A) engage
(B) meander
(C) exhaust
(D) infuriate
(E) dwell

4. ENTOURAGE
(A) cascade
(B) loyalty
(C) attendants
(D) figment
(E) salute

5. ENUNCIATE
(A) babble
(B) articulate
(C) deceive
(D) enlarge
(E) beseech

6. EQUILIBRIUM
(A) fickleness
(B) epiphany
(C) fiasco
(D) poise
(E) epitome

7. EQUITABLE
(A) unreasonable
(B) impartial
(C) fiscal
(D) biased
(E) dauntless

8. EQUIVOCAL
(A) flamboyant
(B) ambivalent
(C) vacant
(D) finicky
(E) uncertain

9. EVICT
(A) blandish
(B) brandish
(C) relish
(D) polish
(E) banish

10. EXALT
(A) appease
(B) burgeon
(C) scowl
(D) fulfill
(E) dignify

Answer 1.B 2.D 3.D 4.C 5.B 6.D 7.B 8.E 9.E 10.E

Check-up 4-4

1. EXCRUCIATING
- (A) extreme
- (B) tortuous
- (C) glib
- (D) hypnotic
- (E) impromptu

2. EXCULPATE
- (A) broach
- (B) condone
- (C) dissent
- (D) separate
- (E) excuse

3. EXHILARATE
- (A) fumble
- (B) glower
- (C) excite
- (D) harass
- (E) imitate

4. EXORBITANT
- (A) deferential
- (B) extravagant
- (C) laudatory
- (D) heinous
- (E) juvenile

5. EXPLICATE
- (A) oust
- (B) untangle
- (C) applaud
- (D) convey
- (E) excel

6. EXTOL
- (A) endure
- (B) acclaim
- (C) linger
- (D) speculate
- (E) perjury

7. EXTORT
- (A) mar
- (B) extract
- (C) lubricate
- (D) concede
- (E) blackmail

8. FABRICATE
- (A) intercede
- (B) permeate
- (C) invoke
- (D) falsify
- (E) placate

9. FALLOW
- (A) concise
- (B) unused
- (C) diverse
- (D) finite
- (E) limber

10. FANATIC
- (A) novice
- (B) magistrate
- (C) zealot
- (D) expert
- (E) magnate

Check-up 4-5

Directions   Each of the following questions consists of one word followed by five words or phrases.
You are to select the one word or phrase whose meaning is closest to the word in capital letters.

1. FATIGUE
(A) exhaustion
(B) hovel
(C) genesis
(D) moniker
(E) impediment

2. FEASIBLE
(A) irrelevant
(B) baleful
(C) malicious
(D) truthful
(E) possible

3. FEIGN
(A) holler
(B) mitigate
(C) pretend
(D) cancel
(E) amass

4. FIASCO
(A) failure
(B) artifice
(C) plateau
(D) reverence
(E) hue

5. FICKLE
(A) temporary
(B) ephemeral
(C) obsolete
(D) capricious
(E) self-possessed

6. FINESSE
(A) opulence
(B) maxim
(C) gimmick
(D) alias
(E) pioneer

7. FLAGRANT
(A) impervious
(B) jaded
(C) religious
(D) impassive
(E) obvious

8. FOOLHARDY
(A) pompous
(B) impetuous
(C) conspicuous
(D) itinerant
(E) joyous

9. GARRULOUS
(A) voluble
(B) outlandish
(C) ignorant
(D) sophisticated
(E) ponderous

10. GLUT
(A) gallantry
(B) egress
(C) surplus
(D) repository
(E) fortress

243

201	gregarious	206	haggard
202	grimace	207	hallucination
203	grind	208	haphazard
204	gullible	209	hapless
205	hackneyed	210	haughty

School Motto

"Festina Lente"

(Make haste slowly)

- Madeira School

SSATKOREA.com

gregarious
[gri-**gair**-ee-uhs]

adj. fond of the company of others

사교적인, 다른 사람과 잘 어울리는

He is such a gregarious and outgoing person.

syn. sociable, amiable, affable

grimace
[**grim**-uhs]

n. a ugly or contortion, frown scowl

찡그린 표정

James' face formed a grimace when the dentist drilled into his tooth.

syn. contortion, frown scowl

grind
[grahynd]

v. to reduce to fine particles

갈다, 가루로 만들다

The waiter will grind fresh pepper onto your spaghetti.

syn. crush, gnash, pound

gullible
[**guhl**-uh-b*uhl*]

adj. easily fooled or deceived

남을 잘 믿는, 잘 속아 넘어가는

Sylvia's parents were worried that people might take advantage of their gullible daughter.

syn. credulous, ingenuous, innocent

hackneyed
[**hak**-nced]

adj. repeated too often

진부한, 너무 많이 반복된

She doesn't like the hackneyed plots of television sit-coms.

syn. banal, commonplace, trite, clichéd

haggard
[**hag**-erd]

adj. having a gaunt, wasted, or exhausted appearance

수척한, 삐쩍 마른

The homeless man had a worn-out, haggard appearance.

syn. gaunt, emaciated, worn-looking

hallucination

[huh-loo-suh-**ney**-shuhn]

n. illusory perception

환각, 환영

A person experiencing a hallucination perceives things that aren't really there.

syn. delusion, mirage, illusion

haphazard

[hap-**haz**-erd]

adj. characterized by lack of order or planning

무계획적인, 되는 대로의

Files have been stored in such a haphazard manner that they are impossible to find.

syn. casual, arbitrary, random

hapless

[**hap**-lis]

adj. unlucky or unfortunate

불운한, 불쌍한

Many children are hapless victims of the war.

syn. unlucky, luckless, unfortunate

haughty

[**haw**-tee]

adj. disdainfully proud

거만한, 오만한

She gave him a haughty look and walked away.

syn. pompous, arrogant, pretentious

Sentence Completion 5-1

Directions : Fill in the blanks to complete the sentences.

1. The _____ general was arrogantly superior and disdainful.

2. The kitchen drawers contained a _____ collection of cooking tools.

3. The _____ girl is easily fooled.

4. The plot of this film is a _____ love story.

5. A _____ results from a mental disorder.

6. You can _____ coffee as coarse or as fine as you like.

7. The _____ passengers were stranded at the airport for three days.

8. The students gave a _____ when the teacher told them about a pop quiz.

211 havoc   216 immerse

212 homogenous   217 imminent

213 idiosyncratic   218 impart

214 ignite   219 implicate

215 immaculate   220 implicit

School Motto

"Do It With Thy Might"

- Masters School

SSATKOREA.com

havoc
[**hav**-uhk]

n. great destruction or devastation

대 파괴, 큰 혼란

*The tornado caused havoc
in the small town.*

syn. chaos, confusion, destruction

homogenous
[huh-**moj**-uh-nuhs]

adj. all of the same or similar kind
or nature

같은 종류의, 동질의

*Stir the chemicals in the beaker until
they become a homogenous mixture.*

syn. identical, uniform, akin

idiosyncratic
[id-ee-oh-sin-**krat**-ik]

adj. strange or peculiar

특이한, 특유한, 색다른

*Wearing two different socks was
his idiosyncratic habit.*

syn. quirky, peculiar, eccentric

ignite
[ig-**nahyt**]

v. to set on fire

점화하다, 불을 붙이다

*A lightning strike ignited
the forest fire.*

syn. kindle, set fire

immaculate
[ih-**mak**-yuh-lit]

adj. free from spot or stain

티 하나 없이 깔끔한, 완벽한

*Nancy's room must be immaculate
before she can start studying.*

syn. impeccable, perfect, pure

immerse
[ih-**murs**]

v. to plunge into or place under a liquid

액체에 담그다

*Immerse your sore ankle in a bowl
of cold water.*

syn. submerge, sink, dip

imminent
[**im**-uh-nuhnt]

adj. about to happen

곧 닥칠, 임박한

*Judging by those dark clouds,
rain is **imminent**.*

syn.   impending, approaching,
forthcoming

impart
[im-**pahrt**]

v. to make known

알리다, 전하다

*He **imparts** the secret to me.*

syn.   tell, relate, reveal

implicate
[**im**-pli-keyt]

v. to show to be also involved

(범죄 등에) 연루되었음을 보여주다, 관련시키다

*Fingerprints on the weapon
implicated Harold in the crime.*

syn.   involve, relate to, connect with

implicit
[im-**plis**-it]

adj. implied, rather than expressly stated

암시된, 내포된

*Although they never discussed it,
they had an **implicit** understanding.*

syn.   implied, tacit, involved

Sentence Completion 5-2

Directions : Fill in the blanks to
complete the sentences.

1. The strike was carried out to
prevent an _____ attack.

2. The population of the village
has remained _____.

3. Oscar was dressed in an
_____ white suit.

4. The dreadful hurricanes
wreaked _____.

5. Charlotte cannot help but
_____ herself in her work,
thinking about work all the time.

6. Mia tried to _____ a match
inside a dark room.

7. Isabella wants to _____
me in the planning of a party for
grandparents.

8. My mom likes to _____ the
importance of dressing neatly every
day.

221 impoverished 226 incumbent

222 incarcerate 227 indefatigable

223 incessant 228 indict

224 incite 229 indifferent

225 incompatible 230 indigent

School Motto

"Integritas, Virilitas, Fidelitas"

(Integrity, Virility, Fidelity)

- Mercersburg Academy

SSATKOREA.com

impoverished
[im-**pov**-er-isht]

adj. reduced to poverty

빈곤한, 결핍된

Many families became impoverished during the Great Depression.

syn. destitute, indigent, poor

incarcerate
[in-**kahr**-suh-reyt]

v. to lock up or confine, in or as in a jail

가두다, 투옥하다

After Mr. Smith was found guilty, he became incarcerated.

syn. imprison, confine, jail

incessant
[in-**ses**-uhnt]

adj. continuing without interruption

끊임없는, 계속되는

The incessant chatter among the students gave the teacher a headache.

syn. uninterrupted, ceaseless, unending

incite
[in-**sahyt**]

v. to stir, encourage, or urge on

자극하다, 선동하다

The cheers from the crowd incited the team to perform better.

syn. instigate, provoke, agitate

incompatible
[in-kuhm-**pat**-uh-b*uh*l]

adj. unable to exist together in harmony

공존할 수 없는, 호환성이 없는

Gail and Charlie broke up because they were incompatible.

syn. antagonistic, factious, hostile

incumbent
[in-**kuhm**-buhnt]

adj. holding an indicated position or role currently

현직의, 재직중인

The incumbent senator hopes to maintain her position.

syn. official, current, in office

indefatigable
[in-di-**fat**-i-guh-b*uh*l]

adj. incapable of being tired out

지치지 않는, 포기할 줄 모르는

The indefatigable guide walked all day long.

syn. untiring, tireless, unflagging

indict
[in-**dahyt**]

v. to accuse formally of a crime

기소하다, 법원에 심판을 요구하다

The grand jury indicted him for murder.

syn. accuse, arraign, charge

indifferent
[in-**dif**-er-uhnt]

adj. showing no interest

무관심한

People have become indifferent to the suffering of others.

syn. apathetic, disinterested, aloof

indigent
[in-di-juhnt]

adj. lacking food or clothing because of poverty

가난한, 빈곤한

Because she was indigent, the court appointed a lawyer to defend her.

syn. impoverished, needy, poor

Sentence Completion 5-3

Directions : Fill in the blanks to complete the sentences.

1. The country became _____ after a devastating war.

2. For Diane, it's tough to tolerate the _____ crying of a baby.

3. Benjamin's _____ mom did hundreds of tasks a day.

4. Harsh words can _____ violent actions.

5. In a race for governor, the _____ governor faces two challengers.

6. The dishonest manager was _____ for fraud.

7. Ross felt _____ about politics.

8. Lea founded the institution to help the needy or _____ people.

Answers

1. impoverished
2. incessant
3. indefatigable
4. incite
5. incumbent
6. indict
7. indifferent
8. indigent

UPPER LEVEL Lesson 5-4

231	indulge	236	innocuous
232	infallible	237	insightful
233	inferior	238	integral
234	ingenious	239	interim
235	ingenuous	240	intermittent

School Motto

"Fides, Veritas, Labor"

(Faith, Truth, Effort)

- Middlesex School

SSATKOREA.com

indulge
[in-**duhlj**]

v. to yield to, satisfy, or gratify desires

원없이 하다, 마음껏 하다

She never indulges children with plenty of pocket money.

syn. favor, gratify, satisfy

infallible
[in-**fal**-uh-b*uh*l]

adj. absolutely trustworthy or sure

틀림없는, 절대 확실한

No one is completely infallible.

syn. certain, irrefutable, sure

inferior
[in-**feer**-ee-er]

adj. lower in quality, rank, or status

하위의, ~보다 못한, 질이 낮은

He felt he was inferior to his superior brother.

syn. lesser, secondary, less in rank

ingenious
[in-**jeen**-yuhs]

adj. very clever or creative

기발한, 독창적인

Jerry came up with an ingenious plan to raise funds for charity.

syn. inventive, creative, clever

ingenuous
[in-**jen**-yoo-uhs]

adj. naturally simple and artless

순진한, 솔직한, 꾸밈없는

The ingenuous man was tricked by the quack selling fake medicine.

syn. artless, innocent, naive

innocuous
[ih-**nok**-yoo-uhs]

adj. not harmful or injurious

무해한, 악의 없는

These mushrooms look innocuous but are in fact deadly.

syn. harmless, innocent, inoffensive

insightful
[**in**-sahyt-f*uh*l]

adj. characterized by or displaying insight, perceptive

통찰력 있는

The points in your essay were very insightful.

syn. discerning, perceptive, astute

integral
[**in**-ti-gr*uh*l]

adj. essential to the whole

필수적인, 필수불가결한

A strong thesis and clear topic sentences are integral to a successful essay.

syn. essential, vital, indispensable

interim
[**in**-ter-uhm]

adj. an intervening time

일시적인, 잠정적인

He only holds the post on an interim basis.

syn. meantime, interval

intermittent
[in-ter-**mit**-nt]

adj. alternately ceasing and beginning again

간헐적인, 간간이 일어나는

We will have intermittent surprise quizzes in this class.

syn. sporadic, episodic, periodic

Sentence Completion 5-4

Directions : Fill in the blanks to complete the sentences.

1. Chloe is an _____ part of our team, and we need her.

2. Even the world-class experts are not _____.

3. A corporal is _____ to a general in the army.

4. This _____ man's nickname is Einstein in this town.

5. That was the only _____ remark in this criticizing interview.

6. Because their homeroom teacher leaves mid-year, they will have an _____ teacher.

7. Lisa has to _____ her craving for chocolate by eating many pieces.

8. The professor expects an _____ analysis of students.

Answers

1. integral
2. infallible
3. inferior
4. ingenious
5. innocuous
6. interim
7. indulge
8. insightful

241 intervene	246 isolated
242 intrepid	247 jeer
243 intricate	248 jovial
244 intuition	249 judicious
245 invigorate	250 jurisdiction

School Motto

"Non Sibi Sed Cunctis"

(Not for oneself, but for all)

- Millbrook School

SSATKOREA.com

intervene
[in-ter-**veen**]

v. to come between disputing people or groups

끼어들다, 개입하다

He intervened in a heated argument between two of his friends.

syn. mediate, arbitrate, interlope

intrepid
[in-**tre**-pid]

adj. resolutely fearless

용감한, 두려움을 모르는

My intrepid grandfather was always brave and bold.

syn. valiant, dauntless, courageous

intricate
[**in**-tri-kit]

adj. hard to understand, work, or make

복잡한, 난해한

The plot of that novel was too intricate to keep track of.

syn. complicated, complex, difficult

intuition
[in-too-**ish**-uhn]

n. direct perception of truth

직관, 직각

Tara made decisions based on her intuition rather than on known facts.

syn. instinct, hunch, insight

invigorate
[in-**vig**-uh-reyt]

v. to give strength or energy to something or someone

기운나게 하다, 활기차게 하다

Drinking cold water invigorated him.

syn. stimulate, energize, enliven

isolated
[**ahy**-suh-ley-tid]

adj. separated from other persons or things

외떨어진, 외딴, 고립된

He was isolated from all the other prisoners.

syn. alone, solitary, separated

jeer
[jeer]

v. to speak or shout derisively

조소하다, 조롱하다

The crowd jeered him when he missed several shots in a row.

syn. sneer, ridicule, scoff

jovial
[**joh**-vee-*uhl*]

adj. endowed with or characterized by a joyous humor

쾌활한, 명랑한, 즐거운

Santa Claus is depicted as a large, jovial man with a white beard.

syn. cheerful, happy, jolly

judicious
[joo-**dish**-uhs]

adj. showing good judgment

현명한

We should make judicious use of the resources available to us.

syn. prudent, sensible, discreet

jurisdiction
[joor-is-**dik**-shuhn]

n. the extent of right or power to administer justice

관할권, 사법권

A police officer from Canada does not have jurisdiction to arrest someone in America.

syn. power, authority, control

Sentence Completion 5-5

Directions : Fill in the blanks to complete the sentences.

1. The government has _____ over the country or territory.

2. Helen had made a _____ decision after she considered many aspects.

3. The film has an _____ plot that I had a hard time following.

4. Joseph can't explain how he knew - he just had an _____.

5. The new baseball coach will _____ the team.

6. Josh has always been the most _____ explorer.

7. The new coach was a _____ figure with his constant smiles.

8. The spectators cheer at the home team and _____ at the visiting team.

Answers

1. jurisdiction
2. judicious
3. intricate
4. intuition
5. invigorate
6. intrepid
7. jovial
8. jeer

Analogy 15. List & Collection

하나하나가 모여 만들어진 전체를 연결시키는 문제입니다. 문제가 많이 나오지는 않아도 빠지지 않고 출제되는 유형이지요.

menu : food
메뉴 : 음식

catalog : goods
카탈로그 : 물건

cookbook : recipe
요리책 : 조리법

atlas : map
지도책 : 지도

receipt : item
영수증 : 물품

lexicon : word
사전 : 단어

suite : tune
모음곡 : 음악, 곡

anthology : work
문집, 작품 모음집 : 작품

manifest : cargo
화물 목록, 승객 명단 : 화물

ledger : transaction
거래장부 : 거래

inventory : merchandise
재고목록 : 상품

index : topic
색인 : 주제

roster : name
명단 : 이름

tally : sum
(총계나 총액을 누적해나가는) 기록 : 총합

POP QUIZ

1. Suite is to tunes as

    (A) anthology is to works
    (B) inventory is to debt
    (C) roster is to transaction
    (D) tally is to tale
    (E) cookbook is to deed

2. Index is to topic as

    (A) menu is to diner
    (B) receipt is to customer
    (C) catalogue is to shopper
    (D) atlas is to chart
    (E) lexicon is to word

Check-up 5-1

Directions Each of the following questions consists of one word followed by five words or phrases. You are to select the one word or phrase whose meaning is closest to the word in capital letters.

1. GREGARIOUS
(A) sociable
(B) abject
(C) callous
(D) enervated
(E) hapless

2. GRIMACE
(A) empathy
(B) contortion
(C) retaliation
(D) surfeit
(E) travesty

3. GRIND
(A) trek
(B) weather
(C) crush
(D) sedate
(E) placate

4. GULLIBLE
(A) pithy
(B) noxious
(C) credulous
(D) magnanimous
(E) lithe

5. HACKNEYED
(A) complicit
(B) algid
(C) envious
(D) banal
(E) gluttonous

6. HAGGARD
(A) irascible
(B) harrowing
(C) familial
(D) divisive
(E) gaunt

7. HALLUCINATION
(A) indignation
(B) delusion
(C) modicum
(D) penchant
(E) repose

8. HAPHAZARD
(A) reprehensible
(B) static
(C) arbitrary
(D) uniform
(E) vivacious

9. HAPLESS
(A) laminated
(B) helpless
(C) dismayed
(D) sumptuous
(E) unlucky

10. HAUGHTY
(A) arrogant
(B) histrionic
(C) fatuous
(D) benign
(E) acute

255

Check-up 5-2

1. HAVOC
  - (A) acumen
  - (B) harmony
  - (C) chaos
  - (D) iniquity
  - (E) maxim

2. HOMOGENOUS
  - (A) meager
  - (B) obdurate
  - (C) novel
  - (D) identical
  - (E) placid

3. IDIOSYNCRATIC
  - (A) precarious
  - (B) quirky
  - (C) remiss
  - (D) scathing
  - (E) complicit

4. IGNITE
  - (A) kindle
  - (B) concede
  - (C) abbreviate
  - (D) mediate
  - (E) ratiocinate

5. IMMACULATE
  - (A) seminal
  - (B) impeccable
  - (C) tortuous
  - (D) ubiquitous
  - (E) voluminous

6. IMMERSE
  - (A) rectify
  - (B) wane
  - (C) abhor
  - (D) submerge
  - (E) berate

7. IMMINENT
  - (A) truculent
  - (B) winsome
  - (C) impending
  - (D) accommodating
  - (E) boisterous

8. IMPART
  - (A) aggregate
  - (B) conduct
  - (C) tell
  - (D) forsake
  - (E) manifest

9. IMPLICATE
  - (A) obfuscate
  - (B) demolish
  - (C) revise
  - (D) satisfy
  - (E) involve

10. IMPLICIT
  - (A) calm
  - (B) scathing
  - (C) overwhelming
  - (D) redoubtable
  - (E) tacit

Check-up 5-3

Directions   Each of the following questions consists of one word followed by five words or phrases. You are to select the one word or phrase whose meaning is closest to the word in capital letters.

1. IMPOVERISHED
(A) destitute
(B) formidable
(C) pervasive
(D) malevolent
(E) judicious

2. INCARCERATE
(A) urge
(B) praise
(C) imprison
(D) diminish
(E) combine

3. INCESSANT
(A) cogent
(B) apparent
(C) pellucid
(D) uninterrupted
(E) flexible

4. INCITE
(A) ratiocinate
(B) satiate
(C) moderate
(D) trek
(E) instigate

5. INCOMPATIBLE
(A) poised
(B) antagonistic
(C) radiant
(D) significant
(E) original

6. INCUMBENT
(A) truculent
(B) unvarying
(C) official
(D) vicarious
(E) charming

7. INDEFATIGABLE
(A) untiring
(B) reprehensible
(C) indistinct
(D) hostile
(E) frenetic

8. INDICT
(A) enlighten
(B) shorten
(C) accuse
(D) enhance
(E) bid

9. INDIFFERENT
(A) numerous
(B) apathetic
(C) reserved
(D) spectral
(E) baleful

10. INDIGENT
(A) brazen
(B) unpredictable
(C) cogent
(D) agreeable
(E) impoverished

257

Check-up 5-4

1. INDULGE
(A) abridge
(B) favor
(C) amble
(D) blandish
(E) coax

2. INFALLIBLE
(A) complicit
(B) impulsive
(C) superficial
(D) certain
(E) daunting

3. INFERIOR
(A) lesser
(B) harmful
(C) abandoned
(D) despondent
(E) transparent

4. INGENIOUS
(A) diligent
(B) exhausted
(C) urgent
(D) fatuous
(E) inventive

5. INGENUOUS
(A) distinct
(B) mistaken
(C) artless
(D) elated
(E) fertile

6. INNOCUOUS
(A) untamed
(B) harmless
(C) fickle
(D) astounded
(E) hopeless

7. INSIGHTFUL
(A) extraordinary
(B) discerning
(C) hapless
(D) dramatic
(E) idolatrous

8. INTEGRAL
(A) immutable
(B) penetrated
(C) angered
(D) essential
(E) jubilant

9. INTERIM
(A) meantime
(B) judicious
(C) intricate
(D) admiring
(E) improper

10. INTERMITTENT
(A) lethargic
(B) vulgar
(C) sporadic
(D) lawless
(E) generous

Check-up 5-5

Directions   Each of the following questions consists of one word followed by five words or phrases.
You are to select the one word or phrase whose meaning is closest to the word in capital letters.

1. INTERVENE
(A) accentuate
(B) interlope
(C) gratify
(D) mollify
(E) exclude

2. INTREPID
(A) noble
(B) valiant
(C) patent
(D) fruitful
(E) indecent

3. INTRICATE
(A) eager
(B) abundant
(C) soiled
(D) fixed
(E) complicated

4. INTUITION
(A) instinct
(B) partiality
(C) irritability
(D) repose
(E) conflict

5. INVIGORATE
(A) abscond
(B) reserved
(C) pacify
(D) stimulate
(E) flourish

6. ISOLATED
(A) celestial
(B) arranged
(C) solitary
(D) viable
(E) intimidating

7. JEER
(A) sneer
(B) approach
(C) defame
(D) fortify
(E) manifest

8. JOVIAL
(A) sarcastic
(B) cheerful
(C) habitual
(D) sentimental
(E) morose

9. JUDICIOUS
(A) negligent
(B) rustic
(C) prudent
(D) enormous
(E) compassionate

10. JURISDICTION
(A) capability
(B) outcast
(C) sympathy
(D) tragedy
(E) authority

251 juxtapose	256 lampoon
252 kindle	257 languid
253 kinetic	258 latent
254 lackluster	259 laudable
255 lament	260 lavish

School Motto

"Dare to be True"

- Milton Academy

SSATKOREA.com

juxtapose
[**juhk**-stuh-**pohz**]

v. to place close together or side by side

옆으로 나란히 늘어놓다

Juxtaposed against a red backdrop, your blue painting really stands out.

syn. appose, bring near, pair

kindle
[**kin**-dl]

v. to start a fire

불을 피우다, 불 붙이다

Knowing how to kindle a fire is an important survival skill.

syn. ignite, inflame, set fire

kinetic
[ki-**net**-ik]

adj. caused by motion

운동의, 운동에 의해 생기는

A roller coaster has a lot of kinetic energy when it rolls down the big dip.

syn. moving, active, energetic

lackluster
[**lak**-luhs-ter]

adj. lacking brilliance or vitality

광택이 없는, 흐리멍덩한

His lackluster life was without brilliance, shine, or vitality.

syn. dull, lifeless, flat

lament
[luh-**ment**]

v. To feel or express sorrow or regret for

슬퍼하다, 애도하다

Josh lamented not studying harder when he received a C on his test.

syn. grieve, mourn, sorrow

lampoon
[lam-**poon**]

n. a sharp, often virulent satire

풍자시, 풍자문

Stacey and Helen performed a lampoon making fun of the school principal.

syn. farce, parody, satire

languid
[**lang**-gwid]

adj. lacking in vigor or vitality

나른한, 움직임에 힘이 없는

Helen felt languid from the heat and humidity.

syn. shiftless, listless, torpid

latent
[**leyt**-nt]

adj. present but not visible

잠재하는, 숨어 있는

Without training, his musical talent remained latent.

syn. hidden, dormant, inert

laudable
[**law**-duh-b*uh*l]

adj. deserving praise

칭찬할 만한

His noble ideas and polite behavior are laudable.

syn. commendable, estimable, praiseworthy

lavish
[**lav**-ish]

adj. extremely generous

풍성한, 호화로운, 후한

The mayor threw a lavish party for his daughter on her 16th birthday.

syn. luxuriant, munificent, opulent

Sentence Completion 6-1

Directions : Fill in the blanks to complete the sentences.

1. The exhibition plans to _____ the early drawings with some later works.

2. Harper enjoys throwing _____ parties with unusual themes.

3. Any object in motion possesses _____ energy.

4. The principal mentioned Veronica's _____ efforts to start a recycling program in her community.

5. Patrick will _____ the mistake he made.

6. In this camp, Rosy discovered her _____ math talents.

7. The golf champion gave a disappointingly _____ performance.

8. Hannah's _____ voice is slow and relaxed.

Answers

1. juxtapose
2. lavish
3. kinetic
4. laudable
5. lament
6. latent
7. lackluster
8. languid

SSAT UPPER LEVEL 261

261	legacy	266	liberal
262	legible	267	lineage
263	legitimate	268	literate
264	lethargic	269	lubricate
255	liaison	270	ludicrous

School Motto

"Discere et Vivere"

(To Learn and to Live)

- Northfield Mount Hermon School

SSATKOREA.com

legacy
[**leg**-uh-see]

n. anything handed down from the past
(선조 등이 남긴) 유산

He received a large legacy from his uncle.

syn. bequest, estate, gift

legible
[**lej**-uh-b*uh*l]

adj. easy to read
글자를 알아 볼 수 있게 쓰여진, 또렷한

His handwriting is clearly legible.

syn. clear, distinct, understandable

legitimate
[li-**jit**-uh-mit]

adj. according to law
합법의, 정당한

I hope you had a legitimate reason for missing yesterday's science class.

syn. lawful, legible, licit

lethargic
[luh-**thahr**-jik]

adj. affected with lethargy
무기력한, 축 처진

Because he had the flu, he felt lethargic.

syn. lifeless, drowsy, sluggish

liaison
[lee-ey-**zawn**]

n. a link between people or groups
연락, 연락 담당자, 연락책

The negotiator provided a liaison with the guerrillas.

syn. contact, channel, connection

liberal
[**lib**-er-*uh*l]

adj. giving and generous in temperament or behavior
관대한, 후한

I like it sweet, so pour a liberal amount of sugar into my lemonade.

syn. abundant, extravagant, plentiful

lineage
[**lin**-ee-ij]

n. lineal descent from an ancestor
혈통

Dave's lineage includes Charles Dickens.

syn. pedigree, ancestry, family tree

literate
[**lit**-er-it]

adj. able to read and write
읽고 쓸 수 있는

I hope that someday all people on Earth can become literate.

syn. educated, erudite, learned

lubricate
[**loo**-bri-keyt]

v. to apply oil in order to diminish friction
윤활유를 바르다, 기름을 치다

It is important to lubricate the metal parts in an engine so they do not get too hot.

syn. grease, oil, wax

ludicrous
[**loo**-di-kruhs]

adj. causing laughter because of absurdity
우스꽝스러운, 터무니없는

The whole idea is absolutely ludicrous!

syn. ridiculous, absurd, laughable

Sentence Completion 6-2

Directions : Fill in the blanks to complete the sentences.

1. Emma is a _____ who aids communication between two companies.

2. Helen was very proud of her ancient royal _____.

3. The retiring coach left a _____ of diligence and integrity.

4. The army gave power back to the _____ government.

5. This _____ play is funny, absurd, and nonsensical.

6. Even though Grace looks old, she is computer _____.

7. Hank will _____ a rusted bolt to unscrew it.

8. Lily's parents are very _____ , so they allow her a lot of freedom.

271 lull	276 mar
272 magnificent	277 meander
273 malady	278 meddle
274 mandatory	279 mediocre
275 manifest	280 meditate

School Motto

"Lumen, Fides, Labor, Facta"

(Light, Faith, Work, and Deeds)

- Eaglebrook School

SSATKOREA.com

lull
[l*uh*l]

n. a pause during which things are calm

소강상태, 잠잠한 시기, 고요해진 상태

Then came the lull before the storm.

syn. pause, calm, hiatus

magnificent
[mag-**nif**-uh-suhnt]

adj. making a splendid appearance

매우 훌륭하고 멋진

The view from the top of the Empire State Building is magnificent.

syn. extraordinary, glorious, grand

malady
[**mal**-uh-dee]

n. any disorder or disease

병, 병폐

Manuel's aunt has a malady that causes her pain in her knees.

syn. ailment, disease, affliction

mandatory
[**man**-duh-tawr-ee]

adj. authoritatively ordered

의무적인, 법에 정해진

Attendance at the meeting is mandatory.

syn. required, compulsory, obligatory

manifest
[**man**-uh-fest]

adj. readily perceived by the eye or the understanding

명백한, 분명한

It is manifest that Jack is in love with Diane.

syn. evident, obvious, apparent

mar
[mahr]

v. to make imperfect

흠집을 내다, 손상시키다

The pen mark mars his crisp, white shirt.

syn. hurt, stain, taint

meander

[mee-**an**-der]

v. to wander aimlessly

거닐다, 구불구불하다

He meandered through the playground and then the mall instead of coming directly home from school.

syn. ramble, saunter, wander

meddle

[**med**-l]

v. to involve oneself in a matter without invitation

간섭하다

Susan always meddles in other people's business.

syn. interlope, interfere, intervene

mediocre

[mee-dee-**oh**-ker]

adj. neither good nor bad

보통 밖에 안 되는, 썩 좋지는 않은

He knew his essay only deserved a mediocre grade.

syn. average, commonplace, ordinary

meditate

[**med**-i-teyt]

v. to engage in transcendental meditation

명상하다

He meditated over what he should major in at college.

syn. ruminate, ponder, deliberate

Sentence Completion 6-3

Directions : Fill in the blanks to complete the sentences.

1. The pen mark will _____ Penelope's white dress.

2. There has been a _____ in a long and tedious conversation.

3. The plot is unoriginal and _____.

4. My boss always has to _____ in other employers' affairs.

5. The Pyramids look _____ when you see with your naked eyes.

6. A _____ minimum is a sentence which the court must give to a person convicted of a crime.

7. Stella surprisingly did not _____ on a winding roundabout course.

8. _____ regularly, and you might become less distracted.

Answers

1. mar
2. lull
3. mediocre
4. meddle
5. magnificent
6. mandatory
7. meander
8. meditate

SSAT UPPER LEVEL **265**

281	memento	286	mesmerize
282	mentor	287	meticulous
283	mercenary	288	minuscule
284	mercurial	289	minute
285	meritorious	290	misconstrue

School Motto

"Non Sibi"

(Not for Self)

- Phillips Academy/ Phillips Exeter Academy

SSATKOREA.com

memento
[muh-**men**-toh]

n. an object item that serves to remind past

기념물, 기념품

Elisa bought a colorful shell as a memento of her trip to Hawaii.

syn.   keepsake, souvenir, memorabilia

mentor
[**men**-tawr]

n. a wise and trusted counselor or teacher

정신적 스승, 조언자

Todd's mentor taught him how to be a good person.

syn.   advisor, role model

mercenary
[**mur**-suh-ner-ee]

adj. working merely for money

돈 버는 데만 관심이 있는, 돈이 목적인

The mercenary soldiers were only loyal to the person who paid them.

syn.   venal, avaricious, greedy

mercurial
[mer-**kyoor**-ee-*uhl*]

adj. changeable and erratic

변덕스러운

Debra's mercurial mood swings always kept Ray on his toes.

syn.   capricious, fickle, whimsical

meritorious
[mer-i-**tawr**-ee-uhs]

adj. deserving praise, reward, esteem

칭찬할 만한

He was praised for his meritorious contributions to the city.

syn.   praiseworthy, admirable, heroic

mesmerize
[**mez**-muh-rahyz]

v. to compel by fascination

매혹시키다, 마음을 사로잡다

The cat was mesmerized by the feather on a string.

syn.   fascinate, captivate, enchant

meticulous
[muh-**tik**-yuh-luhs]

adj. taking extreme care about minute details

꼼꼼한, 세심한

I want my surgeon to be meticulous.

syn. fastidious, precise, thorough

minuscule
[**min**-uh-skyool]

adj. very small

아주 작은

There is a miniscule chance you will pass the test without studying.

syn. tiny, insignificant, infinitesimal

minute
[**min**-it]

adj. extremely small

극히 작은, 매우 상세한

Compared to an elephant, a mouse is a minute creature.

syn. infinitesimal, microscopic, minuscule

misconstrue
[mis-kuhn-**stroo**]

v. to misunderstand the meaning of

오해하다, 잘못 이해하다

She misconstrued her brother's intentions.

syn. misinterpret, distort, misunderstand

Sentence Completion 6-4

Directions : Fill in the blanks to complete the sentences.

1. Liam's bravery is _____ deserving of praise or a reward.

2. The painter paints detailed portraits using _____ paint brushes.

3. Eleanor would often _____ her husband's silence as neglect.

4. Harris was a great _____ who gave young students much help and advice.

5. Ellie kept the seashell as a _____ of her honeymoon.

6. Violet's beauty continued to _____ him for a long time.

7. Many hours of _____ preparation have gone into writing this book.

8. Audrey ate just two _____ pieces of bread.

Answers

1. meritorious
2. minute
3. misconstrue
4. mentor
5. memento
6. mesmerize
7. meticulous
8. minuscule

291	miser	296	muddle
292	monotonous	297	mundane
293	moor	298	munificent
294	morose	299	mutual
295	mourn	300	myriad

School Motto

"Finis andorigine pendet"

(The end is the beginning)

- Phillips Academy/ Phillips Exeter Academy

━━━━━ SSATKOREA.com

miser
[**mahy**-zer]

n. a person who hoards wealth and spends as little money as possible

구두쇠

Scrooge, from Dickens' A Christmas Carol, is a famous miser from literature.

syn. penny pincher, hoarder, scrooge

monotonous
[muh-**not**-n-uhs]

adj. tediously unvarying

단조로운, 변함없는

Students complain about the teacher's uninteresting and monotonous lectures.

syn. tedious, boring, dull

moor
[moor]

v. to secure a ship or boat in a particular place

(배를) 정박시키다, 잡아매다

You'd better moor the canoe to shore so it doesn't float away.

syn. anchor, berth, dock

morose
[muh-**rohs**]

adj. gloomily as a person or mood

시무룩한, 뚱한

You seem morose today; is something wrong?

syn. gloomy, melancholy, somber

mourn
[mawrn]

v. to feel or express sorrow or grief

애도하다, 슬퍼하다

He mourned the loss of a beloved pet.

syn. grieve, sorrow, lament

muddle
[**muh**-dl]

v. to mix up in a confused or bungling manner

혼란스럽게 만들다, 갈피를 못 잡게 하다

She felt muddled when she first woke from a deep sleep.

syn. jumble, confuse, disorganize

mundane
[muhn-**deyn**]

adj. common or ordinary

평범한, 일상적인, 재미없는

When I feel like my life is becoming too mundane, I like to take a small trip.

syn. boring, banal, pedestrian

munificent
[myoo-**nif**-uh-suhnt]

adj. very generous

매우 인자한, 아낌없이 주는

My munificent friend is very lavish when it comes to giving gifts.

syn. lavish, philanthropic, unsparing

mutual
[**myoo**-choo-*uhl*]

adj. experienced by each of two or more with respect

상호간의, 서로의

The two competing nations have a mutual distrust.

syn. reciprocal, communal, bilateral

myriad
[**mir**-ee-uhd]

adj. of an indefinitely great number

무수한, 무수히 많은

We could see the myriad stars of a summer night.

syn. innumerable, countless, untold

Sentence Completion 6-5

Directions : **Fill in the blanks to complete the sentences.**

1. Because Mary was angry at her husband, she gave only _____ responses to his questions.

2. The parents face a _____ of problems bringing up seven children.

3. Why are you so _____ today?

4. The _____ has a strong wish to save money and hates to spend it.

5. Superman hid his identity by posing as his _____ alter ego, Clark Kent.

6. The families still _____ over their neighbor's death.

7. The agreement was terminated by _____ consent.

8. Whenever teachers meet the twins, they always _____ up their names.

  Answers

1. monotonous	5. mundane
2. myriad	6. mourn
3. morose	7. mutual
4. miser	8. muddle

Analogy 16. Place

장소와 장소에 보관되거나 장소에서 하는 일이 연결되는 유형도 자주 출제됩니다. 문제문 풀 때 'A에 B가 있다'라고 생각하지 말고 [A는 B를 보관하기 위해 만든 공간] 또는 [A는 B를 하기 위해 만든 공간]으로 장소의 '목적'에 집중해서 풀어보세요. 더 답이 확실하게 보일 것입니다.

A는 B를 보관하기 위해 만든 장소

library : book
도서관 : 책

morgue : corpse
시체보관소 : 시체

archive : record
기록 보관소 : 기록

silo : fodder
가축 사료 보관소 : 사료

pantry : food
식료품 저장실 : 음식

armory : ammunition
무기고 : 탄약

A를 하기 위해 만든 장소 B

tennis : court
테니스 : 테니스 코트

golf : course
골프 : 골프 코스

hockey : field
하키 : 하키 필드

baseball : diamond
야구 : 야구장

bowling : lane
볼링 : 레인

skate : rink
스케이트 : 아이스 링크장

chess : board
체스 : 체스보드

basketball : court
농구 : 농구 코트

POP QUIZ

1. Court is to tennis as
(A) rink is to billiard
(B) pool is to table
(C) club is to golf
(D) puck is to hockey
(E) diamond is to baseball

2. Pantry is to food as
(A) museum is to curator
(B) silo is to fodder
(C) exhibit is to painter
(D) recital is to pianist
(E) galley is to kitchen

Check-up 6-1

Directions Each of the following questions consists of one word followed by five words or phrases. You are to select the one word or phrase whose meaning is closest to the word in capital letters.

1. JUXTAPOSE
(A) appose
(B) rant
(C) spurn
(D) pander
(E) oscillate

2. KINDLE
(A) mitigate
(B) harbinger
(C) ignite
(D) foster
(E) corrupt

3. KINETIC
(A) hackneyed
(B) active
(C) frugal
(D) eloquent
(E) docile

4. LACKLUSTER
(A) congenial
(B) expendable
(C) ineffable
(D) kinetic
(E) dull

5. LAMENT
(A) incite
(B) sever
(C) patent
(D) grieve
(E) abolish

6. LAMPOON
(A) shrewdness
(B) censure
(C) distend
(D) farce
(E) expedite

7. LANGUID
(A) obtuse
(B) shiftless
(C) cryptic
(D) fastidious
(E) gratuitous

8. LATENT
(A) dubious
(B) hidden
(C) generic
(D) humane
(E) indignant

9. LAUDABLE
(A) judicious
(B) ambiguous
(C) commendable
(D) relevant
(E) trivial

10. LAVISH
(A) opulent
(B) caustic
(C) sage
(D) insignificant
(E) obdurate

271

Check-up 6-2

Each of the following questions consists of one word followed by five words or phrases. You are to select the one word or phrase whose meaning is closest to the word in capital letters.

1. LEGACY
- (A) odyssey
- (B) amity
- (C) bequest
- (D) praise
- (E) ephemeral

2. LEGIBLE
- (A) genetic
- (B) hypocritical
- (C) indolent
- (D) listless
- (E) clear

3. LEGITIMATE
- (A) laconic
- (B) mobile
- (C) haphazard
- (D) lawful
- (E) narcissistic

4. LETHARGIC
- (A) nonchalant
- (B) observable
- (C) affording
- (D) precise
- (E) lifeless

5. LIAISON
- (A) motive
- (B) contact
- (C) sharpness
- (D) equality
- (E) probity

6. LIBERAL
- (A) queasy
- (B) reciprocal
- (C) abundant
- (D) firm
- (E) sardonic

7. LINEAGE
- (A) pedigree
- (B) stimulus
- (C) tangent
- (D) venality
- (E) brevity

8. LITERATE
- (A) refined
- (B) educated
- (C) venerable
- (D) convivial
- (E) affable

9. LUBRICATE
- (A) provoke
- (B) usurp
- (C) seditious
- (D) premeditated
- (E) grease

10. LUDICROUS
- (A) opaque
- (B) ironic
- (C) hideous
- (D) ridiculous
- (E) greedy

Check-up 6-3

Directions   Each of the following questions consists of one word followed by five words or phrases.
You are to select the one word or phrase whose meaning is closest to the word in capital letters.

1. LULL
(A) pause
(B) fidelity
(C) liveliness
(D) accolade
(E) blunder

2. MAGNIFICENT
(A) stable
(B) churlish
(C) extraordinary
(D) bizarre
(E) decorous

3. MALADY
(A) drawback
(B) ailment
(C) edict
(D) foible
(E) genre

4. MANDATORY
(A) complimentary
(B) refractory
(C) decrepit
(D) compulsory
(E) brazen

5. MANIFEST
(A) vigorous
(B) habitual
(C) evident
(D) tolerant
(E) ineffective

6. MAR
(A) hurt
(B) dispose
(C) seize
(D) dwindle
(E) control

7. MEANDER
(A) destroy
(B) jeer
(C) incline
(D) ramble
(E) perceive

8. MEDDLE
(A) replete
(B) placate
(C) abdicate
(D) belittle
(E) interlope

9. MEDIOCRE
(A) humane
(B) overt
(C) vulgar
(D) copious
(E) average

10. MEDITATE
(A) ponder
(B) cull
(C) exile
(D) nag
(E) taint

273

Check-up 6-4

1. MEMENTO
(A) nostalgia
(B) counterbalance
(C) keepsake
(D) oblivion
(E) parity

2. MENTOR
(A) dictum
(B) speech
(C) advisor
(D) quality
(E) hybrid

3. MERCENARY
(A) innocuous
(B) unrestrained
(C) blatant
(D) venal
(E) apocryphal

4. MERCURIAL
(A) capricious
(B) bucolic
(C) occupied
(D) didactic
(E) erudite

5. MERITORIOUS
(A) expendable
(B) famished
(C) germane
(D) insolent
(E) praiseworthy

6. MESMERIZE
(A) fascinate
(B) alleviate
(C) provoke
(D) deviate
(E) rebuke

7. METICULOUS
(A) efficient
(B) distant
(C) gullible
(D) fastidious
(E) irrefutable

8. MINUSCULE
(A) languid
(B) tiny
(C) mournful
(D) dreadful
(E) aloof

9. MINUTE
(A) harmonious
(B) evanescent
(C) infinitesimal
(D) fallow
(E) conspicuous

10. MISCONSTRUE
(A) misinterpret
(B) rugged
(C) disprove
(D) kindle
(E) levitate

Check-up 6-5

Directions Each of the following questions consists of one word followed by five words or phrases. You are to select the one word or phrase whose meaning is closest to the word in capital letters.

1. **MISER**
   (A) philanthropist
   (B) misery
   (C) jury
   (D) penny pincher
   (E) filibuster

2. **MONOTONOUS**
   (A) unnerving
   (B) revitalizing
   (C) poised
   (D) bewildered
   (E) tedious

3. **MOOR**
   (A) declare
   (B) evoke
   (C) ruffle
   (D) hinder
   (E) anchor

4. **MOROSE**
   (A) furtive
   (B) appropriate
   (C) gloomy
   (D) spontaneous
   (E) unyielding

5. **MOURN**
   (A) retract
   (B) lament
   (C) disavow
   (D) scour
   (E) pollute

6. **MUDDLE**
   (A) unveil
   (B) jumble
   (C) oust
   (D) crave
   (E) expel

7. **MUNDANE**
   (A) willful
   (B) omnipresent
   (C) superior
   (D) magnificent
   (E) pedestrian

8. **MUNIFICENT**
   (A) boisterous
   (B) hectic
   (C) lavish
   (D) miserable
   (E) dormant

9. **MUTUAL**
   (A) superb
   (B) exasperating
   (C) deft
   (D) reciprocal
   (E) ample

10. **MYRIAD**
    (A) nagging
    (B) beloved
    (C) innumerable
    (D) baleful
    (E) deported

275

301 naive	306 neutralize
302 nebulous	307 nonchalant
303 negate	308 noncommittal
304 negligible	309 nostalgia
305 nemesis	310 nuance

School Motto

"Certa Viriliter"

(Strive Valiantly)

- Pomfret School

SSATKOREA.com

naive
[nah-**eev**]

adj. lacking sophistication or street smarts

세상 물정을 너무 모르는, 잘 속는

It's naive of you to believe he'll do what he says.

syn.   credulous, childlike, ignorant

nebulous
[**neb**-yuh-luhs]

adj. hazy, vague, indistinct, or confused

흐릿한, 모호한

He has only a nebulous idea about what he'd like to study at college.

syn.   ambiguous, unclear, hazy

negate
[ni-**geyt**]

v. to deny the existence, evidence, or truth of

효력이 없게 만들다, 무효화하다

Shipping charges for heavy items may negate your savings.

syn.   contradict, countermand, annihilate

negligible
[**neg**-li-juh-b*uh*l]

adj. not worth considering

무시해도 될 정도로 작은

There is a negligible difference in meaning between these two words.

syn.   inconsequential, insignificant, paltry

nemesis
[**nem**-uh-sis]

n. something that a person cannot conquer or achieve

이길 수 없는 상대, 피할 수 없는 벌

Inward suffering is the worst of nemesis.

syn.   foe, adversary, opponent

neutralize
[**noo**-truh-lahyz]

v. to make something ineffective

무효화시키다, 상쇄시키다

Acids neutralize alkalis and vice versa.

syn.   counteract, nullify, offset

nonchalant

[non-shuh-**lahnt**]

adj. coolly unconcerned, indifferent, or unexcited

무심한, 태연한 척하는

Tyler always seems nonchalant about his assignments.

syn. indifferent, apathetic, casual

noncommittal

[non-kuh-**mit**-l]

adj. not committing oneself to a particular view

주장을 밝히지 않는, 태도가 애매한

The White House spokesman was noncommittal on this question.

syn. indefinite, vague, equivocal

nostalgia

[no-**stal**-juh]

n. pleasant remembrances

향수 (고향이나 지난 과거를 그리워하는 마음)

Photos of my favorite childhood bring on nostalgia.

syn. wistfulness, longing, hapless

nuance

[**noo**-ahns]

n. a subtle differnce

미묘한 차이, 뉘앙스

This painting is famous in part for its nuances of shading.

syn. hint, inkling, subtlety

Sentence Completion 7-1

Directions : Fill in the blanks to complete the sentences.

1. The tax increases proved to be the president's political _____.

2. Her _____ of the academics resulted in poor grades.

3. On a foggy morning, the trees all have a hazy or _____ look.

4. Acids _____ alkalies and vice versa.

5. Be careful not to let parking fees and gas costs _____ any savings.

6. Looking back at old photographs always brings back a sense of _____ .

7. As Benjamin wants to keep all his options open, he stays _____.

8. Oliver was _____, acting aloof or unconcerned.

 Answers

1. nemesis
2. negligence
3. nebulous
4. neutralize
5. negate
6. nostalgia
7. noncommittal
8. nonchalant

311 null 316 obstinate

312 oblique 317 obstruct

313 obliterate 318 occupy

314 oblivious 319 officious

315 obsessive 320 ominous

School Motto

"Veritas"

(Truth)

- Portsmouth Abbey School

SSATKOREA.com

null
[n*uh*l]

adj. without value, effect, consequence, or significance

아무 가치, 영향, 중요성 등이 없는

The contract was proved to be null and void.

syn. zero value, ineffectual, valueless

oblique
[uh-**bleek**]

adj. indirectly stated or expressed

비스듬한, 완곡한 표현을 하는

Not directly stating their names, the principal made an oblique reference.

syn. indirect, roundabout, slanting

obliterate
[uh-**blit**-uh-reyt]

v. to remove or destroy all

없애다

Our school soccer team obliterated the other team by a score of 7-0.

syn. eliminate, decimate, eradicate

oblivious
[uh-**bliv**-ee-uhs]

adj. lacking remembrance, memory, or mindful attention

의식하지 못하는

Absorbed in her work, she was totally oblivious of her surroundings.

syn. unmindful, unconscious, unaware

obsessive
[uhb-**ses**-iv]

adj. being, pertaining to, or resembling an obsession

(어떤 생각에 심하게) 사로잡혀 있는, 강박적인

Dave is so obsessive about baseball.

syn. neurotic, compulsive, addictive

obstinate
[**ob**-stuh-nit]

adj. firmly or stubbornly adhering to one's purpose

고집 센, 완강한

I was confused by her obstinate refusal to comply with my request.

syn. dogmatic, stubborn, unwilling

obstruct
[uhb-**struhkt**]

v. to block or close up with an obstacle

막다, 차단하다

*The accident is **obstructing** traffic on Main Street.*

syn. block, hinder, impede

occupy
[**ok**-yuh-pahy]

v. to take or fill up

차지하다

*The paintings of Andy Warhol **occupied** a prominent place on her walls.*

syn. inhabit, reside, use

officious
[uh-**fish**-uhs]

adj. objectionably aggressive in offering one's unrequested and unwanted services

거들먹거리는, 위세를 부리는

*His clients are mostly rude and **officious**.*

syn. intrusive, self-important, dictatorial

ominous
[**om**-uh-nuhs]

adj. portending evil or harm

불길한, 나쁜 징조의

*Those **ominous** clouds means we might get a storm soon.*

syn. foreboding, threatening, inauspicious

Sentence Completion 7-2

Directions : Fill in the blanks to complete the sentences.

1.   Roman legion invaded the country to _____ its territory.

2.   _____ is zero.

3.   Absorbed in the movie, Logan was _____ to his surroundings.

4.   The missile will _____ the target.

5.   The _____ man does not hold opinions, but they hold him.

6.   Do not park your car by the exit door; you _____ everybody's way out.

7.   She was _____ about keeping her kitchen clean.

8.   The summon was _____, unpleasant ,and threatening.

Answers

1. occupy
2. null
3. oblivious
4. obliterate
5. obstinate
6. obstruct
7. obsessive
8. ominous

321 onerous   326 orthodox

322 opinionated   327 outlandish

323 optimum   328 outrageous

324 opulent   329 overbearing

325 oratory   330 overlook

School Motto

"Ea discamus in terris quorum scientia perseveret in coelis"
(Let us learn those things on Earth the knowledge of which continues in Heaven)
- St.Paul's School

SSATKOREA.com

onerous
[**on**-er-uhs]

adj. burdensome, oppressive, or troublesome

아주 힘든, 부담되는

Ms. Han gave us an onerous amount of homework this weekend.

syn.   arduous, burdensome, demanding

opinionated
[uh-**pin**-yuh-ney-tid]

adj. conceitedly dogmatic

자기 의견을 고집하는, 독선적인

William is very opinionated when it comes to politics.

syn.   bigoted, dogmatic, stubborn

optimum
[**op**-tuh-muhm]

adj. the best quality and quantity

최고의, 최적의

The optimum result on my report card would be straight A's.

syn.   best, ideal, peak

opulent
[**op**-yuh-luhnt]

adj. abundant or plentiful

부유한, 풍부한, 풍족한

The president usually stays in opulent hotels when she travels.

syn.   rich, affluent, profuse

oratory
[**awr**-uh-tawr-ee]

n. skill or eloquence in public speaking

웅변술

During her speech on third-world poverty, Lisa moved her classmates with her oratory.

syn.   rhetoric, speaking skill, articulation

orthodox
[**awr**-thuh-doks]

adj. usually approved

정통의, 전통적인

Unlike Mr. Cooper and his cutting-edge ideas, Mr. Baker has rather orthodox views about education.

syn.   accepted, approved, conventional

outlandish

[out-**lan**-dish]

adj. freakishly or grotesquely strange or odd

이상한, 기이한

Donna's outlandish outfit drew stares from the other students.

syn.   bizarre, weird, eccentric

outrageous

[out-**rey**-juhs]

adj. greatly exceeding bounds of reason

너무나 충격적인, 터무니 없는

The culprit's outrageous remarks caused public outrage.

syn.   extreme, egregious, wanton

overbearing

[oh-ver-**bair**-ing]

adj. haughty or rudely arrogant

고압적인, 남을 지배하려 드는

The coach can sometimes be overbearing toward his athletes.

syn.   haughty, dictatorial, domineering

overlook

[oh-ver-**look**]

v. to fail to notice, perceive, or consider

못 보고 넘어가다, 간과하다

Making to-do list prevent you from overlooking any details.

syn.   disregard, neglect, omit

Sentence Completion 7-3

Directions : Fill in the blanks to complete the sentences.

1. It was an _____ task of finding a peaceful solution.

2. Don't _____ the cost of car insurance when you're planning to rent a car.

3. My _____ math tutor criticizes every question I attempt.

4. Runners measure their _____ weight before running a marathon.

5. Sebastian lived an _____ lifestyle that included sports cars and luxurious mansions.

6. This is _____ ! I will not put up with such treatment.

7. Henry is an _____ vegetarian; he never eats meat.

8. The speaker has a high reputation for powerful _____.

Answers

1. onerous
2. overlook
3. overbearing
4. optimum
5. opulent
6. outrageous
7. orthodox
8. oratory

331	overture	336	parch
332	pacific	337	parody
333	palatable	338	parry
334	paltry	339	patron
335	paramount	340	patronizing

School Motto

"Pistis Kai Episteme"

(Faith and Learning)

- St. Andrew's School

SSATKOREA.com

overture
[**oh**-ver-cher]

n. an opening or initiating move

서곡, 전주곡

The North rejected the South's overture for more discussions about aid.

syn. first step, opening, proposal

pacific
[puh-**sif**-ik]

adj. calm and peaceful

평화로운

Bruce always feels pacific after a long bike ride.

syn. halcyon, serene, tranquil

palatable
[**pal**-uh-tuh-b*uh*l]

adj. tasty or savory

맛있는, 맛 좋은

Ian thinks chicken curry is a very palatable dish.

syn. appetizing, delectable, luscious

paltry
[**pawl**-tree]

adj. ridiculously or insultingly small

보잘 것 없는, 쥐꼬리만한

Sarah earned a paltry 66% on her biology quiz.

syn. insignificant, meager, scanty

paramount
[**par**-uh-mount]

adj. chief in importance or impact

최고의, 다른 무엇보다 중요한

It is paramount that students have a variety of extracurricular activities if they want to enter an Ivy League school.

syn. chief, outstanding, supreme

parch
[pahrch]

v. to wither or dry out from exposure to heat

바짝 말리다, 물기 하나 없이 건조시키다

American Indians parched corn to preserve it for the winter.

syn. dry, sear, scorch

parody
[**par**-uh-dee]

n. a humorous or satirical imitation

패러디, 풍자 모방

Matthew's parody of Hamlet's soliloquy is sarcastic but brilliant.

syn. imitation, satire

parry
[**par**-ee]

v. to impede the movement of

(공격하는 무기를) 쳐내다, 막다

The shot was parried by the goalie.

syn. ward off, circumvent, avoid

patron
[**pey**-truhn]

n. a person who supports with money

후원자, 단골 고객

The great patrons of the arts donate money to artists every year.

syn. supporter, benefactor, advocate

patronizing
[**pey**-truh-nahy-zing]

adj. displaying an offensively condescending manner

잘난체하는, 생색내는, 베푸는 척하는

Students don't like it when teachers speak to them in a patronizing tone.

syn. condescending, arrogant, pretentious

Sentence Completion 7-4

Directions : Fill in the blanks to complete the sentences.

1. To _____ is to avoid getting stabbed by blocking a thrust.

2. The Chef's signature desserts are very _____.

3. A _____ of a company supports the business by being a loyal customer.

4. Protecting our nation's security is of _____ importance.

5. When an _____ begins, the actors take their places and wait for the curtain to rise.

6. Solomon's _____ actions create unusual peace in these disturbing regions.

7. The government offered Aiden a _____ reparation, which he refused.

8. The _____ girl acts as though she is smarter, classier, and better than anyone.

  Answers

1. parry
2. palatable
3. patron
4. paramount
5. overture
6. pacific
7. paltry
8. patronizing

UPPER LEVEL Lesson 7-5

341 pedantic	346 pernicious
342 pensive	347 perspicacious
343 perceptible	348 pertain
344 perjury	349 peruse
345 permeate	350 pervade

School Motto

"Sapientia Utriusque Vitae Lumen"
(Wisdom, the light of every life)
- St. George's School

SSATKOREA.com

pedantic
[puh-**dan**-tik]

adj. ostentatious in one's learning
많이 배운 척하는, 학자인 척하는

Nobody likes it when Veronica gets pedantic and shows how much she knows about US history.

syn. academic, bookish, stuffy

pensive
[**pen**-siv]

adj. dreamily or wistfully thoughtful
(슬픔이나 걱정 때문에) 깊은 생각에 잠긴

You look pensive.

syn. thoughtful, introspective, meditative

perceptible
[per-**sep**-tuh-b*uh*l]

adj. capable of being perceived
(규모나 정도 등이) 감지할 수 있는

There is a perceptible hint of vanilla in this new coffee.

syn. noticeable, detectable, obvious

perjury
[**pur**-juh-ree]

n. the willful giving of false testimony under oath
위증, 위증죄

She was charged with perjury when it was discovered she had lied in court.

syn. dishonesty, falsehood, forswearing

permeate
[**pur**-mee-eyt]

v. to be diffused through
스며들다, 침투하다

A sense of anxiety permeated the classroom as the students arrived for their final exam.

syn. pervade, saturate, infiltrate

pernicious
[per-**nish**-uhs]

adj. deadly or fatal
치명적인

AIDS is a pernicious disease affecting millions of Africans.

syn. deadly, fatal, lethal

perspicacious
[pur-spi-**key**-shuhs]

adj. having keen mental perception and understanding

총명한, 명민한

He was perspicacious to realize that things were soon going to change.

syn. discerning, keen, perceptive

pertain
[per-**teyn**]

v. to have reference or relation

(특정한 상황이나 때에) 존재하다, 속하다

Ensure your response pertains to the actual question asked.

syn. belong, relate, refer

peruse
[puh-**rooz**]

v. to read through with thoroughness or care

정독하다, 꼼꼼히 읽다

Rina's mother perused magazines while Rina spoke to the doctor.

syn. cover, examine, scan

pervade
[per-**veyd**]

v. to become spread throughout all parts of

널리 퍼지다, 배어 스며들다

A sense of excitement pervaded the arena as sudden-death overtime began.

syn. diffuse, impregnate, infiltrate

Sentence Completion 7-5

Directions : Fill in the blanks to complete the sentences.

1. Samuel became withdrawn and _____, hardly speaking to anyone.

2. Watching too much TV and playing video games all day is _____ to your brain.

3. Uncle Harmon opened a newspaper and began to _____ it.

4. Carter was sentenced to two years in jail for committing _____.

5. The smell of curry will soon _____ the hallway.

6. His _____ grandfather had bought the land as an investment twenty years ago.

7. Since Owen has too many cats, their horrible smell can easily _____ his house.

8. While didactic can have a neutral meaning,_____ is almost always an insult.

 Answers

1. pensive
2. pernicious
3. peruse
4. perjury
5. permeate
6. perspicacious
7. pervade
8. pedantic

Analogy 17. Verse & Prose

글의 유형은 크게 Prose 산문과 Verse 운문으로 이루어 집니다. 글의 유형과 그 내용을 묻는 문제도 Analogy를 풀기 위해 꼭 알아야 하는 내용입니다.

Prose 산문

fiction 소설, 허구, 지어낸 이야기	nonfiction 전기, 역사, 사건 기록
biography 전기, 위인전	essay 수필
memoir 회고록	narrative 이야기
editorial 사설 (신문이나 잡지에서 글쓴이의 주장이나 의견을 써내는 논설)	propaganda 프로파간다 (사상이나 교의 따위의 선전)

Verse 운문

epic 서사시	lyric 서정시
lampoon 풍자시	limerick 5행의 짧고 재미있는 내용의 시
sonnet 소네트, 소곡, 14행시	haiku 일본 단시 형태를 띤 일상적이고 짧은 시
dirge 비가, 슬픔의 시	ode (특정한 사람, 사물 등에 부치는) 시, 송시
ballad 발라드, 감상적인 유행가	chant 구호, 성가, 주문처럼 반복되는 노래

POP QUIZ

1. Lampoon is to satire as
(A) epic is to hero
(B) haiku is to religion
(C) ballad is to logic
(D) limerick is to grief
(E) sonnet is to moral

2. Memoir is to memory as
(A) journal is to review
(B) editorial is to opinion
(C) autobiography is to criticism
(D) propaganda is to satire
(E) campaign is to mount

3. Haiku is to epic as
(A) ode is to sonnet
(B) obituary is to death
(C) lyric is to emotion
(D) ditty is to opera
(E) memoir is to biography

4. Editorial is to opinion as
(A) propaganda is to misinformation
(B) billboard is to post
(C) narrative is to expository
(D) book is to ledger
(E) volume is t encyclopedia

Check-up 7-1

Directions   Each of the following questions consists of one word followed by five words or phrases.
You are to select the one word or phrase whose meaning is closest to the word in capital letters.

1. NAIVE
(A) laconic
(B) credulous
(C) pithy
(D) inactive
(E) reticent

2. NEBULOUS
(A) succinct
(B) taciturn
(C) bombastic
(D) ambiguous
(E) garrulous

3. NEGATE
(A) waft
(B) reject
(C) annihilate
(D) wander
(E) dumbfound

4. NEGLIGIBLE
(A) terse
(B) colloquial
(C) inconsequential
(D) vital
(E) grandiloquent

5. NEMESIS
(A) negotiator
(B) demon
(C) camaraderie
(D) companion
(E) foe

6. NEUTRALIZE
(A) counteract
(B) hoax
(C) avert
(D) peel
(E) vibrate

7. NONCHALANT
(A) complacent
(B) disdainful
(C) egotistical
(D) indifferent
(E) ostentatious

8. NONCOMMITTAL
(A) indefinite
(B) contemptuous
(C) haughty
(D) presumptuous
(E) supercilious

9. NOSTALGIA
(A) bankruptcy
(B) apologia
(C) wistfulness
(D) empathy
(E) compassion

10. NUANCE
(A) evidence
(B) iniquity
(C) maxim
(D) pariah
(E) inkling

Answer 1.B 2.D 3.C 4.C 5.E 6.A 7.D 8.A 9.D 10.E

Check-up 7-2

Each of the following questions consists of one word followed by five words or phrases. You are to select the one word or phrase whose meaning is closest to the word in capital letters.

1. NULL
(A) zero value
(B) turning point
(C) open
(D) highest
(E) frequent visit

2. OBLIQUE
(A) slanting
(B) tedious
(C) unique
(D) vivacious
(E) winsome

3. OBLITERATE
(A) swagger
(B) eliminate
(C) prattle
(D) rant
(E) digress

4. OBLIVIOUS
(A) stagnant
(B) unmindful
(C) reprehensible
(D) portentous
(E) lithe

5. OBSESSIVE
(A) immaculate
(B) forlorn
(C) exorbitant
(D) conciliatory
(E) addictive

6. OBSTINATE
(A) choreographed
(B) belligerent
(C) dogmatic
(D) abject
(E) hasty

7. OBSTRUCT
(A) ramble
(B) dictate
(C) feign
(D) impede
(E) advance

8. OCCUPY
(A) inhabit
(B) hail
(C) fabricate
(D) narrate
(E) peregrinate

9. OFFICIOUS
(A) dilapidated
(B) fecund
(C) intrusive
(D) profuse
(E) rife

10. OMINOUS
(A) favorable
(B) foreboding
(C) timorous
(D) revered
(E) unilateral

Check-up 7-3

Directions Each of the following questions consists of one word followed by five words or phrases.
You are to select the one word or phrase whose meaning is closest to the word in capital letters.

1. ONEROUS
- (A) arduous
- (B) figurative
- (C) truculent
- (D) compassionate
- (E) bloated

2. OPINIONATED
- (A) amiable
- (B) contemptible
- (C) gracious
- (D) gregarious
- (E) bigoted

3. OPTIMUM
- (A) deceit
- (B) ingenuity
- (C) originality
- (D) ideal
- (E) fidelity

4. OPULENT
- (A) innocuous
- (B) affluent
- (C) venerated
- (D) pervasive
- (E) redoubtable

5. ORATORY
- (A) criterion
- (B) dominion
- (C) repose
- (D) guile
- (E) articulation

6. ORTHODOX
- (A) reserved
- (B) enervated
- (C) accepted
- (D) magical
- (E) invariable

7. OUTLANDISH
- (A) copious
- (B) diminutive
- (C) scandalous
- (D) bizarre
- (E) heinous

8. OUTRAGEOUS
- (A) susceptible
- (B) facile
- (C) egregious
- (D) dreary
- (E) marvelous

9. OVERBEARING
- (A) impecunious
- (B) haughty
- (C) jubilant
- (D) tedious
- (E) earnest

10. OVERLOOK
- (A) oblige
- (B) raze
- (C) stuff
- (D) disregard
- (E) astound

Answer 1.A 2.E 3.D 4.B 5.E 6.C 7.D 8.C 9.B 10.D

Check-up 7-4

Directions Each of the following questions consists of one word followed by five words or phrases. You are to select the one word or phrase whose meaning is closest to the word in capital letters.

1. OVERTURE
- (A) surplus
- (B) wonder
- (C) opening
- (D) vitality
- (E) presage

2. PACIFIC
- (A) grateful
- (B) incisive
- (C) harrowing
- (D) flabbergasted
- (E) serene

3. PALATABLE
- (A) growled
- (B) comatose
- (C) appetizing
- (D) viable
- (E) reproachful

4. PALTRY
- (A) vital
- (B) baleful
- (C) audacious
- (D) plentiful
- (E) insignificant

5. PARAMOUNT
- (A) cosmopolitan
- (B) transparent
- (C) divisive
- (D) outstanding
- (E) extravagant

6. PARCH
- (A) petrify
- (B) dry
- (C) scavenge
- (D) acknowledge
- (E) perch

7. PARODY
- (A) credulity
- (B) libel
- (C) imitation
- (D) folklore
- (E) indignation

8. PARRY
- (A) put off
- (B) turn off
- (C) ward off
- (D) take off
- (E) get off

9. PATRON
- (A) advocate
- (B) pathfinder
- (C) vanguard
- (D) entrepreneur
- (E) magnate

10. PATRONIZING
- (A) sophisticated
- (B) diverse
- (C) brusque
- (D) condescending
- (E) abject

Check-up 7-5

Directions Each of the following questions consists of one word followed by five words or phrases. You are to select the one word or phrase whose meaning is closest to the word in capital letters.

1. PEDANTIC
(A) clumsy
(B) histrionic
(C) bookish
(D) supportive
(E) gloomy

2. PENSIVE
(A) pricey
(B) thoughtful
(C) wooden
(D) stilted
(E) radiant

3. PERCEPTIBLE
(A) tranquil
(B) sound
(C) anxious
(D) obvious
(E) shrewd

4. PERJURY
(A) hierarchy
(B) salutation
(C) fib
(D) tendency
(E) dishonesty

5. PERMEATE
(A) search
(B) urge
(C) compel
(D) pervade
(E) extort

6. PERNICIOUS
(A) inveterate
(B) deadly
(C) furious
(D) chronic
(E) lethargic

7. PERSPICACIOUS
(A) malicious
(B) discerning
(C) insane
(D) benign
(E) frigid

8. PERTAIN
(A) groan
(B) defame
(C) construct
(D) belong
(E) contrive

9. PERUSE
(A) scan
(B) extol
(C) impede
(D) mislead
(E) examine

10. PERVADE
(A) clarify
(B) stroll
(C) promote
(D) infuse
(E) diffuse

291

351 petition   356 poignant

352 petty   357 polish

353 philanthropy   358 pompous

354 plagiarize   359 ponder

355 plummet   360 porous

School Motto

"Age Quod Agis"

(Drive because you are driven)

- St. Mark's School

SSATKOREA.com

petition
[puh-**tish**-*uh*n]

n. a formally drawn request

탄원서, 진정서

We're collecting signatures for a petition.

syn. appeal, plea, request

petty
[**pet**-ee]

adj. not important and not worth giving attention to

사소한, 하찮은, 중요하지 않은

Students complain about too many petty rules and restrictions.

syn. trivial, trifling, insignificant

philanthropy
[fi-**lan**-thruh-pee]

n. the activity of helping the poor, especially by giving them money

자선활동, 박애주의

She has been acclaimed by people for his works of public philanthropy.

syn. humanitarianism, altruism, charity

plagiarize
[**pley**-juh-rahyz]

v. to take and use ideas or passages from another's work

표절하다

He was accused of plagiarizing his roommate's writing.

syn. forge, paraphrase, steal

plummet
[**pluhm**-it]

v. drop sharpy

곤두박질치다

Share prices plummeted to an all-time low.

syn. plunge, collapse, dive

poignant
[**poi**-nuhnt]

adj. causing a very sharp feeling of sadness

슬픔으로 가슴 아픈, 가슴 저린

The photograph awakens poignant memories of refugees.

syn. heartrending, painful, touching

polish
[pol-ish]

v. to make smooth and glossy

광택내다, 윤을 내다

It was her job to polish the silverware.

syn. shine, brighten, burnish

pompous
[pom-puhs]

adj. Showing arrogance and conceit

거만한, 잘난 척 하는

He was a little pompous when he talks about film directing.

syn. arrogant, overbearing, imperious

ponder
[pon-der]

v. to think carefully about something, especially for a noticeable length of time

깊이 생각하다, 숙고하다

He sat back to ponder his next chess move.

syn. contemplate, meditate, speculate

porous
[pawr-uhs]

adj. full of pores

구멍이 많이 나 있는, 다공성의

The word "osteoporosis" means porous bone.

syn. absorbent, absorptive, penetrable

Sentence Completion 8-1

Directions : Fill in the blanks to complete the sentences.

1. _____. your shoes regularly to protect the leather.

2. Dylan was a _____, arrogant, and conceited person.

3. The student should not _____ someone's idea as if they own it.

4. Eagles _____ to earth seeking prey.

5. Watching a _____ film gave me a lump in my throat.

6. Claire is focusing on _____ things like picking a napkin design.

7. Savannah is devoted to _____ like donating money to a charity.

8. The _____ border between the two countries allows residents to move easily between them.

361	posterity	366	preamble
362	posthumous	367	precocious
363	posture	368	premonition
364	potable	369	preposterous
365	potent	370	pretentious

School Motto

"Poteris Modo Velis"

(You Can If You Will)

- Fay School

SSATKOREA.com

posterity
[po-**ster**-i-tee]

n. the people who will exist in the future

후손, 후대

Natural habitats must be left to posterity.

syn. descendants, progeny, offspring

posthumous
[**pos**-chuh-m*uhs*]

adj. arising after one's death

사후의

His posthumous work has just been published.

syn. post-mortem, after death, post-obituary

posture
[**pos**-cher]

n. the relative disposition of the parts of something

자세

The model is practicing her walking posture.

syn. stance, aspect, pose

potable
[**poh**-tuh-b*uhl*]

adj. fit or suitable for drinking

마셔도 되는, 음용이 가능한

This tap water is potable.

syn. drinkable, safe to drink

potent
[**poht**-nt]

adj. powerful or mighty

강한, 강력한

The nation has a potent weapons system.

syn. effective, powerful, forceful

preamble
[**pree**-am-b*uhl*]

n. an introduction of books

(책의) 서론, (헌법) 서문

The aims of the treaty are stated in its preamble.

syn. introduction, preface, foreword

precocious

[pri-**koh**-sh*uh*s]

adj. unusually advanced
or mature in development

조숙한, 아이 같지 않은

*The child is too precocious
for her age.*

syn. mature, advanced, intelligent

premonition

[pree-**muh**-nish-*uh*n]

n. a feeling that something, especially
something unpleasant, is going to
happen

예감, 특히 안 좋은 일이 일어날 것 같은 예감

*He had a premonition of what the
future might bring.*

syn. foreboding, forewarning, omen

preposterous

[pri-**pos**-ter-*uh*s]

adj. very silly or stupid

말도 안되는, 터무니 없는, 어리석은

*Her claims are absolutely
preposterous!*

syn. ridiculous, absurd, ludicrous

pretentious

[pri-**ten**-sh*uh*s]

adj. characterized by assumption
of dignity or importance

허세부리는, 가식적인

*He has a pretentious style of writing,
using very difficult words.*

syn. snobbish, conceited, exaggerated

Sentence Completion 8-2

Directions : Fill in the blanks to
complete the sentences.

1. Mark's _____ publication of
a book received a rave review from
critics.

2. The _____ sixth-grader
asked about organic chemistry.

3. The ballerinas have an elegant,
graceful _____.

4. Don't be _____; just act
naturally.

5. We have to save our Earth for
our _____.

6. That was a ridiculous and
_____ suggestion.

7. This powerful magic potion is
_____ and might have side-
effects.

8. The _____ is a brief
introduction to the Constitution.

 Answers

1. posthumous	5. posterity
2. precocious	6. preposterous
3. posture	7. potent
4. pretentious	8. Preamble

371	prevalent	376	prudent
372	pristine	377	prune
373	procrastinate	378	pseudonym
374	prolific	379	pugnacious
375	promenade	380	pun

School Motto

"Suaviter in Modo Fortiter in Re"
(resolute in execution, gentle in manner)
- Stevenson School

SSATKOREA.com

prevalent
[**prev**-uh-lu*h*nt]

adj. widespread or in general use
일반적인

This condition is more prevalent in men than in women.

syn. accepted, widespread, common

pristine
[**pris**-teen]

adj. uncorrupted or unsullied
완전 새것 같은, 아주 깨끗한

The car is in pristine condition.

syn. clean, immaculate, intact

procrastinate
[proh-**kras**-tuh-neyt]

v. to delay
미루다

You procrastinated.
You should have done it little by little.

syn. delay, suspend, dawdle

prolific
[pruh-**lif**-ik]

adj. highly fruitful
생산성이 많은, 다량을 생산하는, 다작의

She is a prolific writer of novels.

syn. fruitful, productive, breeding

promenade
[prom-*uh*-**neyd**]

n. a stroll or walk as for pleasure or a path for walkingn. the original model
산책, 산책로

The girls strolled along on the promenade eating ice creams.

syn. leisurely walk, boardwalk, stroll

prudent
[**prood**-nt]

adj. wise or judicious in practical affairs
신중한

I don't think he is prudent in his behavior.

syn. wise, discreet, cautious

prune
[proon]

v. to cut or lop off

잘라내다, 가지를 치다

*When should we **prune** our rose bushes?*

syn. trim, crop, shave

pseudonym
[**sood**-n-im]

n. a fictitious name to conceal his or her identity

필명, 가명

*Robert Galbraith is a **pseudonym** for J.K. Rowling*

syn. nickname, pen name, alias

pugnacious
[puhg-**ney**-sh*uh*s]

adj. inclined to quarrel or fight readily

싸우기 좋아하는, 공격적인

*English sparrows are **pugnacious** birds.*

syn. belligerent, combative, aggressive

pun
[puhn]

n. the humorous use of a word or phrase

말장난

*A good **pun** brings the smaller excellencies of conversation.*

syn. joke, play on words, witticism

Sentence Completion 8-3

Directions : Fill in the blanks to complete the sentences.

1. Dr. Seuss was the _____ of Theodore Seuss Geisel.

2. Gardeners _____ trees, cutting dead branches off.

3. A _____ writer can write five novels a day.

4. When Amelia writes papers, she always likes to _____.

5. Please don't spill anything on my _____ white carpet.

6. Drug use is _____ among criminals.

7. Phil's _____ brother is always ready to use his fists to settle an argument.

8. A _____ can be quite witty, but it often comes off as silly.

Answers

1. pseudonym
2. prune
3. prolific
4. procrastinate
5. pristine
6. prevalent
7. pugnacious
8. pun

381	pungent	386	quell
382	puzzle	387	quench
383	quaint	388	quixotic
384	qualm	389	rancorous
385	quarantine	390	ratify

School Motto

"Esse Quam Videri"

(To be, rather than to seem)

- Suffield Academy

SSATKOREA.com

pungent
[**puhn**-*juh*nt]

adj. sharply affecting the organs of taste or smell

(맛이나 냄새가) 심하게 자극적인

Garlic has a pungent taste and odor.

syn. highly flavored, sharp, seasoned

puzzle
[**puhz**-*uhl*]

v. be a mystery or bewildering to

어리둥절하게 만들다

What puzzles me is why he left the country without telling anyone.

syn. baffle, confuse, frustrate

quaint
[kweynt]

adj. having an old-fashioned attractiveness or charm

진기한, 매력 있게 예스러운

He has a quaint way of speaking.

syn. bizarre, strange, odd

qualm
[kwahm]

n. an uneasy feeling of conscience as to conduct

양심의 가책, 거리낌

He had been working very hard so he had no qualms about taking a few days off

syn. misgiving, anxiety, suspicion

quarantine
[**kwawr**-*uh*n-teen]

n. a strict isolation

격리

This is a biohazard quarantine area.

syn. isolation, detention, separation

quell
[kwel]

v. to stop something, especially by using force

진압하다, 평정하다, 가라앉히다

The troops quelled the rebellion quickly.

syn. suppress, defeat, extinguish

quench
[kwench]

v. to satisfy a need or wish

(갈증을) 풀다, 해소하다

His thirst for knowledge will never be quenched.

syn. satisfy, sate, satiate

quixotic
[kwik-**sot**-ik]

adj. extravagantly chivalrous or romantic

비현실적

The heroes are quixotic and romantic.

syn. idealistic, foolish, unrealistic

rancorous
[**rang**-ker-*uh*s]

adj. showing hatred or resentment

원한이 있는, 악의에 불타는

The debate became bitter and rancorous.

syn. resentful, bitter, frowning

ratify
[**rat**-uh-fahy]

v. to confirm by expressing consent

승인하다, 허가하다

All the members have voted to ratify the treaty.

syn. affirm, authorize, approve

Sentence Completion 8-4

Directions : Fill in the blanks to complete the sentences.

1. Police in riot gear were called in to _____ the riot.

2. Ethan was _____ about his henchman's betrayal.

3. When you have a fever, please put yourself in _____ so that you don't infect others.

4. New technologies continually _____ my grandfather.

5. The only thing he wanted was a nice big glass of ice water to _____ his thirst.

6. Don Quixote's _____ task is challenging to achieve.

7. Even if Zoe devised a plan for a family vacation, her parents must _____ it first.

8. The _____ little store sells tea cozies and antique tea services.

Answers

1. quell
2. rancorous
3. quarantine
4. puzzle
5. quench
6. quixotic
7. ratify
8. quaint

391	rational	396	rectify
392	ravenous	397	recuperate
393	recalcitrant	398	refute
394	reciprocal	399	reiterate
395	recluse	400	relegate

School Motto

"Vincit Semper Veritas"

(Truth Always Conquers)

- Tabor Academy

SSATKOREA.com

recalcitrant
[ri-**kal**-si-tr*uh*nt]

adj. resisting authority or control

반항하는, 다루기 힘든

At last, the recalcitrant leader engaged in talks towards reconciliation.

syn. obstinate, disobedient, uncontrollable

reciprocal
[ri-**sip**-ruh-k*uh*l]

adj. given or felt by each toward the other

상호적인, 서로간의

She was hoping for some reciprocal respect.

syn. mutual, alternate, exchanged

rational
[**rash**-uh-nl]

adj. having its source in or being guided by the intellect

합리적인

Don't jump to conclusions. Be rational.

syn. sensible, reasonable, judicious

recluse
[**rek**-loos]

n. a person living in seclusion or apart from society

은둔자

He has led the life of a recluse since his wife died.

syn. hermit, solitaire

ravenous
[**rav**-uh-n*uh*s]

adj. extremely hungry

몹시 굶주린, 게걸스러운, 탐욕스러운

The lions have not eaten for four days and are ravenous.

syn. gluttonous, greedy, voracious

rectify
[**rek**-t*uh*-fahy]

v. to correct something or make something right

바로잡다, 정정하다, 고치다

We must rectify any mistakes before the book is printed.

syn. correct, fix, amend

recuperate

[ri-**koo**-*puh*-reyt]

v. to recover from sickness or exhaustionv.

회복하다, 건강을 되찾다

He spent several months recuperating after the operation.

syn. convalesce, recover, get well

refute

[ri-**fyoot**]

v. to prove to be false

반박하다

It was the kind of rumor that it is impossible to refute.

syn. contradict, oppose, rebut

reiterate

[ree-**it**-*uh*-reyt]

v. to say or do again or repeatedly

반복하다, 되풀이하다

The president reiterated refusal to compromise with terrorists.

syn. repeat, echo, restate

relegate

[**rel**-i-geyt]

v. to send or consign to an inferior position

좌천하다, 계급을 떨어뜨리다, 강등시키다

He was relegated to the role of assistant.

syn. demote, downgrade, dismiss

Sentence Completion 8-5

Directions : Fill in the blanks to complete the sentences.

1. Scarlet was hoping for some _____ gestures.

2. A _____ person feels like they haven't eaten in days.

3. His _____ dad won't budge on an issue.

4. This photo of a crime scene could not _____ the evidence.

5. The editor should _____ all the mistakes in a manuscript before printing.

6. A _____ person is someone who is sensible, making decisions based on intelligent thinking rather than on emotion .

7. David was a millionaire _____ who donates anonymously.

8. The negotiator has to _____ its compromise between two parties.

Answers

1. reciprocal
2. ravenous
3. recalcitrant
4. refute
5. rectify
6. rational
7. recluse
8. reiterate

Analogy 18. Figure of Speech

01. Life is a roller coaster.

Metaphor 은유법
A figure of speech that identifies something as being the same as some unrelated thing for rhetorical effect, thus highlighting the similarities between the two

02. The king was as brave as a lion.

Simile 직유법
A figure of speech involving the comparison of one thing with another thing of a different kind, used to make a description more emphatic or vivid. "As" and "like" are used

03. The pen is mightier than the sword.

Metonymy 환유법
A figure of speech in which a thing or concept is called not by its own name but rather by the name of something associated in meaning with that thing

04. The stars dance in the sky.

Personification 의인법
A rhetorical device in which a thing or animal is given human characteristics

05. The traffic cop got his license suspended for unpaid parking tickets.

Irony 반어법
The expression of one's meaning by using language that normally signifies the opposite, typically for humorous or emphatic effect

06. To ensure peace, the two countries must continue to build weapons.

Paradox 역설법
A statement that apparently contradicts itself and yet might be true

07. Bam! Splash!! Slam!!!

Onomatopoeia 의성어
A word that phonetically imitates, resembles or suggests the source of the sound that it describes

08. Peter Piper Picked a Peck of Pickled Peppers.

Alliteration 두운법
A stylistic literary device identified by the repeated sound of the first consonant in a series of multiple words at the beginning of words

09. Humpty Dumpty sat on a wall Humpty Dumpty had a great fall.

Rhyme 각운법
Correspondence of sound between words or the endings of words, especially when these are used at the ends of lines of poetry

10. Life is short, but art is long.

Contrast 대조법
Device used to describe difference(s) between two or more entities

Check-up 8-1

Directions Each of the following questions consists of one word followed by five words or phrases. You are to select the one word or phrase whose meaning is closest to the word in capital letters.

1. PETITION
(A) plea
(B) elixir
(C) glut
(D) connoisseur
(E) repose

2. PETTY
(A) forlorn
(B) innate
(C) sensible
(D) insignificant
(E) temperate

3. PHILANTHROPY
(A) despotism
(B) altruism
(C) euphemism
(D) aristocracy
(E) epiphany

4. PLAGIARIZE
(A) chatter
(B) abstain
(C) steal
(D) nod
(E) indulge

5. PLUMMET
(A) abdicate
(B) disparage
(C) hinder
(D) immerse
(E) plunge

6. POIGNANT
(A) pithy
(B) reserved
(C) irate
(D) heartrending
(E) saved

7. POLISH
(A) burnish
(B) tether
(C) wander
(D) revere
(E) appease

8. POMPOUS
(A) humble
(B) beneficial
(C) overdue
(D) unassuming
(E) overbearing

9. PONDER
(A) bellow
(B) contemplate
(C) rehearse
(D) clasp
(E) escalate

10. POROUS
(A) minute
(B) ponderous
(C) dumbfounded
(D) impromptu
(E) absorbent

303

Check-up 8-2

1. POSTERITY
(A) progeny
(B) boor
(C) cooper
(D) bumpkin
(E) erudite

2. POSTHUMOUS
(A) assailant
(B) tepid
(C) after death
(D) shallow
(E) poach

3. POSTURE
(A) rivulet
(B) leniency
(C) augment
(D) stance
(E) solace

4. POTABLE
(A) lukewarm
(B) strewn
(C) vigilant
(D) laconic
(E) drinkable

5. POTENT
(A) powerful
(B) pliable
(C) illegible
(D) pungent
(E) amusing

6. PREAMBLE
(A) escort
(B) nomad
(C) throng
(D) introduction
(E) battalion

7. PRECOCIOUS
(A) superficial
(B) forethought
(C) advanced
(D) repulsive
(E) contradictory

8. PREMONITION
(A) forewarning
(B) pitfall
(C) pinnacle
(D) hilarious
(E) luminescence

9. PREPOSTEROUS
(A) exotic
(B) absurd
(C) pernicious
(D) narcissistic
(E) floundering

10. PRETENTIOUS
(A) headstrong
(B) conceited
(C) muddled
(D) enthusiastic
(E) pecuniary

Check-up 8-3

Each of the following questions consists of one word followed by five words or phrases. You are to select the one word or phrase whose meaning is closest to the word in capital letters.

1. PREVALENT
(A) common
(B) phlegmatic
(C) treasonous
(D) culinary
(E) shared

2. PRISTINE
(A) ecumenical
(B) distasteful
(C) stubborn
(D) abominable
(E) intact

3. PROCRASTINATE
(A) remit
(B) sprinkle
(C) sully
(D) delay
(E) tarnish

4. PROLIFIC
(A) reluctant
(B) confident
(C) courageous
(D) productive
(E) concerned

5. PROMENADE
(A) stroll
(B) turncoat
(C) claim
(D) finale
(E) apostate

6. PRUDENT
(A) ornate
(B) eminent
(C) discreet
(D) despicable
(E) lithe

7. PRUNE
(A) rustle
(B) bellow
(C) grieve
(D) trim
(E) misconstrue

8. PSEUDONYM
(A) memorandum
(B) insomnia
(C) dissertation
(D) strongbox
(E) alias

9. PUGNACIOUS
(A) combative
(B) complimentary
(C) amiable
(D) ingenuous
(E) fair-minded

10. PUN
(A) sonnet
(B) word play
(C) syntax
(D) amnesia
(E) brawl

MIDDLE 1 2 3 4 5 6 7 8 9 10

UPPER 1 2 3 4 5 6 7 8 9 10

Check-up 8-4

1. PUNGENT
- (A) exemplary
- (B) gentle
- (C) sharp
- (D) mild
- (E) predictable

2. PUZZLE
- (A) retract
- (B) abbreviate
- (C) baffle
- (D) withdraw
- (E) misjudge

3. QUAINT
- (A) bizarre
- (B) avaricious
- (C) mortified
- (D) delighted
- (E) humiliated

4. QUALM
- (A) rampage
- (B) subpoena
- (C) obeisance
- (D) misgiving
- (E) royalty

5. QUARANTINE
- (A) swarm
- (B) din
- (C) mob
- (D) understatement
- (E) isolation

6. QUELL
- (A) broach
- (B) suppress
- (C) elicit
- (D) blackmail
- (E) loom

7. QUENCH
- (A) direct
- (B) motivate
- (C) satisfy
- (D) vitalize
- (E) weld

8. QUIXOTIC
- (A) earnest
- (B) recurrent
- (C) nimble
- (D) idealistic
- (E) diligent

9. RANCOROUS
- (A) antithetical
- (B) comparable
- (C) malnourished
- (D) resentful
- (E) identical

10. RATIFY
- (A) scatter
- (B) rectify
- (C) extinguish
- (D) coordinate
- (E) approve

Check-up 8-5

Directions   Each of the following questions consists of one word followed by five words or phrases. You are to select the one word or phrase whose meaning is closest to the word in capital letters.

1. RATIONAL
(A) overblown
(B) vivid
(C) sensible
(D) withdrawn
(E) obscure

2. RAVENOUS
(A) reserved
(B) vibrant
(C) arcane
(D) gluttonous
(E) prudish

3. RECALCITRANT
(A) obstinate
(B) habitable
(C) tranquil
(D) docile
(E) gullible

4. RECIPROCAL
(A) palatable
(B) olfactory
(C) mutual
(D) illustrious
(E) boorish

5. RECLUSE
(A) anarchist
(B) iconoclast
(C) stipend
(D) burglar
(E) hermit

6. RECTIFY
(A) snoop
(B) commence
(C) aggravate
(D) reassure
(E) fix

7. RECUPERATE
(A) convalesce
(B) reminisce
(C) remit
(D) repudiate
(E) chastise

8. REFUTE
(A) skitter
(B) glance
(C) rebut
(D) exonerate
(E) exempt

9. REITERATE
(A) reproduce
(B) confiscate
(C) purloin
(D) repeat
(E) chide

10. RELEGATE
(A) impound
(B) demote
(C) jabber
(D) scrutinize
(E) renounce

401	relentless	406	replica
402	relinquish	407	reproach
403	reminisce	408	repulse
404	remorse	409	requisite
405	reparation	410	rescind

School Motto

"Non ut sibi ministretur sed ut ministret"

(Not to be served but to serve)

- Taft School

SSATKOREA.com

reminisce
[rem-uh-**nis**]

v. to recall past experiences or events

추억에 잠기다, 회상하다

She likes to reminisce about her childhood.

syn.   retrospect, recollect, recall

remorse
[ri-**mawrs**]

n. a feeling of deep regret

후회, 회상

She felt remorse when she saw the outcome of her action.

syn.   penitence, penance, compunction

relentless
[ri-**lent**-lis]

adj. unyieldingly severe, strict, or harsh

끈질긴, 수그러들지 않는

This relentless pressure began to wear down their resistance.

syn.   persistent, harsh, cruel

reparation
[rep-uh-**rey**-sh*uh*n]

n. the making of amends for wrong or injury done

배상, 보상

Offenders must make reparation for their crimes.

syn.   compensation, amends

relinquish
[ri-**ling**-kwish]

v. to renounce or surrender

(마지못해 소유권 등을) 포기하다, 내주다

No one wants to relinquish power once they have it.

syn.   give up, renounce, abandon

replica
[**rep**-li-kuh]

n. an exact copy

복사, 복제품

She made a 1:5 scale replica of a real ship.

syn.   facsimile, copy, duplicate

reproach
[ri-**prohch**]

v. to find fault with

비난하다, 야단치다

*Do not **reproach** yourself, it was not your fault.*

syn.   reprove, reprimand, reprehend

repulse
[ri-**puhls**]

v. to drive back

(호의를) 거부하다, 뒤쫓아버리다

*The armed forces were prepared to **repulse** any attacks.*

syn.   repel, drive back, resist

requisite
[**rek**-wuh-zit]

n. a required or necessary thing for a particular purpose

필수품, 꼭 필요한 것

*Self-confidence is the first **requisite** to great undertakings.*

syn.   need, necessity, precondition

rescind
[ri-**sind**]

v. to invalidate an act or measure

(법률, 계약 등을) 폐지하다, 철회하다

*You cannot **rescind** the contract simply because our payment is delayed by one day.*

syn.   annul, revoke, repeal

Sentence Completion 9-1

Directions : Fill in the blanks to complete the sentences.

1. The "Mona Lisa" in the suite room is a _____.

2. A defeated nation was forced to pay _____ to its victorious enemy.

3. The convict felt _____ for his misdeed.

4. Isaac will _____ control of the army when you resign as general.

5. The government has decided to _____ all the national tests.

6. Jaxon's grandmother should _____ him for his poor manners.

7. The foul smell and disgusting sight of the dead corpse _____ the detectives.

8. The prince showed a _____ pursuit of wealth and power.

Answers

1. replica
2. reparation
3. remorse
4. relinquish
5. rescind
6. reproach
7. repulse
8. relentless

411	resilient	416	retort
412	restitution	417	retract
413	restrain	418	retribution
414	resuscitate	419	retrospect
415	retaliate	420	revere

School Motto

"Non sibi sed aliis"

(Not for self, but for others)

- The Governor's Academy

SSATKOREA.com

resilient
[ri-**zil**-y*uh*nt]

adj. returning to the original form

회복력이 있는, 탄성이 있는

He was so resilient that he could recover quickly from unfortunate circumstances.

syn. elastic, bouncy, flexible

restitution
[res-ti-**too**-sh*uh*n]

n. the act of restoring something to the rightful owner

배상, 보상

He had to make restitution for the broken window, paying for its replacement.

syn. compensation, repayment

restrain
[**ri**-streyn]

v. to keep under control

저지하다, 제지하다

When she found herself face to face with a dessert case, she had to restrain herself.

syn. hold back, constrain, restrict

resuscitate
[ri-**suhs**-i-teyt]

v. to revive, especially from apparent death

소생시키다, 다시 살리다

Ambulance workers are skilled at resuscitating heart and lungs.

syn. revive, rejuvenate, revitalize

retaliate
[ri-**tal**-ee-eyt]

v. to return like for like, especially evil for evil

보복하다, 앙갚음하다

When Ellen tripped Tanya in the schoolyard, Tanya retaliated by pulling Ellen's hair.

syn. avenge, counter, reciprocate

retort
[ri-**tawrt**]

v. to reply in a sharp or retaliatory way

쏘아붙이다, 대꾸하다

'Mind your own business,' Jamie retorted angrily.

syn. repartee, retaliate, respond

retract
[ri-**trakt**]

v. to draw back or in
(속으로) 들어가다, 움츠리다, 취소하다

A tiger retracts its claw.

syn. pull back, recant, cancel

retribution
[re-truh-**byoo**-sh*uh*n]

n. punishment for offenses
보복, 징벌

She speaks the truth to the public without fear of retribution.

syn. vengeance, reprisal, revenge

retrospect
[**re**-truh-spekt]

n. looking back and contemplating the past
회상, 회고, 추억

In retrospect, she found herself wishing that she had done some things differently.

syn. reminiscence, afterthought, recollection

revere
[ri-**veer**]

v. to regard with respect tinged with awe
숭배하다, 경외하다, 존경하다

Lance reveres his favorite author, Ernest Hemingway.

syn. venerate, worship, exalt

Sentence Completion 9-2

Directions : Fill in the blanks to complete the sentences.

1. Many African Americans _____ Rosa Parks for her bravery.

2. George was so upset that he could not _____ his anger.

3. The terrorists will _____ at the military base with bombs and missiles.

4. Jude apologized saying that she will _____ his allegation.

5. When Abbie's heart had stopped, the doctors were able to successfully _____ her.

6. In _____, I think my childhood was relatively special.

7. Ryan likes to sarcastically_____ everything his little sister says.

8. After Caleb pulled a prank on his brother, he expected _____.

Answers

1. replica
2. reparation
3. remorse
4. relinquish
5. rescind
6. reproach
7. repulse
8. relentless

421	revert	426	ruthless
422	revile	427	sabotage
423	robust	428	sage
424	rotund	429	sanctimonious
425	rue	430	sanguine

School Motto

"Whatsoever things are true."

- The Hill School

SSATKOREA.com

revert
[ri-**vurt**]

v. to return to a former habit or condition
(본래 상태나 습관으로) 되돌아가다

House cats will revert to a wild, feral state if they are left outside.

syn.   backslide, lapse, regress

revile
[ri-**vahyl**]

v. to scold abusively
심하게 꾸짖다, 심하게 욕하다

No one likes spam calls, and they are widely reviled.

syn.   vilify, berate, castigate

robust
[roh-**buhst**]

adj. strong and healthy
원기 왕성한, 건강한

His robust strength made him survive the disaster.

syn.   healthy, strong, vigorous

rotund
[roh-**tuhnd**]

adj. plump or round
둥근, 퉁퉁하게 살찐

My chubby Aunt Margie is rotund like a teapot.

syn.   chubby, stout, plump

rue
[roo]

v. to feel sorry for
후회하다

She rued the day she and her sister had bought such an expensive car without any consideration.

syn.   regret, lament, deplore

ruthless
[**rooth**-lis]

adj. without pity or compassion
잔인한, 무자비한

She is ruthless in her dealings with competitors.

syn.   cruel, merciless, truculent

sabotage

[**sab**-uh-tahzh]

n. a deliberate act of destruction

고의적인 방해, 고의적인 파괴

If you don't believe in yourself, you cause sabotage to yourself.

syn. damage, destruction, vandalism

sage

[seyj]

n. a profoundly wise person

현명한 사람, 지혜로운 사람

Warren Buffett, an American business magnate, is often called the Sage of Omaha.

syn. wise person, mentor, guru

sanctimonious

[sangk-tuh-**moh**-nee-*uh*s]

adj. making a hypocritical show of religious devotion

독실한 체하는

The sanctimonious religious leader preached about morality.

syn. hypocritical, preachy, self-righteous

sanguine

[**sang**-gwin]

adj. cheerfully optimistic, hopeful, or confident

낙관적인, 자신감이 넘치는

He tends to take a sanguine view of the problems involved.

syn. happy, optimistic, cheerful

Sentence Completion 9-3

Directions : Fill in the blanks to complete the sentences.

1. This school has a _____ sports program with great training staff and talented athletes.

2. The policy _____ knew what advice to give politicians.

3. The rebels tried to_____ the gas stations.

4. Alex could not help but _____ to his chronic bad habits.

5. Jim's _____ wife was always optimistic and easygoing.

6. Ben's face is _____ like a vase full of flowers.

7. Though _____ people try to act like saints, their actions are far from holy.

8. You have to be _____ and throw out everything that's not essential.

  Answers

1. robust	5. sanguine
2. sage	6. rotund
3. sabotage	7. sanctimonious
4. revert	8. ruthless

431	sarcasm	436	sedentary
432	satiate	437	segregate
433	scrutinize	438	sequel
434	secede	439	sequester
435	sedate	440	shirk

School Motto

"Virtus Scientia"

(Virtue through knowledge)

- The Hockaday School

SSATKOREA.com

sarcasm
[**sahr**-kaz-*uh*m]

n. a mocking remark

빈정댐, 비꼼

She said "Oh, you're so clever!" with sarcasm.

syn. banter, bitterness, satire

satiate
[**sey**-shee-yet]

v. to satisfy fully

(욕구를 충분히) 채우다

The more the heart is satiated with joy, the more it becomes insatiable.

syn. satisfy, gratify, indulge

scrutinize
[**skroot**-n-ahyz]

v. to examine in detail with careful attention

세심히 살피다, 면밀히 조사하다

Be sure to scrutinize your essays for spelling and grammar errors.

syn. examine, inspect, observe

secede
[si-**seed**]

v. to withdraw from an alliance, federation, or association

(동맹, 연합, 협회 등에서) 탈퇴하다, 분리 독립하다

Britain decided to secede from the European Union.

syn. pull away, split from, separate

sedate
[si-**deyt**]

adj. calm, quiet, or composed

차분한, 조용한

We set off again at a more sedate pace.

syn. calm, collected, placid

sedentary
[**sed**-n-ter-ee]

adj. characterized by or requiring a sitting posture

주로 앉아서 하는, 좌식의

Humans adopted a sedentary rather than a mobile lifestyle after learning how to farm.

syn. fixed, immobile, inactive

segregate
[**seg**-ri-geyt]

v. to separate from the main body or group

분리하다, 차별하다

The goal of Dr. Martin Luther King is to give Black people a chance to sit in a segregated restaurant beside the same white man who had brutalized them for 400 years.

syn. separate, isolate, discriminate

sequel
[**see**-kw*uhl*]

n. an event following something

(책이나 영화 등의) 속편, 후편

The sequel to last year's most exciting movie is opening this weekend.

syn. continuation, follow-up, progression

sequester
[si-**kwes**-ter]

v. to remove or withdraw into solitude or retirement

격리시키다, 떨어뜨려 놓다

The jury is expected to be sequestered for at least two months.

syn. isolate, seclude, quarantine

shirk
[shurk]

v. to get out of responsibility

(의무를) 피하다, 안 하려하다

If you shirk your responsibilities duties now, the situation will just be that much harder.

syn. avoid, evade, elude

Sentence Completion 9-4

Directions : Fill in the blanks to complete the sentences.

1. I will not _____ from my duties.

2. Thomas must _____ the men's faces carefully.

3. Many popular movies have at least one _____.

4. The South wanted to _____ during the U.S. Civil War.

5. The food at the all-you-can-eat buffet could not _____ her hunger .

6. My doctor warned me about my _____ lifestyle.

7. Doctors usually tell patients to have a _____ evening the day before a big surgery.

8. New pedestrian lanes are designed to _____ walkers from auto traffic.

Answers

1. shirk
2. scrutinize
3. sequel
4. secede
5. satiate
6. sedentary
7. sedate
8. segregate

---

441 simultaneous 446 sneer

442 skirmish 447 snub

443 slander 448 sojourn

444 smear 449 speculate

445 smother 450 stipulation

School Motto

"Moniti Meliora Sequamur"

(Guided by each other, let us seek better paths)

- The Hotchkiss School

SSATKOREA.com

simultaneous
[sahy-m*uhl*-**tey**-nee-*uhs*]

adj. existing , occurring, or operating at the same time

동시의, 동시에 일어나는

The explosion was almost simultaneous with the announcement.

syn. concurrent, contemporaneous, concomitant

skirmish
[**skur**-mish]

n. a fight between small bodies of troops

소규모 접전, 충돌

Today, every skirmish in every part of the planet is broadcast straight into your living room live.

syn. brief fight, scuffle, altercation

slander
[**slan**-der]

n. the act of making a false or negative statement

악의적인 소문을 퍼뜨림, 비방

She does not care about rumors full of slander.

syn. defamation, libel, smear

smear
[smeer]

v. to tarnish a reputation

(명예나 명성을) 더럽히다, 실추시키다

His arm was smeared with dirt.

syn. sully, tarnish, taint

smother
[**smuhth**-er]

v. to deprive of oxygen and prevent from breathing

질식 시키다

The criminal tried to smother him with a pillow.

syn. extinguish, choke, suffocate

sneer
[sneer]

v. to express through a scornful smile

비웃다, 조롱하다

Although some may sneer, working as a secretary is for many the fastest route to career success.

syn. mock, condemn, jeer

snub
[snuhb]

v. to rebuff, ignore, or spurn disdainfully

모욕하다, 무시하다

I tried to be friendly, but she snubbed me completely.

syn. ignore, disregard, boycott

sojourn
[**soh**-jurn]

n. a temporary stay

체류, 일시적인 머무름

Next weekend, we're going to take a sojourn into Nicaragua.

syn. rest, stay, visit

speculate
[**spek**-yuh-leyt]

v. to think about deeply and theorize

추측하다, 짐작하다

I wouldn't like to speculate on the reasons for her resignation.

syn. contemplate, think, surmise

stipulation
[stip-yuh-**ley**-shuhn]

n. a condition, demand, or promise in an agreement or contract

(계약이나 법률상의) 조항, 조건

You must be careful of any stipulation before accepting it.

syn. condition, clause, specification

Sentence Completion 9-5

Directions : **Fill in the blanks to complete the sentences.**

1. Leo attempted to draw me into a conversation, but I wanted to _____ him.

2. After a brief _____ in Korea to study Korean, he moved to England.

3. The magnate left all his money to the town with the _____ that it should be used to build a new library.

4. The children could easily _____ chocolate on the white sofa.

5. Terrorists made several _____ explosions in a city.

6. The arrogant women _____ at Dorothy's shoes.

7. There was a short _____ between the two nations.

8. The plastic bags _____ ocean life.

MIDDLE 1 2 3 4 5 6 7 8 9 10

UPPER 1 2 3 4 5 6 7 8 9 10

Analogy 19. Styles of Passage

Reading 문제를 풀 때 지문의 유형을 묻는 문제를 종종 만나게 되실 겁니다. 지문 유형은 다양한 단서를 찾아내어 알아 볼 수 있는데요, 이 때 제일 중요한 것이 글쓴이가 감정을 표현하는 단어를 사용했는가 여부 입니다. 이 것만 찾아내더라도 글이 객관적 정보인지, 주관적 감정인지를 판단할 수 있고, 이 후 정확한 글의 유형을 파악할 수 있게 되지요.

A는 B의 내용이나 감정을 담은 작품

hymn : praise
찬송가 : 찬양

elegy : grief
애가, 비가 : 슬픔

eulogy : praise
찬양하는 연설 : 찬양

lampoon : satire
풍자시 : 풍자

tribute : admiration
헌사, 바치는 글 : 존경, 감탄

obituary : sorrow
부고기사 : 슬픔

Types of Written Documents

manuscript 원고, 필사본

manual 설명서

anthology 시선집, 문집

atlas 지도책

almanac 연감

screenplay 영화대본, 시나리오

script 연극 대본

advertisement 광고

blurb 과장 광고

diatribe 심한 비판의 글

memoir 회고록

dissertation 학위 논문

contract 계약서

journal 학술지, (전문분야를 다루는) 저널

manifesto 성명서, 선언문

editorial 사설

encyclopedia 백과사전

lexicon 어휘 사전

glossary 용어사전

catalog 상품 목록

log 일지, 일기

petition 탄원서, 진정서

propaganda 선전문

ledger 거래내역을 적은 거래 장부

deed (토지나 건물의 소유권을 증명하는) 증서

summons 소환장

POP QUIZ

1. Cookbook is to recipe as
(A) diatribe is to criticism
(B) brochure is to folktale
(C) manual is to trade
(D) ledger is to instruction
(E) glossary is to opinion

2. Tribute is to praise as
(A) petition is to appeal
(B) memoir is to word
(C) encyclopedia is to review
(D) periodical is to magazine
(E) harangue is to advertisement

Check-up 9-1

Directions   Each of the following questions consists of one word followed by five words or phrases.
You are to select the one word or phrase whose meaning is closest to the word in capital letters.

1. RELENTLESS
(A) innate
(B) persistent
(C) incredible
(D) genuine
(E) inflammable

2. RELINQUISH
(A) moor
(B) hoax
(C) renounce
(D) envelop
(E) insist

3. REMINISCE
(A) gaze
(B) stare
(C) dissent
(D) retrospect
(E) glimpse

4. REMORSE
(A) penitence
(B) habitat
(C) malfunction
(D) route
(E) fatigue

5. REPARATION
(A) expedition
(B) boycott
(C) caliber
(D) aplomb
(E) compensation

6. REPLICA
(A) vitality
(B) facsimile
(C) onslaught
(D) budget
(E) recital

7. REPROACH
(A) captivate
(B) renounce
(C) corrode
(D) deceive
(E) reprimand

8. REPULSE
(A) applaud
(B) convalesce
(C) inspire
(D) repel
(E) elude

9. REQUISITE
(A) crusade
(B) pantomime
(C) reputation
(D) need
(E) misgiving

10. RESCIND
(A) loom
(B) err
(C) contend
(D) annul
(E) detract

Check-up 9-2

Each of the following questions consists of one word followed by five words or phrases. You are to select the one word or phrase whose meaning is closest to the word in capital letters.

1. RESILIENT
(A) elastic
(B) heedful
(C) solitary
(D) meager
(E) rational

2. RESTITUTION
(A) integrity
(B) fidelity
(C) oracle
(D) compensation
(E) liability

3. RESTRAIN
(A) associate
(B) constrain
(C) devour
(D) galvanize
(E) disseminate

4. RESUSCITATE
(A) soar
(B) recede
(C) debunk
(D) revitalize
(E) agitate

5. RETALIATE
(A) mediate
(B) commence
(C) devastate
(D) avenge
(E) compromise

6. RETORT
(A) recourse
(B) replenish
(C) resort
(D) repartee
(E) renovate

7. RETRACT
(A) perceive
(B) compel
(C) implicate
(D) cancel
(E) involve

8. RETRIBUTION
(A) prowess
(B) vengeance
(C) garland
(D) maneuver
(E) proximity

9. RETROSPECT
(A) era
(B) debut
(C) recollection
(D) locomotion
(E) component

10. REVERE
(A) repulse
(B) ebb
(C) annihilate
(D) wax
(E) venerate

Check-up 9-3

Directions Each of the following questions consists of one word followed by five words or phrases.
You are to select the one word or phrase whose meaning is closest to the word in capital letters.

1. REVERT
(A) petrify
(B) hover
(C) backslide
(D) flourish
(E) enlighten

2. REVILE
(A) vilify
(B) dominate
(C) eliminate
(D) dispatch
(E) enroll

3. ROBUST
(A) formidable
(B) haughty
(C) dilapidated
(D) fluctuate
(E) vigorous

4. ROTUND
(A) grueling
(B) chubby
(C) illiterate
(D) benevolent
(E) drastic

5. RUE
(A) educe
(B) hover
(C) discuss
(D) mention
(E) regret

6. RUTHLESS
(A) invincible
(B) lucrative
(C) truculent
(D) polyglot
(E) sacred

7. SABOTAGE
(A) jest
(B) destruction
(C) ecstasy
(D) revelry
(E) theme

8. SAGE
(A) a wise person
(B) a sense of pride
(C) an antique jewelry
(D) a massive attack
(E) a streaming cold

9. SANCTIMONIOUS
(A) restful
(B) curious
(C) hypocritical
(D) tedious
(E) religious

10. SANGUINE
(A) colossal
(B) toxic
(C) pathetic
(D) ultimate
(E) cheerful

Answer 1.C 2.A 3.E 4.B 5.E 6.C 7.B 8.A 9.C 10.E

Check-up 9-4

1. SARCASM
   (A) trek
   (B) vocation
   (C) satire
   (D) whim
   (E) plumage

2. SATIATE
   (A) locate
   (B) ponder
   (C) fascinate
   (D) satisfy
   (E) unveil

3. SCRUTINIZE
   (A) depart
   (B) lurk
   (C) perish
   (D) examine
   (E) consent

4. SECEDE
   (A) ensure
   (B) don
   (C) scoff
   (D) manipulate
   (E) separate

5. SEDATE
   (A) tropical
   (B) intrepid
   (C) credulous
   (D) gullible
   (E) calm

6. SEDENTARY
   (A) impetuous
   (B) fixed
   (C) epidemic
   (D) ravenous
   (E) dismal

7. SEGREGATE
   (A) separate
   (B) meddle
   (C) overlook
   (D) saunter
   (E) purge

8. SEQUEL
   (A) continuation
   (B) distinction
   (C) oasis
   (D) figment
   (E) exhilaration

9. SEQUESTER
   (A) intervene
   (B) fathom
   (C) quarantine
   (D) dissuade
   (E) gratify

10. SHIRK
   (A) inherit
   (B) elude
   (C) intimidate
   (D) oppress
   (E) procure

Check-up 9-5

Directions   Each of the following questions consists of one word followed by five words or phrases.
You are to select the one word or phrase whose meaning is closest to the word in capital letters.

1. SIMULTANEOUS
(A) intermittent
(B) concurrent
(C) veteran
(D) dreadful
(E) privileged

2. SKIRMISH
(A) sovereign
(B) jest
(C) scuffle
(D) revelry
(E) comfort

3. SLANDER
(A) defamation
(B) collusion
(C) drought
(D) poverty
(E) indifference

4. SMEAR
(A) sully
(B) table
(C) suspend
(D) ruminate
(E) exude

5. SMOTHER
(A) extinguish
(B) waft
(C) dispute
(D) convert
(E) reprove

6. SNEER
(A) impede
(B) condemn
(C) sink
(D) thrive
(E) flourish

7. SNUB
(A) subjugate
(B) ignore
(C) elevate
(D) deflate
(E) conscientious

8. SOJOURN
(A) abhor
(B) confer
(C) visit
(D) distinguish
(E) cull

9. SPECULATE
(A) endure
(B) muffle
(C) think
(D) plead
(E) suffocate

10. STIPULATION
(A) query
(B) rabble
(C) salvage
(D) condition
(E) stipend

323

451 **sublime**	456 **summit**
452 **submissive**	457 **sumptuous**
453 **substantiate**	458 **supercilious**
454 **succumb**	459 **superfluous**
455 **sully**	460 **supple**

School Motto

"Ne Cede Malis"

(Yield not to evil)

- The Loomis Chaffee School

SSATKOREA.com

sublime
[suh-**blahym**]

adj. impressing the mind with a sense of grandeur or power

숭고한, 절묘한

There is but one step from the sublime to the ridiculous.

syn. exalted, divine, magnificent

submissive
[suhb-**mis**-iv]

adj. unresistingly or humbly obedient

순종적인, 고분고분한

When animals live in packs, one animal is usually the dominant leader, while the others fall into more submissive roles.

syn. compliant, meek, obedient

substantiate
[suhb-**stan**-shee-eyt]

v. to establish by proof or competent evidence

입증하다

If you accuse someone of committing a crime, you should have proof to substantiate the claim.

syn. authenticate, confirm, corroborate

succumb
[suh-**kuhm**]

v. to yield to or surrender

굴복하다, 무릎을 꿇다

She tried to study all night, but eventually succumbed to sleep around 3 a.m.

syn. surrender, yield, accede

sully
[**suhl**-ee]

v. to try to ruin one's reputation

(명예나 이미지를) 훼손하다, 더럽히다

Joan's good reputation was sullied by the false rumors.

syn. mar, defile, deface

summit
[**suhm**-it]

n. the highest point

꼭대기, 절정, 최고점

It took us hours to climb to the summit of the mountain, but the view was worth it.

syn. apex, pinnacle, peak

sumptuous

[**suhmp**-choo-uhs]

adj. rich and superior in quality

호화로운, 화려한

The chefs prepared a sumptuous meal for the wedding.

syn.   lavish, luxurious, deluxe

supercilious

[soo-per-**sil**-ee-uhs]

adj. having arrogant superiority

거만한, 남을 얕보는

Her supercilious sister acts snobby by raising her eyebrow.

syn.   haughty, arrogant, rude

superfluous

[soo-**pur**-floo-uhs]

adj. being more than is sufficient or required

(더 이상) 필요치 않은, 불필요한

Since each student will be carrying his or her own supplies, try not to bring anything superfluous.

syn.   excessive, unnecessary, needless

supple

[**suhp**-*uhl*]

adj. limber and flexible

유연한, 탄력 있는

The belt was made of a soft, supple leather.

syn.   limber, pliant, malleable

Sentence Completion 10-1

Directions : Fill in the blanks to complete the sentences.

1.   Jacob felt he indeed had not reached the _____ of his career.

2.   Kelly will _____ to the temptation of chocolate cake.

3.   The Countess spoke in a haughty, _____ voice.

4.   No speck of dirt could ever _____ her hands.

5.   The celebrity guests enjoyed the _____ banquet.

6.   The police have evidence to _____ the allegations against him.

7.   I need the thickest shoes; beyond these, all else seems _____ to me.

8.   The dancer is so _____ that she can use her body freely.

461 surmise   466 taint

462 susceptible   467 tarnish

463 tacit   468 taut

464 taciturn   469 tenacious

465 tactful   470 tenure

School Motto

"Honor. Virtue. Humility."

- The Pennington School

SSATKOREA.com

surmise
[ser-**mahyz**]

n. a matter of conjecture
추측, 추정

Her surmise turned out to be right.

syn.   guess, conjecture, assumption

susceptible
[suh-**sep**-tuh-b*uh*l]

adj. easily affected by
민감한, 예민한

The operation had left her susceptible to infection.

syn.   impressionable, sensitive, vulnerable

tacit
[**tas**-it]

adj. not openly said but implied
암묵적인, 무언의

Your silence implies tacit consent to these proposals.

syn.   implied, implicit, understood

taciturn
[**tas**-i-turn]

adj. inclined to silence
과묵한, 말수가 적은

The ship's captain was a taciturn man who spoke only to give orders.

syn.   reserved, laconic, quiet

tactful
[**takt**-f*uh*l]

adj. having or manifesting tact
수완이 좋은, 요령 있는, 눈치가 좋은

She is extremely tactful in dealing with the finance.

syn.   diplomatic, thoughtful, careful

taint
[teynt]

v. to sully or tarnish
(평판 등을) 더럽히다, 오염시키다

The warm weather will taint the food.

syn.   stain, sully, tarnish

tarnish
[**tahr**-nish]

v. to dull the luster of something
(광택을 잃고) 흐려지다, 변색되다

*The affair could **tarnish** the reputation of the prime minister.*

syn.   smear, spoil, corrupt

taut
[tawt]

adj. tightly stretched
팽팽한

*The skin of the drum is **taut**.*

syn.   tight, drawn, tense

tenacious
[tuh-**ney**-sh*uh*s]

adj. stubborn or persistent
집요한, 완강한

*He is regarded as a **tenacious** and persistent interviewer.*

syn.   unyielding, persistent, stubborn

tenure
[**ten**-yer]

n. time in position of responsibility
재임 기간

*During his **tenure** as dean, he had a real influence on the students.*

syn.   regime, reign, term

Sentence Completion 10-2

Directions : **Fill in the blanks to complete the sentences.**

1. Helen's _____ brother is good at negotiations.

2. Silver tends to _____ easily.

3. Jude's _____ father is reserved, not loud and talkative.

4. Holding hands might be _____ acknowledgement.

5. A clingy child had a _____ grip on his mother's hand.

6. If you use the plastic bottle again, you might _____ your drinking water.

7. Your _____ as a student ends when you graduate high school.

8. Eric isn't very_____ to flattery.

 Answers

1. tactful
2. tarnish
3. taciturn
4. tacit
5. tenacious
6. taint
7. tenure
8. susceptible

471	tepid	476	trite
472	torrid	477	trivial
473	trait	478	tumult
474	tranquil	479	unanimous
475	transcend	480	unattainable

School Motto

"Principes non Homines"

(Leaders, not Ordinary Men)

- The Webb School of California

SSATKOREA.com

tepid
[**tep**-id]

adj. characterized by a lack of force or enthusiasm

미지근한, 열의 없는, 성의 없는

He got a tepid response to his suggestion.

syn. lukewarm, halfhearted, unenthusiastic

torrid
[**tawr**-id]

adj. extremely hot

몹시 덥고 건조한

She was sitting on the rocks in the torrid sun.

syn. blazing, parched, sweltering

trait
[treyt]

n. distinguishing characteristic of one's personal nature

특색, 특성

Persistence is the common trait of anyone who has had a significant impact on the world.

syn. disposition, attribute, characteristic

tranquil
[**trang**-kwil]

adj. free from commotion or tumult

평온한, 고요한

She stared at the tranquil surface of the water.

syn. calm, pacific, placid

transcend
[tran-**send**]

v. to rise above or go beyond

초월하다, 능가하다

The best novels are those which transcend national or cultural barriers.

syn. surpass, exceed, outdo

trite
[trahyt]

adj. lacking in freshness because of excessive repetition

진부한, 독창적이지 못한

Her remarks sounded trite and ill-informed.

syn. hackneyed, stale, stereotyped

trivial

[triv-ee-*uhl*]

adj. of very small importance

사소한, 하찮은

She showed her inexperience by asking lots of trivial questions.

syn. insignificant, trifling, paltry

tumult

[**too**-m*uh*lt]

n. a state of great commotion, confusion or disturbance

소란, 혼란

They waited for the tumult to die down.

syn. agitation, disturbance, commotion

unanimous

[yoo-**nan**-uh-m*uh*s]

adj. in complete agreement

만장일치의, 모든 찬성표를 받은

The jury reached a unanimous verdict of 'not guilty'.

syn. in agreement, uncontested, unified

unattainable

[un-uh-**tey**-nuh-b*uh*l]

adj. hard to be achieved

달성하기 어려운, 불가능한

This is not an unattainable ideal, but a goal which you must pursue.

syn. impossible, inaccessible, unreachable

Sentence Completion 10-3

Directions : Fill in the blanks to complete the sentences.

1. It would be nice to _____ the narrow limits.

2. _____ love songs are silly and overused.

3. The manager didn't want to examine _____ details.

4. It was a _____ decision to get pizza.

5. Don Quixote pursues an _____ dream.

6. Nate's mother has said that he got his best _____ from her.

7. The pop star is greeted with a _____ of fan's voices.

8. Johan and Sally had a _____ romance before they got married.

Answers

1. transcend
2. trite
3. trivial
4. unanimous
5. unattainable
6. trait
7. tumult
8. torrid

481	undermine	486	verify
482	unflinching	487	vicious
483	unprecedented	488	vie
484	venerate	489	vigilant
485	verbose	490	vindictive

School Motto

"Dat Deus Incrementum"

(God Gives the Increase)

- Westminster School

SSATKOREA.com

undermine
[uhn-der-**mahyn**]

v. to injure or destroy

(자신감이나 권위 등을) 약화시키다

He constantly tried to undermine her self-confidence.

syn.   weaken, blunt, injure

unflinching
[uhn-**flin**-ching]

adj. not shrinking from danger

위축되지 않는, 수그러들지 않는

They are strong, brave and unflinching to fight again this disaster.

syn.   resolute, courageous, steadfast

unprecedented
[uhn-**pres**-i-den-tid]

adj. having no precedent

전례 없는, 최초의

Such a move is rare, but not unprecedented.

syn.   exceptional, original, novel

venerate
[**ven**-uh-reyt]

v. to regard or treat with reverence

숭배하다, 경외하다, 존경하다

The monk was venerated as a saint.

syn.   revere, respect

verbose
[ver-**bohs**]

adj. using or containing too many words

수다스러운, 말이 많은

His writing is often unclear and verbose.

syn.   wordy, loquacious, talkative

verify
[**ver**-uh-fahy]

v. to prove the truth of

진실을 밝히다, 입증하다

Are you able to verify your allegation?

syn.   confirm, substantiate, authenticate

vicious
[**vish**-*uh*s]

adj. addicted to or characterized by vice

잔인한, 포악한, 사악한

They were the victims of a vicious racist attack.

syn. wicked, vile, evil

vie
[vahy]

v. to strive in competition or rivalry with another

경쟁하다, 다투다

The state champions will vie for the national title.

syn. compete, contend, strive

vigilant
[**vij**-uh-l*uh*nt]

adj. keenly watchful to detect danger

경계하는, 조심하는

He warned the public to be vigilant and report anything suspicious.

syn. watchful, wary, chary

vindictive
[vin-**dik**-tiv]

adj. disposed or inclined to revenge

앙심을 품은, 보복하려 하는

A vindictive man will look for occasions for resentment.

syn. vengeful, hateful, revengeful

Sentence Completion 10-4

Directions : **Fill in the blanks to complete the sentences.**

1. Harsh criticisms about Alicia's book _____ her confidence.

2. Many students get trapped in a _____ cycle of cell phone games.

3. This environmental destruction is on an _____ scale.

4. We are now witnessing an _____ crisis.

5. After the attacks, all the staff have been warned to be extra _____.

6. These numbers are suspiciously high, and you need to _____ them with the doctor.

7. The two children tend to _____ with each other for their mother's attention.

8. A _____ former prisoner threatens the lawyer.

Answers

1. undermine
2. vicious
3. unprecedented
4. unflinching
5. vigilant
6. verify
7. vie
8. vindictive

491	vociferous	496	wither
492	vulnerable	497	wrath
493	wail	498	writhe
494	waive	499	zany
495	wince	500	zealous

School Motto

"Cogitare Agere Esse"

(To think, to do, to be)

- Westover School

SSATKOREA.com

vociferous
[vo-**sif**-er-*uh*s]

adj. conspicuously and offensively loud

소리 높여 표현하는, 강하게 외치는

Max was vociferous in his support of the proposal.

syn. clamorous, strident, boisterous

vulnerable
[**vuh**l-ner-uh-b*uh*l]

adj. capable of being physically or emotionally wounded

상처받기 쉬운, 연약한

Jack was very vulnerable after his divorce.

syn. assailable, susceptible, defenseless

wail
[weyl]

v. to express sorrow audibly

울부짖다, 통곡하다, 흐느끼다

The child started wailing after she stumbled and fell.

syn. cry, howl, grieve

waive
[**weyv**]

v. to give up

(권리 등을) 포기하다

Many banks waive online transaction fees.

syn. forgo, let go, give up

wince
[wins]

v. to shrink back involuntarily as from pain

움찔하고 놀라다, 움찔하다

Tom winced as the nurse gave him an injection.

syn. cower, cringe, flinch

wither
[**with**-er]

v. to become dry and sapless

시들다, 말라죽다

The plants withered and died.

syn. shrivel, wilt, droop

wrath
[rath]

n. strong vengeful anger or indignation

심한 분노, 노여움

When the critic wrote a harsh review of the play, he earned the wrath of the playwright's fans.

syn. fury, rage, indignation

writhe
[rahyth]

v. to twist into coils or folds

비비 꼬다, 온몸을 비틀다

She lay on the floor, writhing in pain.

syn. contort, wrest, squirm

zany
[zey-nee]

adj. ludicrously or whimsically comical

엉뚱한, 괴짜 같은

There's a fine line between zany and crazy.

syn. funny, eccentric, comical

zealous
[zel-uhs]

adj. marked by active interest and enthusiasm

열성적인, 열광적인

No one was more zealous than her in that work.

syn. ardent, passionate, fervent

Sentence Completion 10-5

Directions : **Fill in the blanks to complete the sentences.**

1. A right-wing politician is well-known as a _____ opponent of human rights.

2. The candidate's _____ supporters worked tirelessly.

3. Sometimes it might be helpful to _____ as loudly as possible.

4. Stephanie continued to _____ in discomfort at what Jayden said.

5. It was strange, surprising, and _____ ideas, indeed.

6. Test fee waivers _____ some or all of the test fee.

7. Don't speak harshly to her; she's very _____ today.

8. Noah saw the flood as a sign of the _____ of God.

Answers

1. vociferous
2. zealous
3. wail
4. wince
5. zany
6. whimsical
7. vulnerable
8. wrath

Analogy 20. Math Terms

Math Section 고득점을 위해서는 Math 용어를 정확히 익히고 문제를 충분히 풀어야 합니다. 본문에는 Arithmetic/ Algebra/ Geometry 핵심 어휘와 Math Lexicon 수학용어사전까지 포함되어 있습니다. 수학 용어가 약하다면 본문을 꼼꼼히 익히고 연습문제를 풀어야 합니다.

absolute value 절대값	average 평균값
digit 숫자	distinct digit 다른 숫자
even number 짝수	odd number 홀수
decimal 소수	fraction 분수
sequence 순서	consecutive number 연속하는 수
factor 인수	integer 정수
greatest common factor 최대공약수	least common multiple 최소공배수
in terms of x x로 나타내면	whole number 0을 포함한 양의 정수
prime number 소수	factorization 인수분해
numerator 분자	denominator 분모
lowest term 기약분수	mixed number 대분수
average 평균	reciprocal 역수
median 중간 값	mode 최빈수, 가장 자주 나오는 수
ratio 비, 비율	rate 속도, 비율
rounding off 반올림	x-axis | y-axis x 축 | y 축
slope 기울기	x-intercept | y-intercept x 절편 | y 절편
set 집합	subset 부분집합
union 합집합	null set 공집합
intersection 교집합	sum of sets 합집합
perimeter 둘레길이	circumference 원의 둘레길이
radius 반지름	diameter 지름
diagonal 대각선	vertex 꼭지점
Pythagorean theorem 피타고라스의 정리	scalene triangle 부등변 삼각형
isosceles triangle 이등변 삼각형	parallelogram 평행사변형

Check-up 10-1

Directions Each of the following questions consists of one word followed by five words or phrases. You are to select the one word or phrase whose meaning is closest to the word in capital letters.

1. SUBLIME
(A) patient
(B) exalted
(C) frigid
(D) dormant
(E) aghast

2. SUBMISSIVE
(A) obedient
(B) visible
(C) stupendous
(D) aloof
(E) eloquent

3. SUBSTANTIATE
(A) alleviate
(B) captivate
(C) employ
(D) inflict
(E) authenticate

4. SUCCUMB
(A) illuminate
(B) slither
(C) relieve
(D) surrender
(E) apologize

5. SULLY
(A) scold
(B) exist
(C) mar
(D) vacate
(E) accelerate

6. SUMMIT
(A) cacophony
(B) terrain
(C) apex
(D) hangar
(E) adversary

7. SUMPTUOUS
(A) lavish
(B) unfeeling
(C) arranged
(D) frugal
(E) elaborate

8. SUPERCILIOUS
(A) circumspect
(B) viable
(C) desperate
(D) puny
(E) haughty

9. SUPERFLUOUS
(A) ravenous
(B) unnecessary
(C) elusive
(D) lethargic
(E) minute

10. SUPPLE
(A) limber
(B) complicit
(C) ferocious
(D) grim
(E) efficient

335

Check-up 10-2

1. SURMISE
(A) kindle
(B) despise
(C) conjecture
(D) employ
(E) adopt

2. SUSCEPTIBLE
(A) lavish
(B) momentous
(C) nomadic
(D) vulnerable
(E) inevitable

3. TACIT
(A) understood
(B) rare
(C) inhibited
(D) banned
(E) occupied

4. TACITURN
(A) transparent
(B) vacant
(C) threadbare
(D) reserved
(E) scarce

5. TACTFUL
(A) level
(B) accurate
(C) furious
(D) humble
(E) diplomatic

6. TAINT
(A) overwhelm
(B) sully
(C) perturb
(D) slaughter
(E) abduct

7. TARNISH
(A) rejoice
(B) burnish
(C) halt
(D) smear
(E) abate

8. TAUT
(A) mediocre
(B) tight
(C) perpetual
(D) extravagant
(E) brisk

9. TENACIOUS
(A) ignorant
(B) keen
(C) esteemed
(D) unyielding
(E) intelligent

10. TENURE
(A) chamber
(B) tempo
(C) meter
(D) entourage
(E) term

Check-up 10-3

Directions Each of the following questions consists of one word followed by five words or phrases. You are to select the one word or phrase whose meaning is closest to the word in capital letters.

1. TEPID
(A) lukewarm
(B) conspicuous
(C) trepid
(D) exotic
(E) impromptu

2. TORRID
(A) immaculate
(B) laden
(C) sweltering
(D) rancorous
(E) pensive

3. TRAIT
(A) diction
(B) visage
(C) homage
(D) disposition
(E) stance

4. TRANQUIL
(A) paltry
(B) unctuous
(C) discreet
(D) placid
(E) inept

5. TRANSCEND
(A) muffle
(B) dissent
(C) incinerate
(D) surpass
(E) decimate

6. TRITE
(A) hackneyed
(B) marvelous
(C) tranquil
(D) enormous
(E) flimsy

7. TRIVIAL
(A) insignificant
(B) accurate
(C) mysterious
(D) grandiose
(E) untamed

8. TUMULT
(A) token
(B) umpire
(C) trek
(D) commotion
(E) turncoat

9. UNANIMOUS
(A) traumatic
(B) ubiquitous
(C) tenable
(D) unified
(E) cardinal

10. UNATTAINABLE
(A) irate
(B) obsolete
(C) mere
(D) impossible
(E) lethargic

Answer 1.A 2.C 3.D 4.D 5.D 6.A 7.A 8.D 9.D 10.D

Check-up 10-4

1. UNDERMINE

(A) injure
(B) classify
(C) accelerate
(D) beseech
(E) restrain

2. UNFLINCHING

(A) steadfast
(B) daunted
(C) jubilant
(D) deft
(E) indistinct

3. UNPRECEDENTED

(A) intermittent
(B) exceptional
(C) malicious
(D) dynamic
(E) valiant

4. VENERATE

(A) hibernate
(B) revere
(C) intimidate
(D) compel
(E) assimilate

5. VERBOSE

(A) comprehensive
(B) loquacious
(C) secondary
(D) considerable
(E) exclusive

6. VERIFY

(A) authenticate
(B) boycott
(C) provoke
(D) capsize
(E) entrust

7. VICIOUS

(A) holistic
(B) evil
(C) brawny
(D) graceful
(E) condensed

8. VIE

(A) concede
(B) enrage
(C) modify
(D) compete
(E) entice

9. VIGILANT

(A) wary
(B) ambivalent
(C) ephemeral
(D) feasible
(E) superior

10. VINDICTIVE

(A) fatigued
(B) amiable
(C) spontaneous
(D) revengeful
(E) condescending

Check-up 10-5

Directions Each of the following questions consists of one word followed by five words or phrases. You are to select the one word or phrase whose meaning is closest to the word in capital letters.

1. VOCIFEROUS
(A) austere
(B) impulsive
(C) clamorous
(D) fatigued
(E) revengeful

2. VULNERABLE
(A) assailable
(B) humorous
(C) integrated
(D) flamboyant
(E) stagnant

3. WAIL
(A) slander
(B) excavate
(C) cry
(D) fortify
(E) depict

4. WAIVE
(A) daunt
(B) remunerate
(C) intimidate
(D) rejoice
(E) forgo

5. WINCE
(A) fumble
(B) cower
(C) grope
(D) furnish
(E) sharpen

6. WITHER
(A) shrivel
(B) nourish
(C) renovate
(D) hinder
(E) inhale

7. WRATH
(A) retribution
(B) feint
(C) havoc
(D) indignation
(E) distinction

8. WRITHE
(A) harry
(B) pester
(C) badger
(D) contort
(E) consecrate

9. ZANY
(A) comical
(B) fastidious
(C) gargantuan
(D) complimentary
(E) ferocious

10. ZEALOUS
(A) hollow
(B) futile
(C) conceited
(D) fervent
(E) sympathetic

339

한세희의 SSAT
HIT VOCABULARY

초판 발행 2020년 6월.5일
개정 2쇄 2023년 8월 31일

지은이 한세희
감수자 이준, 박세영, 이지은, Phillip Lim
펴낸이 최영민
디자인 이연수
Contributors Yewon Lee, Jeongwon Han

펴낸곳 헤르몬하우스
출판등록 제406-2015-31호
주소 경기도 파주시 신촌로 16
전화 031-8071-0088
Fax 031-942-8688
이메일 hermonh@naver.com

ISBN 979-11-91188-46-2 (13740)

■ 헤르몬하우스는 피앤피북의 임프린트입니다.
■ 책값은 뒤표지에 있습니다. 잘못된 책은 구입하신 곳에서 교환해드립니다.